Privatization

PRIVATIZATION
The Provision of Public Services
by the Private Sector

Edited by
Roger L. Kemp

McFarland & Company, Inc., Publishers
Jefferson, North Carolina, and London

To Jill and Jonathan,
my travelling companions

Grateful acknowledgment is made to the following organizations and publishers for granting permission to reprint the articles in this volume: American Society for Public Administration; Callaghan & Company, Inc.; Congressional Quarterly, Inc.; Communication Channels, Inc.; Government Finance Officers Association; International City Management Association; McGraw-Hill, Inc.; National Civic League; Texas Municipal League; The Academy of Political Science; The Privatization Council; The Urban Institute; University of Cincinnati; University of Hartford; and Water Pollution Control Federation.

British Library Cataloguing-in-Publication data are available

Library of Congress Cataloguing-in-Publication Data

Kemp, Roger L.
    Privatization : the provision of public services by the
private sector / edited by Roger L. Kemp.
        p.   cm.
    Includes bibliographical references and index.
    ISBN 0-89950-619-4 (lib. bdg. : 50 # alk. paper) ∞
    1. Municipal services—United States. 2. Privatization—United
States. I. Title.
HD4605.K45   1991
338.973—dc20
                                                            91-52599
                                                            CIP

Manufactured in the United States of America

McFarland & Company, Inc., Publishers
  Box 611, Jefferson, North Carolina 28640

Contents

Part One: The Need

Part Two: The Process

Part Three: The Application

Part Four: The Precautions

Part Five: The Future

Foreword

Many changes have taken place in our cities and towns since the so-called "taxpayers' revolt" of the 1980s. During the past decade, nearly every state has implemented some form of self-imposed or citizen-mandated taxing or spending limitation. Such financial constraints, coupled with the limited growth of revenues, increased citizen demand for services, continued economic inflation, soaring energy costs, and fewer state and federal grants, have focused national attention on ways to improve services, reduce costs, and hold down taxes in our local governments.

The private marketplace has recently begun to provide public services, primarily by contract, to the citizens of our municipalities. This trend has been called the "privatization" of public services. In order to improve planning for service delivery, make every effort to hold down costs, and to ensure the competitiveness of government services, public officials must understand the dynamics of the evolving field of privatization. Elected officials and administrators alike are now reviewing and evaluating existing public programs, and scrutinizing new services, with a philosophy of fiscal conservatism. The era of unlimited revenues, brought about by the routine upward adjustment of tax rates, has come to an end. This is now a political and operational fact of life in cities and towns throughout America.

All public officials, because of this new fiscal environment, must understand ways to lower costs and increase productivity. While the privatization option is not a panacea, it is in the best interest of taxpayers to compare the cost of government services with those of the private sector. This does not mean that all public services will, or should, be provided by private providers in the future. Rather, it stresses that government should maintain control over both the quality and competitiveness of their services.

Privatization examples now exist in many cities throughout the nation. Most decisions to contract for public services have been diverse, fragmented, and piecemeal in their development and application. For the most part, each municipality is "doing its own thing" in this dynamic and rapidly expanding field. The purpose of this book is to demonstrate the need to explore privatization options in our cities, to review different privatization processes and guidelines useful to local public officials, and to describe proven and successful privatization applications. The longest section of this book deals with practical privatization applications for those public services generic to most local governments.

Careful attention is also given to an examination of the precautions that public officials should take when considering the privatization option for public services. When public services are contracted to the private sector, government becomes the adminstrator of contracts with private sector companies. These companies—the private providers of public services— must be continually monitored and held accountable to make sure that they serve in the public interest. Public officials must ensure that public contracts for private services are in the best interest of taxpayers—using both service equity and cost criteria.

The privatization guidelines, examples, and precautions outlined in this book will help public officials and citizens across the land develop sound and prudent processes for coping in an era of limited financial resources. The passage of the Gramm-Rudman-Hollings legislation at the federal level will continue to exacerbate the financial plight of our local governments. Politically and administratively sound privatization strategies must be developed to foster public confidence in government. The level of public trust in local governments can only be enhanced through the application of prudent and financially sound privatization practices— practices that ensure proper public accountability. It is hoped that this book will achieve this goal.

Roger L. Kemp
Clifton, New Jersey
January, 1991

1. Introduction

Roger L. Kemp

While the private marketplace has been in existence since the beginning of time, it has only recently begun to provide public services. An increasing number of local governments are contracting with the private sector for public services. External conditions such as inflation, revenue shortages, soaring energy costs, and fewer grants from higher levels of government have altered traditional methods for providing public services. These factors, when coupled with rising public expectations for more services and fewer taxes, set the contemporary context in which municipalities operate. In order to improve planning for service delivery, and in an effort to hold down costs and taxes, public officials must understand the dynamics of the evolving field of privatization.

Gone are the more predictable days for local governments. When revenues were plentiful and public officials could merely adjust tax rates to balance budgets, life was relatively simple and routine. The private sector did not pose signficant challenges, opportunities, or threats. Public programs were merely increased in response to citizen demands for more services. In addition to the basic public services, most cities now provide many recreational, cultural, and social services. Currently, both the scale and mix of public services are being reevaluated in response to increasing fiscal constraints. Traditional methods of providing public services, designed during more stable periods of steady growth and predictable revenues, are now outdated.

Public officials, because of the new fiscal environment, must understand ways to lower costs and increase productivity. While privatization is not a panacea, it is in the best interest of taxpayers to compare the cost of government services with those of the private sector. This book does not emphasize replacing all public service with private providers. Rather, it stresses that government should maintain control over both the quality and competitiveness of their services. Privatization examples now exist in many

1

cities throughout the nation. Most decisions to contract for public services have been diverse and piecemeal in their development and application. For the most part, each city is "doing its own thing" in this dynamic and rapidly expanding field. The purpose of this book is to demonstrate the need for privatization in our cities, to review different privatization processes useful to local governments, to describe successful privatization applications, to examine the precautions that should be taken when contracting for public services, and to review the future direction of privatization in America's cities. These topics are highlighted in the following pages.

Part One: The Need

Part One examines the need for the privatization of public services. Private delivery systems, with proper controls, provide an alternative to traditional ways of providing public services. Several of the authors discuss how to safeguard the public interest when privatizing services. The private provision of public services is a new tool available to public managers. A national survey revealed that over 60 types of public services are already being contracted to the private sector. One author challenges local public officials to conduct "make" or "buy" decisions for all of their services. Other authors comment on the most radical form of privatization—service shedding. Another study revealed that one-fourth of all cities have "shed" one or more of their services to the private sector. While service shedding is one option, other forms of privatization are also reviewed. Another national survey revealed that nearly 80 percent of public officials believe that contracting out will increase in importance during the coming decade. It is also emphasized that privatization should not be treated as a threat, but rather as a tool to better manage government productivity. All authors agree that public/private partnerships represent a wave of the future.

Local governments across the nation are facing a common dilemma— an enormous need for services and public facilities, without the means to finance them. Decreases in federal and state-funded programs are shifting a greater amount of responsibility to local public officials, who will have to determine local program needs and priorities. Harvey Goldman and Sandra Mokuvos, in "Dividing the Pie Between Public and Private," note that "while some municipal officials are stymied in their desires to provide citizens with needed services, many others are looking at privatization, a financing and service delivery approach with potential advantages over traditional funding alternatives."

Goldman and Mokuvos go on to state "the privatization concept— private sector involvement in the financing, design, construction, owner-ship and/or operation, and delivery of services—is based on an emerging trend of public/private partnerships." The authors analyze the advantages of private sector construction and operation of public facilities, and also discuss how to safeguard the public's interest in the process. While the methodologies necessary to accomplish this are new to most local governments, the authors conclude, "they are easily put to use with appropriate guidance and direction."

In "Privatization and America's Cities," David Seader discusses the results of a national survey documenting the growth of privatization in the public sector. The author notes that "privatization is just one management tool available to the public sector." This chapter reviews the various types of public-private partnerships, and examines the results of a survey conducted by the International City Management Association, which revealed that some 60 public services are provided by the private sector. The three most contracted-for services include vehicle towing and storage, legal services, and commercial solid waste collection.

The author concludes by challenging cities to conduct "make" or "buy" decisions for all of their services and facilities. All such decisions must take into account both the direct and indirect costs associated with providing a particular service or facility. "Privatization," Seader emphasizes, "really represents a spirit, an entrepreneurial drive that all can use, take advantage of, and control." The "control" aspects imposed by government include protecting the taxpayers from substandard or non-performance by private sector contractors. Such safeguards ensure that citizens receive high quality services and the most for their limited tax dollars.

Philip E. Fixler, Jr., in "Service Shedding—A New Option" examines the most radical form of privatization—the process of turning over activities from the public sector to the private sector. The author reviews what he refers to as the "micropolitics" of privatization, which involves taking into consideration the political interests supporting the provision of a particular public service, and how those interests may be placated during the privatization process. Fixler documents several successful local government service shedding case studies.

The author concludes by revealing the results of a privatization study. Over one-fourth of all cities have "shed" one or more services to the private sector, as compared to one-fifth of all counties. The primary recipient of service shedding was the private sector (nearly 40 percent) followed by non-profit organizations (16 percent). Cities in Texas, Florida, and California led the nation in the shedding of services to the private sector. Fixler concludes by noting that while service shedding is the most pure form of privatization "it also has the most potential for reducing expenditures."

While service shedding may be one form of privatization, many other options exist for the public provision of public services. Terry Peters, in "Public Services and the Private Sector," analyzes other service options,

including the partial contracting of services, contracts with non-profit organizations, the use of franchises, government subsidies, service vouchers,
and self-help strategies, as well as regulatory and tax incentives. This
chapter identifies and discusses both the advantages and disadvantages of
contracting services to the private sector.

Peters notes that "except in the case of solid waste collection, no
systematic comparisons of government service delivery with private service
delivery have been reported." While local governments are contracting a
growing number of services with the private sector, the surveys done so far
are not definitive enough to declare it a major trend. The services that appear to be the best candidates for contracting include new services, services
for which outputs can be clearly specified, services that require specialized
skills and or equipment, seasonal services, and services with a large number
of providers. "Other forms of privatization," Peters concludes, "are less
widely practiced than contracting and have not been the subject of intensive
research."

There are clearly two sides to the privatization issue. Thomas Darr
points out in "Privatization May Be Good for Your Government" that advocates say privatization saves tax dollars and increases public-sector productivity. Opponents, on the other hand, argue that privatization raises
serious issues of accountability, quality, flexibility, and integrity. Despite
these reservations, Darr notes "it is clear that more and more functions
traditionally performed by public employees are increasingly being turned
over to the private sector." Moreover, nearly 80 percent of local government officials believe that privatization will be a primary tool to provide
local government services and facilities in the coming decade.

Darr emphasizes that while not a panacea, privatization may prove to
be more of a powerful "management tool." One of the primary benefits of
privatization may be that it forces public officials to analyze and cost-out
their services and programs, and compare these costs with those of the
private sector. The best public managers don't look at privatization as a
threat, but rather as another tool to better manage productivity. One important safeguard in privatization is to consider the quality of the service
and not just the price. The lowest bid may offer neither the best quality of
service nor the quality to which citizens are accustomed. The quality of service, however, may be controlled through the development of accurate
specifications and an appropriately worded service agreement.

Local governments in the United States, more than anywhere else in
the world, are serving as laboratories for privatization. Philip E. Fixler, Jr.,
and Robert W. Poole, Jr., in "Status of Local Privatization," note that
"virtually every type of service performed by local governments is being
provided privately in one form or another somewhere in the United States."
For many public services, the authors note, "private provision is probably

more common than government provision. And the extent of privatization appears to be growing rapidly."

Fixler and Poole conclude that "there is moderately strong quantitative evidence that privatization has grown dramatically and that it has yielded significant cost savings for a variety of services." While privatization has caused some problems, adequate legal safeguards exist to minimize the shortcomings of contracting public services to the private sector. The authors conclude by emphasizing that "empirical conclusions again and again point to the superior flexibility, responsiveness, and cost-effectiveness of privatization."

Part Two: The Process

Part Two reviews, in detail, several analytical processes for contracting public services to the private sector. Different options also exist for privatizing different components of public services. The need exists for public officials to compare the cost of their services with those of the private sector. The bottom line is the lowest cost to taxpayers, since they must ultimately foot the bill. Several models set forth the necessary steps that must be undertaken to help properly evaluate whether or not to contract a particular service to the private sector. Most authors agree that many variables exist in the privatization equation. Contracting out, however, is one way to inject private sector market competition into the provision of public services. Since any decision to contract a public service is a highly political one, the politics of privatization are also examined. Several authors agree that, while local government must be responsible for providing a service, the actual service provision may be performed by the private sector. One author examines the coproduction alternative for providing public services, and the need to get citizens more involved in the provision of their community programs. Some of the pitfalls of privatization are also discussed, along with ways to eliminate them through proper contract performance measurements.

There are several variations to the traditional approach of the public sector merely buying services from the private sector. Ted Kolderie and Jody Hauer, in "Contracting as an Approach to Public Management," explore these program options. Cities can purchase a service, or they can break it down into its different components and buy only selected portions of the service. These various components, according to the authors, include "pieces of the work itself, support services for the work, the supervision of the work or of the support services, or the equipment and facilities needed for the work." This chapter also explores how the "purchase of service" arrangement can create incentives for improved program management and performance.

Kolderie and Hauer also examine other issues concerning the contracting of services. One of the most important ones is that it forces a public agency to determine its costs to deliver a service. It may also "leverage the alternative producers (whether the public agency itself or other, competing contractors) into improving their price and performance." Another important benefit is the pressure that the contract relationship can stimulate for better program management and for more creative and innovative approaches to delivering a public service. These benefits can make public managers more creative and innovative, and can help save scarce tax dollars in the process.

America's industrial leaders have come to realize that to be competitive in the global economy they must demonstrate to the buying public that their products represent the best value. John Miller and Christopher Tufts indicate, in "A Means to Achieve 'More with Less'," that such a mode of economics-based decision making is now being applied by taxpayers to the goods and services produced by government. The authors stress that "taxpayers and consumers alike are demanding the best quality and value for their hard earned dollars." This chapter examines the concept of downsizing government, specifically focusing on privatization of service delivery as one alternative.

In the view of Miller and Tufts, government downsizing is the selective application of a broad range of management and cost-reduction techniques to streamline operations and eliminate unnecessary costs. These techniques are applied to the expansion of government services, the maintenance of service levels, improvement of quality, and reduction of costs. The authors state that "each potential opportunity for downsizing must be approached creatively to ensure the public still receives the best service and the lowest possible costs." To prove their point, Miller and Tufts cite several privatization case studies—both successes and failures. They also review several relevant topics to ensure the success of privatization.

Privatization can take many forms, ranging from a private operation of a small project to a service contract under which a private company designs, constructs, owns, operates, and finances a major facility. Larry Scully and Lisa Cole note, in "Making the Decision," that "there are literally hundreds of privatization options for each project. Selecting the most effective privatization option requires an 'apples-to-apples' comparison of the costs and risks associated with full municipal development, full privatization, and several privatization options." This chapter presents a strategy for making realistic comparisons prior to making the final privatization decision.

The authors set forth a five-step model for analyzing all privatization decisions. These steps include: (1) define the project scope, (2) develop options, (3) define engineering and financing assumptions, (4) estimate costs, and (5) analyze management and risk factors, This analysis is intended to illustrate the key issues facing a municipality in the decision to involve private firms in the financing, design, construction, and operation of a public facility or service. It is emphasized that "the most cost-effective option . . . may evolve quite differently for each city." The final privatization decision should be based on a clear understanding of all the costs and risks associated with a particular project or service.

Edward Hayes, in "Contracting for Services," notes that "contracting for services provides cities with a method for injecting marketplace competition into service delivery." Stressing a systematic approach, Hayes examines an eight-step model that should be used when making a decision to privatize a municipal service. These steps involve analyzing the alternatives to contracting-out, making a comparison between public versus private service delivery, reviewing the program design and avoidable costs, writing objective performance indicators, deciding upon penalties and incentives, soliciting bids and writing the contract, administering and monitoring the contract, and the closing or renewing the contract.

The author also emphasizes that "contracting has its pitfalls. The greatest of these is a service provider who does a shoddy job, or who raises prices halfway through the contract." These problems can be all but eliminated by writing into the contract measurable performance indicators. Hayes also warns public agencies not to contract out 100 percent of their service capacity. By doing this, if the contractor does not live up to performance expectations, or raises the costs, a public agency may perform some of the service. In taking this approach, "a contractor knows you can step back into service delivery and is very unlikely to horse you around with demands for money, or to ignore citizen complaints." These words of wisdom may be especially applicable to a first-time contractor that may not have a proven track record of established service.

Frances Winslow, in "The Politics of Advocacy," examines the politics of privatizing public services. In addition to possibly reducing costs, "privatization may solve problems of obsolescence, technological innovation, and capital-intensive development." Limited financial resources force administrators to evaluate services and select areas where funds can be saved. Privatization offers an alternative to service cutbacks, elimination, or a marked decline in the quality of service. Winslow states "the logic of privatization seems compelling to the staff that is forced to balance a municipal budget with decreasing revenue sources, but making this sensible solution obvious and palatable to the politicians . . . is sometimes difficult." In such a case "the municipal administrator," in the author's words, "must become a politician."

The remainder of this chapter analyzes how to gain political and community support for a privatization proposal. A four-point program is set forth to achieve this goal. The steps involved include ways to analyze a community, different avenues to present the privatization issue, identification of special interest groups, and techniques for the development of a successful media campaign to support a privatization proposal. Lastly, several successful options are examined on how to best present the privatization issue to a city's elected officials. Winslow concludes by stressing that "privatization is a new issue for many voters and local politicians. It may be met with concern and fear. A solid political strategy can develop a strong base of public support for the program, resulting in a successful realignment of public resources for the good of the community."

Other program options, in addition to privatization, are available to the public sector to decrease government's involvement in the provision of services. Jeffrey Brudney, in "Coproduction and Local Governments," notes that "while local governments must be involved in the provision of services, production is not inherently a governmental task and can be accomplished through a number of mechanisms, depending upon the type of service." The author stresses the need for local governments to increase citizen participation in the production of community services. Service delivery approaches premised on citizen involvement require "coproduction," the joint provision of a service by both a government and its citizens.

Brudney goes on to analyze the concept of coproduction and the costs and benefits involved in making this decision to provide a public service. "It would be unfortunate," the author states, "if consideration of alternatives went no further than contracting or similar devices that increase reliance on the private sector for the production of services." The benefits of coproduction are threefold — the enhancement of jobs of public employees, cost-efficiency in service delivery, and restoration of the traditional values of citizenship and community service. Prior to making the decision to privatize, depending upon the nature of the service involved, consideration should be given to the possibility of coproduction of the service.

Part Three: The Application

Part Three cites actual applications of privatization techniques in cities throughout the United States. Details are provided concerning contracting out of such diverse public services as fire protection, information resources, parks and recreation programs, prisons and jail facilities, public works operations, refuse collection, street sweeping, transit services, and wastewater treatment facilities. For example, one private company has been providing public fire protection services since 1951. They now provide services to some 50 communities in 5 states. There is also a growing trend to contract for information resources, enabling public agencies to avoid the large one-time expenses associated with computer hardware acquisition. Many public/private partnerships are developing for parks and recreational services, as well as for jails and prisons. Various aspects of public works operations are also successfully being provided by the private sector. One national study revealed that a savings of nearly 30 percent can be achieved through private refuse collection. Street sweeping is another popular area for contract services. Another major study revealed that local governments can save as much as 60 percent by providing public transit services through private contractors. The privatization of wastewater treatment plants also has a proven track record of savings. Concrete examples are provided for each of these public services.

A few years ago New York's Governor Mario Cuomo said, "It's not government's obligation to provide services, but to see that they're provided." John Turner, in "Fire Protection," examines one company's efforts to provide private fire protection and emergency services to America's municipalities. Rural/Metro Corporation provides a range of private emergency services, including fire protection, to some 50 communities in 5 states. The first contract Rural/Metro had in 1951 was with the City of Phoenix, Arizona. Other cities and special districts have been added through the years. Actual case studies are provided for other cities in different states. Municipal fire departments, with their traditional strong employee unions, make it difficult for cities to convert from a paid employee to a contract fire service.

Nonetheless, Rural/Metro started with one fire truck and four men back in 1948. They celebrated their 40th anniversary in 1988 with a fleet of over 300 vehicles and over 1,700 employees. Its contracts range from $160,000 to over $3 million annually for periods ranging in length from one to ten years. The company has over 95,000 fire subscription and 30,000 ambulance subscription customers including both individual homeowners and businesses. Unusual as it may seem, the company does not seek out municipal fire protection contracts. Instead, they prefer to respond to inquiries from various local government entities interested in their services. This company has been a leader in the privatization of fire and emergency services. As the author states, "privatization has not only arrived . . . it is here to stay."

There is a growing awareness in the public sector that government services do not always need to be supplied by the government. Many public officials have found that it is sometimes more cost-effective for services to be arranged and funded by government, but provided by the private sector. David Krings and Charles Martin indicate, in "Information Resources," that "one of the growing areas for privatization is the management and operation of information resources — data processing, office automation systems, and telecommunications." This field is growing rapidly because the automation of information services can have a dramatic impact on a government's ability to deliver services in a timely and cost-effective manner.

Additionally, improved access to data can provide government executives with the vital information they need to make critical management decisions in this era of changing demographic patterns, rising costs, and declining funding. The authors note that "dozens of cities and counties are already working under such arrangements with private industry partners to increase the efficiency of their information systems." They provide a framework for comparing public versus private provisions for information services. The "external" solution is sometimes easier since private companies are less encumbered by the constraints placed on local governments regarding internal salary restriction, limited career paths, and cumbersome hiring processes. Another advantage is that local governments do not have the high front-end costs associated with the purchase of expensive computer systems.

Joe Morris and Terry Stone, in "Public Parks," comment that "public parks and recreational facilities are being targeted for privatization as they become too costly for local governments to maintain." Skyrocketing costs for personnel and maintenance are forcing many local governments out of the rest-and-relaxation business. Many municipal recreation departments are considering or have instituted public/private partnerships in this important service area. The main impetus to seek alternative delivery systems rests with the high costs of government benefits, such as insurance and pensions. Additionally, some cities allow civic groups to participate in park maintenance, either voluntarily or by contract. In some cases, community involvement has also reduced vandalism.

The authors discuss various contract considerations and other options for the privatization of parks and recreational services. Sometimes it is easier to contract these services since they have traditionally not generated enough revenues to pay their own way. Rather than not have a service, it is more advantageous to contract with the private sector, a nonprofit organization, or another governmental agency to provide the service. This is also one service area where it is easy to identify program beneficiaries and target them with user fees and charges for the services they use. In many cases, the local government provides the space and the sponsorship, while the private contractor provides the service. Frequently, the local government receives a percentage of the revenues. Many privatization options are available and should be considered before any such service is eliminated for lack of funds.

Another vital service, quite different from those in the recreational area, is the provision of prisons and jails by local governments. Kent Chabotar, in "Prisons and Jails," notes that "traditionally, local governments have financed capital improvements with current operating revenues or general obligation bonds." Local governments are now finding it difficult to raise capital for prison and jail construction due to federal aid cutbacks, economic recession, and tax and debt limitations imposed by voters. Increasingly, local governments are turning to the private sector for help and are exploring a variety of lease and lease/purchase agreements. Most privatization arrangements involve contracting for correctional services and facility operations, as well as the financing of new construction.

Chabotar provides several examples and case studies, citing both the advantages and limitations of contracting for prison and jail construction and facility operations. The author also examines public policy considerations that must be taken into account when consideration is given to privatizing these facilities. Key to these considerations is the citizen perception of avoiding voter referenda and public debate through the issuance of revenues bonds and certificates for the long-term debt obligations of a government entity. In New York, for example, a taxpayers' suit was filed against the state's Urban Development Corporation (UDC) to prevent it from issuing revenue bonds after a general obligation bond issue for correctional facilities failed at the polls. While the taxpayers won at the trial court level, the state's highest court dismissed the complaint and allowed the UDC to proceed with the bond issue.

Another important service area common to all municipalities, and used more frequently than prisons and jails, is municipal public works operations. There is a growing trend towards the privatization of the construction, supervision, and maintenance of public works plants. Karen Carter, in "Public Works," examines the growing privatization trends in this area of public service. The major reasons cities are contracting for public works operations include "compliance problems, financial considerations, and staffing problems." Carter states that "the greater flexibility in personnel management is one of the great assets of contract operations." The author goes on to cite several case studies dealing with the privatization of public works facilities.

Several contract options exist for this common municipal service. Many cities find it beneficial to contract for only a portion of their total plant operations. Contract services have been used for liquid and solid waste processing, operations, and or maintenance. Many private contractors have the advantage of already having technically qualified personnel. They can also achieve economies of scale by bulk purchasing since a single operator may manage several public works facilities. Bulk purchases by contract operators can save a city as much as 25 percent on supplies. The author notes, for example, that "[S]everal plants in Oregon, too small to afford sophisticated equipment or expert personnel, individually can share in the costs and benefits collectively." The author concludes by stating "the response to contract operations has been positive and the benefits well documented."

No municipal service is as visible or as regularly provided as refuse collection. Eugene Wingerter, in "Refuse Collection," points out that "two-thirds of all U.S. cities have their residential trash hauled away by trucks owned and operated by for-profit companies." The reasons for this major privatization trend are threefold—private refuse collection is cheaper, there is a proven track record of quality service, and personnel problems are handled by the private company. Another contributing factor is the competitive nature of this business. There are as many as 10,000 private refuse collection companies in the U.S., which results in vigorous competition for municipal service contracts. The savings to taxpayers has also been well documented by the National Solid Wastes Management Association.

Wingerter cites examples of cost-savings using privatization examples from several municipal case studies. A major study of both private and public refuse collection arrangements in over 2,000 cities in 200 metropolitan areas was conducted by Columbia University for the National Science Foundation. This study documented the advantages of private refuse collection. It reveals that "refuse collection by private contractors was found [to be] 29 percent less costly than service using municipal crews." The author concludes by emphasizing that "many other public cleansing services can be successfully shifted to the private sector, with significant savings." These services include the operation of refuse processing and disposal systems, street sweeping, and sewage sludge dewatering plant operations.

More than half of America's cities and towns could also deliver more for less by contracting-out street cleaning services. James Mills, in "Street Sweeping," examines the results of a nationwide study on municipal street cleaning operations. The study revealed that "the primary reasons for improved performance under contracting are greater equipment utilization and repair and maintenance efficiencies.... The movement toward contract street sweeping is catching on at a slow but increasing pace." The author states that "street sweeping is the next most popular stage in the [privatization] movement since private waste collection." The survey also revealed that private contractors would capture between 25 and 35 percent of the municipal market for this service within the next 5 years.

Several case studies of cities on both the West and East coasts document the savings realized through the privatization of municipal street cleaning services. The biggest obstacle to service privatization, Mills states, "is union opposition and conventional interpretations of public and private sector motivation." A statement made by one municipal official in a large city illustrates the typical public sector response to privatization. He states "we have a strong civil service tradition and a union that supports the city's leadership. Private contractors are profit oriented, whereas the civil servant is dedicated to the common good." Generally speaking, the larger the city and the more powerful the unions, the greater the opposition to privatization of any kind, including street sweeping. Such sentiments, however, are not in the best interest of taxpayers, who ultimately foot the bill for public services, and deserve to have them delivered as economically as possible.

Another vitally important and costly service to cities is public transportation. Ralph Stanley, in "Transit," comments that "at the Urban Mass Transit Administration (UMTA), we have reached conclusions which were so positive that we now advocate increased public/private partnerships in the field of mass transportation. UMTA is a catalyst for this policy, and the laboratories are the cities and towns across the nation." Private sector involvement in mass transportation is no longer an abstract idea— it is fast becoming a working reality which produces results. A recent study conducted by the University of California's Institute of Transportation Studies found cost savings ranging from 20 to 60 percent in sampled communities where transit services were contracted with private providers.

Typical contract transportation services include fixed route, demand-responsive, elderly and handicapped, and commuter services. Several municipal case studies are provided which document the savings made through the privatization of public transit services. "Put simply in political terms," Stanley states, "privatization means unleashing free-market forces and using private competition and local initiative to meet local needs." The author concludes by emphasizing that, in addressing transportation problems, "the blending of the profit motive of private business with the public interest responsibilities of government will lead to more efficient solutions than through either public or private provision alone." The most effective approach to improve transit services starts with close coordination between the public and private sectors at all levels of the process, including planning, funding, and operations.

Since 1983, the concept of privatizing wastewater management facilities has progressed from an idea that seemed worthwhile to reality. Douglas Herbst and Lanny Katz, in "Wastewater Treatment," document the advantages of the privatization approach to the construction of wastewater management facilities. Using three recently concluded privatization transactions, the authors compare this approach to the traditional methods of grant funding or local funding. Private options are emerging since "the grant picture has changed markedly. Efforts to curb federal spending have had their effect on both the size and nature of projects." Grant eligibility criteria have been tightened in recent years to exclude collection systems, portions of conveyance systems, and costs for future growth. Federal grant funds have also been reduced from three-quarters to slightly over one-half of eligible project costs.

These changes have made privatization more attractive for this type of municipal service. Using the three examples illustrated, privatization provides new and creative ways to finance and construct wastewater treatment facilities. "Privatization," the authors state, "needs to be brought out of the background and into the forefront as an alternative for state and local governments. When (privatization) is properly evaluated and fully understood, it will present a viable alternative for solving the nation's water pollution problems." Herbst and Katz conclude that the results of privatization — affordable wastewater treatment services, more efficient use of federal and state funds, and in effect, an enhancement of government funding — can be achieved if privatization continues to be economically attractive to both the public and private sectors. "One way to assure this," the authors emphasize, "is for Congress to recognize the clear public purpose nature of privatization and retain current or comparable tax postures for privatization projects."

Part Four: The Precautions

Part Four examines the ideological issues surrounding privatization, and the overly optimistic expectations that some individuals hold for this trend. While the private provision of public services has its advantages, it also has its limitations. Most citizens expect government to be responsible for providing a service, even though it may be produced privately. Public services should not be privatized merely to limit the scope of government. This is not an end in itself. Rather, the most cost-effective method of service delivery should be the goal. Service equity is another important consideration. Both service equity and price competition are integral components in the privatization equation. Many policy-makers agree that the privatization of public services is highly situational. One of the main advantages of contracting is that is makes the public sector more cost-conscious and innovative. Union considerations must also be taken into account when contracting for services. Many experts, and union officials, also agree that it is not always cheaper to contract for a public service. One national survey revealed several legal safeguards that public agencies can take to ensure the performance and responsiveness of private contractors. Also, government officials have a public responsibility to continually administer and monitor the performance of private providers.

The privatization of public services is not a cure-all for local governments and their taxpayers. It only represents one option that should be considered in the delivery of public services. Robert Bailey, in "Uses and

Misuses," examines the limits of privatization. The author notes that "at least four identifiable policy initiatives are associated with privatization . . . and no one of them excludes the others." Bailey goes on to analyze government load-shedding, state-owned enterprises, the sale of government assets, and privatization by contract. The current trend in local government privatization encompasses contract services, whereby the government retains the right to set policy and finance a particular public service. The point is made that "the ideological advocates of privatization so overstate its applicability, or so cloud it as a concept, that practical public managers . . . find themselves on the defensive." The author goes on to cite the differences between public and private management.

Bailey points out that "the monopolistic nature of much of local service delivery is matched by a monopsonist character [which leads to] noncompetitive restraints." This creates a tendency towards internal preference scales and creates an extraordinary imbalance of power between the bureaucracy and the individual. This chapter illustrates that, while privatization may be desirable, it has its shortcomings. Four municipal case studies are provided dealing with commercial refuse collection, proprietary vocational schools, school transportation services, and the management of sports facilities. Ten issues are examined that should be considered before policy-makers and public managers make a commitment to privatize. The author concludes by stating that "Privatization will be applied only to things that the American people are not willing to risk; that includes every policy and program that several generations have put in place to protect themselves from the whims, uncertainties, instabilities, and unintended consequences of the marketplace."

The term "privatization" means many things to different people. The term is also very confusing. Ted Kolderie, in "Two Different Concepts," clarifies this concept very admirably by explaining the difference between "providing" and "producing" a public service. Local governments decide upon which services should be provided as a part of their policy-making process. Local public officials, if it is cost-effective, may decide to have a particular service produced by contract via the private sector. The responsibility for service provision, however, remains with government and its elected officials. This chapter goes on to analyze several important issues that should be resolved before making a decision to privatize a public service. Many of these issue involved ways to safeguard and protect the public against the possible shortcomings of the private sector.

Those who wish to privatize public services merely to limit the scope of government should also take into consideration the costs of providing the service. If government can provide a service more cheaply, then this is in the best interest of the taxpayers to do so. Kolderie notes that "for the moment, however, both the private leadership and the political leadership are mired in the old ways of thinking. Both are bogged down by traditional concepts of government that are insufficiently sensitive to needs for economy and responsiveness and by concepts of a private role that are insufficiently sensitive to the need for equity." A new concept of privatization is needed: one that combines equity in the provision of services with competition in their production. This distinction, the author states, has yet to be articulated politically.

Public officials should periodically consider options for greater use of the private sector for delivering their services. Harry Hatry, in "Problems," notes that "this is good public policy and good public management." Public officials should also examine existing instances of private sector delivery and consider the option of switching back to public employee delivery. Hatry states that "this is also good public policy." For a number of reasons, private delivery can become inefficient or have quality problems. "The appropriateness and success of using a particular privatization option," the author states, "is highly situational." Success depends upon many factors that are individual to the particular public agency.

A government agency may be delivering a service quite efficiently with good quality — leaving little room for improvement. In other situations, the service may be inefficient or of poor quality. The latter situation provides the major opportunity for change. Also, without good implementation, Hatry states, "even the best ideas will go awry." For example, in a switch to contracting, the quality of the request-for-proposal process is key to assuring that a capable contractor is selected. Also, a sound, sustained contract administration and monitoring process is essential to assuring that contractor performance remains up to par. The author emphasizes that "the major advantage of the privatization movement is not that the private sector can reduce costs or improve service to a great extent, but that consideration of privatization encourages public officials and public employees to innovate and to break down obstacles to improving employee efficiency." This chapter goes on to analyze some of the problems and shortcomings of privatization.

One of the major problems encountered with privatization is union opposition. Joe Morris, in "The Unions," argues that "despite the emergence of such issues as privatization, most communities have managed to strike a balance with their organized workers." Contracting public services to the private sector is still in the exploratory stages in most areas of the country. The three most commonly contracted services include refuse collection, major construction projects, and landscaping. Other services remain largely in the public sector. Morris goes on to cite several examples of how cities deal with their unions on the issue of privatization. In one city, after receiving bids for private refuse collection, it was determined that this service could be provided more efficiently by city workers. The bottom line is productivity. If the public sector can compete with contract suppliers, traditional control over services may be in the best interest of taxpayers.

Privatization is seen by many public managers as a way to avoid union labor. That thinking does not set well with employee unions, and is likely to cause unnecessary confrontations at the bargaining table. "Privatization," Morris states, "seems destined to become more the rule than the exception, but with proper boundaries, it should not threaten union labor." If used correctly, some of the money saved by contracting could be used to grant other union requests for their employees, such as higher salaries and better health benefits. One cannot categorically state that it is always cheaper to have a public service provided by the private sector. The costs of privatizing a service should always be compared with the cost to provide the same service by city employees. This process of cost comparison also forces public unions and their employees to be more productive and cost-conscious. Each municipality must seek its own balance concerning the privatization of their services.

Some experts believe that the privatization of public services is not a fad but a permanent trend. Susan Brown, in "A Cautionary Note," states that "[This] trend is likely to continue given the current administration's push to invite further private sector participation in delivery of public services and the nonstop fiscal pressure on government budgets at all levels." The author points out that privatization "should proceed with caution. Administrators need to assess each case separately." Although privatization may reduce costs, it can also become inefficient and result in quality problems. This chapter examines some of the possible shortcomings to the private delivery of public services. These potential problems include corruption, maintaining service quality, ensuring public access and accountability, and protecting the public against service interruptions.

The likelihood of the success of privatization depends upon several situational variables. These include the performance of the current delivery system, special circumstances such as the number and quality of potential service providers, government absorption of displaced employees, and the relationship between employee associations and the government. "A capable contractor and a sound, sustained contract administration and monitoring process," Brown remarks, "are essential to ensure successful implementation [of a privatization project]." One of the main advantages of the privatization movement is that competition by the private sector encourages public employees to be more innovative and efficient. The message to the public sector is clear, public services need to be effective and efficient, or they may be replaced with a private provider. The net result should be less costly and higher quality services for the public.

A number of sound management practices are emerging that enable cities to contract more effectively for public services. Harper Roehm,

Joseph Castellano, and David Karns, in "A Survey of Management Practices," discuss the results of a national privatization survey of cities having populations greater than 50,000. This study focused on methods for selecting contractors and the types of contracts used, the means for providing initial capital financing, the management of displaced workers' problems, and how cities monitor the quality of contract services. The main method used to select contractors was "the lowest bid among qualified companies." The "lowest bid" approach was seldom used. Typical agreements with private providers were based on either a "firm fixed price" or "unit price" approach to contract costs. The initial capitalization for the service was typically provided by the contractor, enabling governments to avoid the large up front costs associated with some services.

This study also revealed that most contracting occurs for new services. In nearly 70 percent of all cases involving contract services, no government workers were displaced. When government workers were involved, they were given a priority for other available jobs within the government. In nearly all cases, the formal agreement requires that citizen complaints be made to the government as a way to tract the contractor's performance. In order to protect the public against service interruptions, performance bond and termination penalty provisions were frequently included in contracts. The study revealed that, in a great majority of the cases, public officials were "very satisfied" with their contract services. The authors conclude by emphasizing that privatization can be successful when appropriate legal safeguards are taken to ensure the pricing and quality of the services provided, and when public officials take an active part in monitoring the performance of the private providers.

Part Five: The Future

Part Five explains and clarifies some of the future trends surrounding privatization. Competition prevails in the marketplace, and is becoming an important force in the public sector. The private provision of public services fits nicely with the American values of freedom of choice and self-reliancy. Many citizens believe that government should provide only the basics, and leave the extras to private service providers. Other citizens believe that privatization will enable public agencies to discard those services that only bear indirectly on their mission. The public versus private dichotomy has created a great deal of controversy and has clouded the true meaning of privatization. The most efficient delivery of public services is in the best interest of taxpayers, not necessarily reducing the size of government. Many public officials base the level of public services on political decisions, rather than on economic realities. The public deserves more professional decisions regarding their public services. Some experts believe that government should be provided the opportunity to be more productive before any decision is made to contract for a public service. Also, market values do not solely determine the price of public services. Civic values are also important when making a decision to price public services. Many public services fall short of being cost-covering and will never be provided by the private marketplace.

Privatization appears to echo the American values of competition and the freedom of individual choice. If only government provides a service, a monopolistic condition exists, which is not in the best interest of the tax-payers. Patricia Florestano, in "Considerations for the Future," states that privatization "has challenged profoundly both what government does and how it does it." In this context, privatization has several different meanings. Government should ignore some problems, leaving their resolution to the private sector; government should make more extensive use of market-available solutions to problems; and government should create markets for the production of public services. Florestano concludes that privatization is here to stay. Three factors have stimulated this trend — a concern for the costs and effectiveness of government, a dislike for government intrusiveness, and a growing desire for more individual self-reliance and freedom of choice.

Several major trends have also facilitated the movement towards privatization — self-help and volunteerism, participatory democracy, decentralization, public private partnerships, less federal largesse, more state and local responsibility, and a service-based economy. "In the face of these sorts of trends," the author states, "government will continue to withdraw from selected activities." One of the advantages of privatization is that public agencies will be able to discard responsibility for services that bear only indirectly on their public mission. Because of this, they will be able to concentrate more directly on the essential activities of government. The author concludes by emphasizing that if citizens are forced to think more clearly about which public activities actually produce public benefits, we may be able to concentrate on those things that only government can do and ways to improve upon them.

Contracting-out the delivery of services has become a familiar item on American municipal agendas. Privatizing public services has generally been portrayed as a "public versus private" issue — the assumption being that one mode of delivery is more appropriate than the other. Kate Ascher, in "The Business of Local Government," notes that "such a portrayal carries with it very high political stakes and has therefore prompted a reaction from trade unions, conservative think-tanks, and other lobbying organizations." All too often the participation of these groups in the debate has led to an unsettling, and unnecessary, level of controversy surrounding local service delivery decisions. The author stresses that the "public versus private" dichotomy is not only controversial, but has created a smokescreen. It calls attention to the political symptoms, rather than to the underlying economic causes, of recent shifts in service delivery modes.

"Municipalities," the author states, "have tended to base delivery decisions more on political than on economic realities, and in doing so have failed to make maximum use of new, private approaches to service delivery." This chapter describes the need to change the way we think about contracting-out public services. Rather than view privatization as an isolated political development, we need to see it as part of a broader economic question—one which concerns the relative benefits of internal delivery versus those of external or market provision. Ascher puts the contracting-out debate into appropriate historical and economic perspective in an effort to encourage more professional and less political approaches to this issue on the part of public agencies. Traditionally, the public sector has shied away from performing any rigorous analysis of the competitiveness of their services. The author concludes that "we owe it to ourselves to bring more professional discipline—and less political posturing—to the business of running our cities."

Before transferring a service to the private sector, local governments should have the option of being more competitive and productive in their service delivery. Jerry Frug, in "The Choice Between Privatization and Publicazation," says that "we need to find out why the private sector is cheaper . . . and make government better." Local governments should be reformed to make them more competitive with the private sector. The author also stresses that public services should be provided in such a way that involves members of the public in their planning and management. There ought to be more public participation in the delivery of government services. "Some government services," Frug says, "could be managed by groups formed on a participatory basis." The increased involvement of citizens in the provision of their services is referred to as "publicazation." The effective provision of a service is what counts, not whether it is provided by the public or private sector.

Publicazation and privatization—in the sense of transferring government services to the private sector—need not be thought of as opposites. Both could happen simultaneously. The critical choice between the public or private provision of services, therefore, is not whether government or business should provide public services. "The critical choice instead," according to Frug, "is whether we want public participation in the delivery of public services whoever provides them." Only by taking a share in governance can citizens learn how to deal with people with whom they disagree, how to wield and limit power, and how to affect the complex social process that touches their lives. Additionally, citizens overcome the feelings of insignificance and powerlessness that many times constitute privatization. "The difficult task of reforming government," the author concludes, "can itself become a vehicle for citizen participation." Frug emphasizes that both government and business should be more participatory in nature.

While privatization may be desirable, the private market does have its limits. Robert Kuttner, in "The Private Market Can't Always Solve Public Problems," examines the limits of the private sector in providing public services. "In an organized society," Kuttner states, "we counterpose certain public values to those of a pure market." Maintaining a political democracy in a private economy requires a set of compromises between the two incompatible principles of political equality (one-person-one-vote) and economic inequality (one-dollar-one-vote). Even in the strictly economic realm, our society has decided to stop somewhat short of pure Social Darwinism. Some public services are based on civic values, not market values. If people qualify as citizens for services that they could not afford as consumers, then somebody has to decide who gets what. This is the domain of government. Certain citizens do not have the cash, but still get the product. Part of the role of government is making the social commitment to who gets what in the way of public services.

While privatization may be appropriate for some public services, it is not the only solution. The author cites some examples of contracting-out public services that have not been in the best interests of citizens. Kuttner points out one study, conducted by the conservative Massachusetts Taxpayers Foundation, that concluded that some excesses had resulted from privatization. They concluded that one government had "lost fiscal and program control" to a "provider-dominated system." Beyond a certain point, government-by-contract couples the inefficiencies of the public sector with the less savory aspects of the private sector. "The market," the late economist Arthur Okum wrote, "needs a place, and the market needs to be kept in its place." "We Americans," Kuttner concludes, "are not just buyers and sellers, we are also citizens."

Part One: The Need

2. Dividing the Pie Between Public and Private

Harvey Goldman and Sandra Mokuvos

Local governments across the United States are all facing a common
dilemma—an enormous need for infrastructure facilities, without the
financial wherewithal to fund their construction. Decreases in federally and
state-funded programs are shifting a greater amount of responsibility to
mayors, town councils and others who must decide which project will proceed and which will be indefinitely stalled due to lack of funds. While some
municipal officials are stymied in their desires to provide citizens with
needed services, many others are looking at privatization, a financing and
service delivery approach with potential advantages over traditional funding alternatives.

The privatization concept—private sector involvement in financing,
design, construction, ownership and or operation and delivery of service—is based on an emerging trend of public/private partnerships. Because
the private sector has unique advantages available to it that are not available
to local governments, public officials have the opportunity to capitalize on
situations that could result in savings for the community. The possible
savings result from construction cost and time efficiencies, operational
advantages, and utilization of tax benefits.

A private sector firm undertaking a construction project will generally
proceed at a faster rate and with a less cumbersome approach when compared to an identical project constructed with public monies. The many
regulations and procedures that must be followed during construction of
a publicly funded project typically raise the cost of a project by a significant
amount. Bidding procedures, procurement regulations and other condi-

Harvey Goldman and Sandra Mokuvos, "Dividing the Pie Between Public and Private."
Reprinted with permission from American City & County, Vol. 99, No. 1, January, 1984.
Published by Communication Channels, Inc., Atlanta, Georgia.

tions imposed upon local governments are intended to protect the public. They also delay projects and cost money.

Privatization, coupled with service delivery contracts, have proven to be a cost-effective way of putting projects and services into place while still protecting the public. While the methodologies necessary to accomplish this goal are new to most local government units, they are easily put to use with appropriate guidance and direction.

Operation Efficiencies

After a project is constructed, private sector operation may be more efficient as well. "Contracting out" service delivery or blending public and private work forces to achieve operational and potential tax benefits could be considered in many cases. Contract operations have proven successful in many areas. One source of savings results from economies of scale that come into play when the same private sector firm provides services to multiple customers.

Tax benefits, which are not available to tax-exempt governmental entities, can be used by the private sector to lower service delivery costs even further. Changes made to the tax law in 1981 and carried over in the 1982 changes allow equipment and machinery to be depreciated over five years and structures over 15 years, about half the time previously allowed.

In many instances, investment and energy tax credits are also available. If the private sector entity uses a combination of equity and debt to finance the project, the interest payments on debt are tax deductible.

The privatization approach is applicable to a variety of infrastructure projects. Typically, equipment-intensive projects are more attractive than structurally intensive facilities because of the higher degree of tax credits and tax deductions. However, the feasibility of privatization should be determined on a site-specific basis.

Suitable Projects

Among the types of facilities for which privatization is especially suited are water and wastewater treatment facilities, parking and transit systems, garages, and other general and special purpose facilities.

In addition, privatization concepts also have been used by communities to attract private investment to develop properties which are owned by the public sector, but arc not needed or usable in their current dedicated use. The conversion of vacant land into important new taxable property and the rehabilitation of older structures through the use of privatization concepts has been successfully demonstrated in many situations.

Establishing the economic viability of privatization is important, but there are other matters that need to be addressed, and an orderly, proven methodology is essential. A key concept that governs this approach is that the public and private sectors must work together as partners.

When a privatization transaction is appropriately structured, both partners will benefit, but neither gains at the expense of the other. The private sector group gets an opportunity to pursue a legitimate business opportunity with a public sector client. The public gets a service delivered at a cost which could be far below its own cost of providing such a service. In fact, the public may be getting a service which it could not afford to provide for itself.

Risks Involved

As in any business arrangement, there will be some risks involved in a privatization transaction. If privatization is to be truly a partnership between the public and private sectors, then along with sharing the benefits, risks will also have to be shared. However, it should be noted that by working together, the risks can be minimized.

For example, in a privatized wastewater treatment facility, the private sector firm will most likely be responsible, under penalty of fine, for meeting the discharge requirements of the municipality's National Pollution Discharge Elimination System permit. If the responsibility is to be shared, then it is more than likely that the municipality will guarantee the general quality of the wastewater entering the plant to be treated. Similar types of risk-sharing approaches must be conceived on a site and project specific basis.

Public officials interested in using the privatization concept to help meet their infrastructure needs must understand both the privatization concept and the role that community leaders and the community's work force will play in the concept's implementation.

For example, a privatization feasibility study requires that a determination be made of the needs to be met. While a consultant familiar with the privatization concept, including a thorough understanding of the tax laws, is the most likely to undertake this endeavor, that person would be wise to work with the community's engineer and legal counsel to gain their insights into the situation. At the time a private sector firm begins operation of a facility, the existing public work force may be incorporated into the new one.

Question of Control

Some municipal officials may feel that turning over essential services to the private sector will diminish their control and authority over those services. The issue lies in understanding the difference between production and provision of services.

Although the municipality may no longer be producing the service, it is still providing it; and by structuring an appropriate oversight program, the municipality can still retain control over the timely and cost-effective provision of the service.

The oversight program is most likely to be set out in the contractual agreement between the municipality and the private sector firm. It may include independent financial and operational audits, and quality control reviews. Transactions can also be structured to enable the community to take control of the facilities in future periods.

Privatization offers many potential advantages to the public sector. First and foremost, privatization may provide a means to answer environmental, social and economic development needs to municipalities without the monetary means to finance needed infrastructure facilities. In other cases, it may allow local communities to use their limited debt capacity to finance other essential needs. In comparison to federally funded grant programs, which dictate the ways in which needs are determined, local communities could have more flexibility in determining their own growth and development through a privatization approach.

If privatization is deemed appropriate enough in a specific situation to warrant further study, the key to using it successfully is to approach the process in a thoughtful and organized manner. Communities that are to survive and thrive in the uncertain economic conditions of the 1980s must be alert to new solutions. Privatization is one such solution.

3. Privatization and America's Cities

David Seader

Privatization—the use of private sector resources in service to the public sector—has been gaining increased use and acceptance in recent years. Public jurisdictions have found it advantageous to involve the private sector in the design, building, ownership, financing, and operation of public facilities and services for several reasons:

1. Reduction of direct municipal outlays and extension of municipal general obligation credit
2. Limitation of some risks to government by shifting or sharing the risk with the private provider
3. Reduction of costs to taxpayers through private sector efficiencies and savings in construction costs and time, operations productivity, and economies of scale
4. Maintenance of or increased service levels with no increase in tax rates or user fees

Roles of the Sectors

Too often a tendency exists to make advocacy of privatization the same as denigration of government, as if the two should not coexist. But those advocating privatization should not be saying that the public sector is bad and the private sector is good, or that we need to dismantle the state or do away with the public sector. In fact, if privatization is to succeed, we need a very strong, healthy, and well-managed public sector.

David Seader, "Privatization and America's Cities." Reprinted with permission from Public Management, *Vol. 68, No. 12, December, 1986. Published by the International City Management Association, Washington, D.C.*

Privatization is essentially a public-private partnership. It is putting the business talent and drive of private enterprise at the disposal of the public. To get the most out of this partnership, each of the sectors—public and private—should look at what it does best, and what roles it should take.

The public sector represents, identifies, defends, and expresses the public interest—the will and the needs of the people and the services that they demand. But it does not need to provide all of those services directly. In looking at privatization and how it works in local government, one has to think first of how a city or county delivers its services. The role of the local government is really as a controller, a manager, and a protector. It is not necessarily a direct provider of service and does not have to be an operator.

The city can always be an operator of services—an operator of last resort. In fact, the competitive element in service delivery injected by privatization serves the public employees and the public managers as well as it does the private sector, by forcing everyone to be more efficient.

The essence of privatization is an arrangement in which the private sector provides goods, facilities, and services that traditionally have been provided by the public sector. It could be done through strict contracting out to a profit-making organization and paying a fee, or by just changing regulations and legislation to break up public monopolies of facility operation or services to allow for competition. It could also involve various types of voucher systems or other kinds of alternative service delivery.

Privatization is just one management tool available to the public sector. Cities are using and can use a wide range of other approaches as well. Some are having mixed and some great success. Indeed, privatization has had mixed success, a record that will probably continue in the near future, until the two sectors get more used to dealing with each other.

The Privatization Council focuses mostly on for-profit, private enterprise serving cities, counties, state governments, and authorities at a profit. The council started a year ago as a nonprofit educational group to provide a focus for bringing together the private and the public sectors. The council will develop the tools, techniques, and concepts of privatization in concert with the public sector—the users and the evaluators of the types of services that the private sector wants to provide.

Growth of Privatization

Privatization, which has been going on for some time, has been gaining ground in recent years. In 1982, ICMA identified about 60 services for which some contracting out had been undertaken. The survey indicated

that the national percentages for services turned over to the private sector
included the following:

	Percent
Commercial solid waste collectionn	41
Residential solid waste collection	34
Street repair	26
Street lighting operation	38
Vehicle towing and storage	78
Ambulance service	25
Operation/management of hospitals	25
Legal services	48
Fleet management/maintenance	30
Data processing	22
Building/grounds maintenance	19

More recently, the National Center for Policy Analysis determined
that 80 percent of localities are now using the private sector for vehicle towing, commercial waste collection has risen to 44 percent, 30 percent for ambulance and hospital operations and maintenance, 35 percent for day care
centers, and 42 percent for bus system operation and maintenance. A
myriad of other services are "privatizable," including snow plowing, utility
billing, parks maintenance, rodent control, labor relations, security, job
training, liquor store management, personnel, and secretarial services.

Throughout the country, communities have found that they can save
money by privatizing.

- In St. Paul, Minnesota, private businesses provide sanitation, street
  paving, lighting improvement, and other services.
- Phoenix, Arizona, estimates it saves $2.3 million annually by privatizing
  17 services, including bus system operation, security and crowd control,
  street sweeping, and trash collection.
- Newark, New Jersey, pays private firms for sewer cleaning, vehicle maintenance, printing, data processing, and street repair.
- Los Angeles County has 139 contracts for private services.
- Scottsdale, Arizona, and La Mirada, California, have privately run fire
  departments. In La Mirada, even the police and building inspectors have
  been privatized.
- Hamilton County, Tennessee, has a privately operated prison.
- Private firms run juvenile facilities in eight states.

The Council of State Governments notes that in 1982 $81 billion per
year of services were provided by the private sector through privatization.
That figure was up from $67 billion in 1980 and $27 billion in 1975. The
Privatization Council estimates that within the past year that amount has
probably exceeded $100 billion in services provided annually by the private
sector to the public.

Privatization is no longer an ideological issue. It is not a matter of Democrat versus Republican, left versus right, liberal versus conservative. It is basically an economic efficiency issue. Local governments at all levels need the type of economic relief that can be provided by private enterprise. And the need for such assistance will grow for several reasons.

- Provisions for deficit reduction will continue cutbacks in numerous federal assistance programs, including general revenue sharing, especially under Gramm-Rudman-Hollings.
- Public resistance to new public spending and "taxpayer revolts" will demand new funding methods for traditional service delivery.
- Replacement of aging facilities and provision of new facilities in expanding communities will create a demand for capital.
- The political pendulum swing toward market-oriented solutions set in motion by the current administration will not soon lose momentum.

Yet the federal government still maintains very high requirements for cities and counties, especially regarding environmental facilities, clean water, clean air, waste disposal, and hazardous waste disposal. And so the squeeze.

The states are finding that they cannot fill in the gap. The National Governors Association has warned that states cannot "bail out" localities losing federal aid — 17 states have already been forced to reduce their current budgets, and more will need to do so in the future. States like Texas have been hit hard by the decline in oil prices, on which many of their revenue formulas are based.

Taxpayer resistance to new taxes for expanding public services has been seen throughout the country. Prime examples occurred in California and Massachusetts, but, more dramatically on a local level, bond issues for schools and other facilities have been widely defeated. Polarization is growing between the old and the young in cities and between inner cities and the suburbs. This has resulted in an inability of local governments to develop and provide the types of services and facilities they know are necessary.

Privatization can help alleviate this situation, but it cannot promise miracles. Privatization opens up a realm of resources for use in cities. It creates an infusion of capital from the private sector and makes available private sector flexibility, innovation, efficiency in management, and a controlling mechanism that is very powerful in this country — the profit motive.

An important noneconomic benefit provided by the private sector is that of risk sharing, especially for environmental facilities where the private sector takes responsibility for providing, owning, and operating sewage treatment plants or other environmental control facilities. Businesses then share in significant ways the technological risk of the control technologies, as well as the risk of construction completion and long-term operations.

Types of Privatization

Privatization has three aspects:

1. Public asset divestiture to private firms by all levels of government.
2. Private development of infrastructure facilities — project-based privatization — for provision of services to state, county, and local governments. Examples of such capital projects include environmental control and transportation facilities.
3. Private provision of services to units of government. Examples include street maintenance, health care, and operation of environmental control facilities provided by private firms under contract to the public body.

The first type, asset divestiture, is probably the most controversial. Although it receives the most press coverage, it is the least active and has the least potential for impact at the local level. Most of the proposals have been at the federal level. The Office of Management and Budget and the administration in office look to sell the federal power marketing administrations, FHA loan portfolios, student loan portfolios, the Postal Service, and Conrail. Not all asset divestiture activity has taken place at the national level, however. There is a growing effort by states and localities to identify surplus properties that are underused or undervalued, which, in the hands of the private sector, might prove more productive and beneficial to the community. The University of Connecticut in 1985 undertook a procurement process to contract with a developer who will convert an 1800s residential mansion into a hotel and conference center for both university and outside use; the state of New Jersey is considering a similar step regarding mansions in two state parks. Buffalo, New York, is exploring the potential of selling portions or all of its city-wide parking system to private interests. In the near future, state and local governments may be moved to divest themselves of other functions or assets such as bus systems, hospitals, power generation facilities, or office buildings.

The criticism of asset divestiture is that it comprises only a one-shot infusion of cash, akin to eating one's seed corn. Asset divestiture is justified in those cases where continued ownership is a burden to the community. It may not be justified in cases where the asset is being used to the fullest and is in fact a money-maker for the city, state, or federal government. Divestiture should rely on careful valuation of the asset over its remaining life. Once value and costs are properly identified, a decision can be made.

Divestiture debates divert attention from the more productive current privatization efforts. Prime among them is infrastructure development, where an overwhelming need exists and where the private sector can provide a great deal of help.

The need for capital spending on infrastructure to the year 2000 has

```
┌─────────────────────────────────────────────────────┐
│                    Data Brief                         │
│                                                       │
│  Individuals inside local governments most frequently in- │
│  volved in the early stages of evaluating the feasibility of private │
│  service delivery alternatives:                       │
│                                                       │
│  Manager/CAO............................. 89.1%       │
│  Department heads ......................... 79.5%     │
│  Elected officials........................... 44.1%   │
│  Finance/accounting officer ................. 39.7%   │
│  Assistant Manager/CAO ..................... 38.0%    │
│  Attorney ................................. 30.6%     │
│                                                       │
│            ICMA Newsletter survey, February 1986      │
└─────────────────────────────────────────────────────┘
```

been estimated at $800 billion by the Congressional Budget Office (CBO) and $1 trillion by the Joint Economic Committee. Such spending includes, but is not limited to, facilities for solid waste management, water and wastewater treatment, roads, bridges, mass transit, and institutional buildings (e.g., schools, hospitals, prisons). A wider definition would add to that need by including parking facilities, ports, vehicle maintenance facilities, rolling stock, recreation and convention facilities, etc. Using that broader definition, the Associated General Contractors projects the need to be about $3 trillion.

Yet the CBO estimates spending on infrastructure to be only $39 billion annually, or $624 billion by the end of the century, creating an infrastructure "gap" of between $236 billion and $486 billion. In the area of wastewater treatment, the 1984 EPA needs assessment found that $109 billion of facilities will be required by 2000. At current levels of federal support, local governments would need to increase their spending by 50 percent to meet the need. Similarly, in water resources and supply, CBO found an estimated shortfall of $5.4 billion annually in spending for needed plant and equipment.

Recent developments imply that the gap will become more severe.

- Gramm-Rudman-Hollings cutbacks are reducing levels of federal support for infrastructure.
- Proposed reauthorization of the Clean Water Act includes increased local contributions to project construction funding from 25 percent to 45 percent or more.
- For the first time, legislation for waterway construction projects will require state and local contributions.
- The new tax reform legislation restricts the use of industrial revenue bonds for even purely governmental financings.

Clearly, a prime method to fill the gap is by employing private capital in infrastructure projects. A recent survey in *City and State* magazine found that overall about one-half of responding public officials believe privatization to be useful in developing environmental control and infrastructure projects. Positive responses ranged from 52 percent for solid waste projects, 38 percent for hospitals, and 30 percent for mass transit and sewage treatment, to 22 percent for water mains and 10 percent for roads. The Privatization Council and others are actively working to inform local officials about the benefits and uses of privatization in order to increase those positive responses.

Privatization of infrastructure has already been proving itself viable throughout the country.

- Westchester County, New York; Pittsfield, Massachusetts; Tulsa, Oklahoma; and Baltimore, Maryland, have joined several other communities with private waste-to-energy facilities; dozens more are being planned, developed, and constructed currently.
- Chandler and Gilbert, Arizona; Auburn, Alabama; East Aurora, New York; and Downingtown, Pennsylvania, now have privately owned and operated sewage treatment plants.

One way that the private sector can get involved in developing such facilities is by providing a turnkey service — design-build — turning the facilities over to the locality for operation at completion. Or the private sector can take the turnkey contract and also provide either a short- or long-term operating contract for the facility. A third alternative would involve providing a full-service facility. Full service means that the private entity would design, build, own, operate, and finance the facility. A solid waste facility, sewage treatment plant, water supply and water distribution facility, and even roads and county bridges can be implemented this way, as can public buildings, schools, hospitals, prisons, and other types of facilities.

How does privatization help in these cases? Financing of privately run projects may in fact be cheaper than public financing, even financing with grants. Studies by major accounting firms have shown cases where, even with the combination of federal grants and municipal financing, private financing was cheaper overall. Prior to tax reform, privatized financing was 20 percent to 40 percent cheaper for these types of facilities. Under the new tax reform act, that advantage will be cut in half, but in many cases privatization will still have the edge.

Privatization also provides construction efficiencies that will reduce overall facility cost, savings that can be passed on and shared with the locality. In New York City, for example, the Wollman Skating Rink in Central Park is being rehabilitated. The project has been millions of dollars over budget and years behind schedule. Finally, after the city spent an additional $200,000 to find out what was wrong with the renovation, it gave up and was prepared to start all over again, ripping out the faulty system. Donald Trump, who is a major developer in New York City, wrote a letter to the mayor saying that he could do the work in 4 months rather than the 18 months estimated by the city. An article in the *New York Times* presented a comparison between some of the simplest elements of the job. Both Mr. Trump and the director of capital projects for the city's parks and recreation department agreed that it would take two weeks to put in a new underground piping system for freezing the water and a day or two to pour the concrete slab. Thus, it was agreed that two weeks and two days were required to do the bulk of the physical work. Yet Mr. Trump promised the whole job could be done in 4 months, and the city admitted it could do it in no less than 18 months. Though this is a unique and dramatic case, it is not unusual in the realm of public works projects.

In contracting out, the third type of privatization, recent studies have shown that privately provided services are generally cheaper. A 1984 study by the U.S. Department of Housing and Urban Development found that many services provided by municipalities were more expensive than the same service provided privately. These include:

	Percent more expensive
Street cleaning	43
Janitorial	73
Residential refuse collection	28–42
Traffic signal maintenance	56
Asphalt overlay construction	96
Turf maintenance	40
Street tree maintenance	37

In service provision, basic economics come into play, because the private sector has more flexibility and efficiency in labor deployment, cost control, financing, and overall resource use. Economies of scale that may be available to the private provider may not be available to the public provider, especially if the private provider is a regional or national firm with more buying power and flexibility in the deployment of its resources.

The element of competition also drives down the price. Whether the private sector or the public sector wins a bid doesn't make any difference, because the taxpayers always win. The ultimate aim of privatization is to see that services and facilities are provided at the most efficient level for the constituents.

The Privatization Decision

How does one make a decision to privatize? This is the same type of management decision made by any private sector enterprise — a "make or buy" decision. When planning a new product or service, management breaks it down into components. It will then look at each of the components and make a decision whether it is cheaper or more effective to have some outside firm provide that part or product, or whether the originators should make it themselves. If cities would conduct make-or-buy decisions for all of their services and facilities, they would get the best for their money. And, in most cases, the private sector would win.

Before such a decision can be made, however, the true costs have to be known, and the accounting system has to be able to make valid comparisons, including all indirect and hidden costs. Included in the list of such items are depreciation of the assets that are used in the provision of a service and proper accounting for the overhead.

For example, some local officials have made statements such as "It's costing us only $10 a ton to get rid of the waste at the landfill. Why should we be paying $25 a ton for a private resource recovery plant?" Then, upon analysis, they discover that no management time is allocated for the DPW director to operate the landfill; fringe benefits for all the operators are handled under a different line item; when one of the vehicles breaks down, it goes to a motor pool with a separate budget; and no costs have been allocated for ultimate closure. Sure enough, private business can't compete with something that costs only $10 if somebody else is paying for all the rest.

This strict apples-to-apples cost comparison is not the final decision maker, however. Certainly, cities are not just economic animals — other values have to be served in cities. This type of make-or-buy decision process, however, begins to identify the cost of promoting and maintaining those other values. It gives everyone a clear sense of what it costs to be part of the constituency of the city.

If cities are to privatize effectively, they have to maintain control. The control starts with the request for proposal (RFP) process whereby the city identifies and selects a privatizer. Low bid is not enough, and localities should prequalify responsible bidders — ones who have the financial, technical, and experiential resources to deal with the job at hand. There must be fair and open competition. Clarity is needed, particularly in the requirements for the service provided. Then the selection should be of the most responsive proposer. This approach reflects what lawyers say about a trial: if one selects the right jury, one is nine-tenths of the way home in terms of getting the desired decision. The same holds true with the RFP process — if the right bidder is selected, the community is nine-tenths of the way home.

However, that other tenth is just as important and can really outweigh the selection if it is not handled properly. This 10 percent concerns the service contract that is written with the successful bidder. The contract should always have clarity, clear performance standards, methods of measuring and judging performance, proper incentives for performance, clear penalties for nonperformance, and simple and straightforward dispute resolution procedures so that the service or facility does not get interrupted while the parties argue over whose fault problems are. The city also needs protection. That includes penalties for nonperformance, proper risk allocation known at the outset, proper insurances and credit enhancement where needed, and the ability to replace or remove the operator for nonperformance.

In summary, privatization really represents a spirit, an entrepreneurial drive that all can use, take advantage of, and control. It means increased resources for states, counties, and cities, and it comes with innovation and flexibility. While the private sector does not have a lock on innovation, flexibility, and entrepreneurship, it certainly is the guiding force.

4. Service Shedding— A New Option

Philip E. Fixler, Jr.

Introduction

Since the late 1970s, local governments have faced a variety of fiscal pressures including tax revolts, recession, and cutbacks in some federal-aid programs. In 1986, local governments face even greater threats in the form of proposed tax-reform legislation that could reduce or eliminate the deductibility of local and state taxes, effectively increasing the cost of local and state public services (especially in high-tax states). Also on the horizon is the Gramm-Rudman-Hollings legislation, passed by Congress in 1985, requiring the phasing-in of substantial cuts in the federal deficit beginning in 1986. Federal aid to local governments is a very likely target of these cuts. For these reasons, local policy-makers should be prepared to give serious consideration to one very effective option for reducing expenditures[1] — service shedding[2] — as part of their overall effort to control spending. While service shedding is just one of many possible responses to resource constraint, it is resorted to much less often than other cutback-management techniques.[3]

To the private sector, service shedding is the most radical or "purest" form of what has come to be known as "privatization": the process of turning over activities from the public sector to the private sector (both non-profit and for-profit organizations).[4] Other forms of privatization or quasi-privatization include contracting-out for the delivery of public services and the imposition of user fees to privately finance public services.

Philip E. Fixler, Jr., "Service Shedding—A New Option for Local Governments." Reprinted with permission from The Privatization Review, *Vol. 2, No. 3, Summer, 1986. Published by The Privatization Council, Washington, D.C. (Printed by Maxco Publications, Inc., Little Falls, New Jersey.)*

The essence of service shedding is the manifestation of a theme with a traditionally strong, albeit usually unsuccessful, appeal in the United States—to reduce the size and scope of government. But service shedding represents part of a much more sophisticated strategy (i.e., privatization) than that in which government simply discontinues providing a given service. It involves the relinquishing of an activity, while ensuring that any legitimate needs that government must provide are taken into account. Moreover, privatization incorporates an appreciation of the political interests supporting the provision of services, and how those interests may be placated. The art of implementing service shedding and other forms of privatization is what has been termed micropolitics:

> ... the art of generating circumstances in which individuals will be motivated to prefer and embrace the alternative of private supply, and in which people will make individual and voluntary decisions whose cumulative effect will be to bring about the desired state of affairs.[5]

In light of the relative dearth of scholarly literature examining the service-shedding option,[6] the purpose of this paper is to analyze service shedding and to profile the nature and extent of service shedding by local governments in the United States. It is hoped that this examination will stimulate local policy-makers to incorporate service shedding into their fiscal planning and regard it as a realistic option to reduce expenditures. The importance of including service shedding early in the planning process is best illustrated by the observation of Urban Institute researchers John M. Griener and Harry P. Hatry:

> It is, perhaps, natural for administrators to be reactive rather than proactive during periods of fiscal retrenchment. The emphasis is more on cutting back—and cutting one's losses—than taking the initiative and planning for the future.[7]

The Concept of Service Shedding

The most official definition of service shedding to date is contained in the U.S. Department of Housing and Urban Development's (HUD) *Directory of Alternative Service Delivery Approaches,* which compiles the results of a 1982 International City Management Association survey on alternative service delivery:

> [Service shedding] occurs when a service, which at one time was provided ... by government, has been discontinued. The service may be taken over by another government or authority, for-profit firm, non-profit organiza-

tion or is no longer provided in the community. When a service is "shed" to another government or organization, there may be an initial financial or in-kind contribution by the . . . [involved] government to the new provider, *but there is no continuing financial support.*[8] (Emphasis added.)

The characteristics of service shedding would appear to be that at one time, government provided the service in question, and then relinquished or "shed" the service, either in part or in whole. An implicit form of service shedding can occur when the government either refuses or fails to provide any more of the service[9]; or provides tax incentives to neighborhoods, for example, to agree to forego certain services.[10]

A government could refuse to supply any more of a service, even if it is already providing it, either because of budgetary limitations or a lack of other resources necessary to furnish the service (e.g., qualified personnel). A government might fail to provide any more of a service for reasons such as lack of demand, insufficient resources, or inadequate information. Another reason for failing to provide a service could be simple maladministration.

As a first step in service shedding, local policy-makers must determine which services are most appropriate for relinquishment. Some of the considerations would be the relative importance of the service, and whether the efficiency and effectiveness of service provision would be improved.

Many argue that private-sector organizations can provide many public services more efficiently and effectively.[11] Service-shedding proponents maintain that the private sector can provide services less expensively because private organizations have fewer regulations to comply with, can employ workers at lower salaries, and can more easily recruit committed volunteers. They further argue that private agencies have a higher level of morale and commitment (e.g., religious organizations), which can mean more effective service delivery.[12] Service-shedding proponents also maintain that there are inherent flaws in government provision that are immune to reformist actions.[13]

Some of the drawbacks to service shedding could include service interruptions due to insufficient demand, inadequate service to the poor, unavailability of an organization to assume a given service/function (or enough organizations to offer sufficient competition), and lack of guarantees concerning the future price, quality, and effectiveness of the service.[14]

If, after careful consideration, policy-makers conclude that service shedding of a given activity is both appropriate and feasible, attention must then be directed to the desirability of attaching provisions or conditions to the process. Many incentives could be provided to encourage the private sector to take up a service discontinued by local government. These include tax rebates, credits, and reductions, as well as appropriate deregulation.[15] Tax benefits could be for a limited period of time or permanent.

Provisions might also include some sort of guarantees regarding the service (grants or subsidies up to a certain cutoff date). However, if the guarantees do not include a definite time limit, the concept of service shedding may be lost, or transformed into another mode of alternative service delivery such as "subsidization of a private provider."

Service-shedding provisions may also be based on certain strategic considerations. The first might involve timing—policy-makers might decide to phase out a service over a period of time rather than relinquish it immediately. They could decide to supply the service only during certain periods of time. Or they could determine the optimal time of year to shed the service.

A second set of strategic considerations would be the order in which the service or services could be shed. It might be more appropriate to shed some aspects of a service earlier than others. Moreover, if several related services are involved, policy-makers could determine if certain services should be shed first; or, for that matter, the exact order in which the services should be relinquished.[16]

The third set of strategic questions relates to the area in which service is delivered. Policy-makers could choose to withdraw the service from some areas before others. For example, service would be withdrawn from outer areas before centrally located areas, or wealthier areas before others. Services could be first withdrawn from areas in which nearby firms or agencies could take up the slack. Finally, services might be relinquished on a district-by-district basis.

A fourth set of strategic considerations could be based on socioeconomic characteristics of recipients. For example, services could be withdrawn from higher-income individuals immediately and phased out for lower-income recipients.

As previously suggested, local policy-makers may choose to turn over the service to either a for-profit or non-profit organization. Shedding to one or more for-profit firms should be much more of a straightforward operation. Minimal health and safety regulations could initially be applied to all such providers. These regulations should be directly related to legitimate governmental concerns and should not by intent or effect restrict nor regulate price, entry, or service conditions that might serve to create a private monopoly or government-sanctioned cartel.[17]

If local government turns over a given activity to a non-profit agency, there can be a number of other complexities. An important consideration in determining the feasibility of shedding a particular service could be the anticipated recipient of the service. At least two forms of non-profit associations could inherit services: standard, non-profit voluntary organizations which have had a long history of providing human services (such as the Salvation Army or YMCA)[18]; or one of several types of "micro collectives" such as condominium associations, business complexes (e.g., malls), or neighborhood organizations.[19]

Decisions regarding the appropriateness and feasibility of service shedding are extremely complex and difficult. Those who put forth service shedding as an option should cite the evidence and resources with which to make such assessments. For example, in evaluating the feasibility of service shedding, you should examine whether that is being supplied by the private sector elsewhere, independent of government. In other words, has it been demonstrated that the private can provide this type of service without government involvement such as subsidies or regulatory benefits? Some local policy-makers might be surprised to learn of subscription fire, emergency medical, and even police services furnished to people on an individual (or group) basis.[20]

Another important question to address is whether organizations can be created to take up a given service, or are such organizations already in the vicinity (or could be enticed to come into the area). And finally, has the service been shed by other jurisdictions? How has it been done? Has it been done successfully?

Historical Context of Service Shedding

Although the call for cutting "big government" has been made throughout American history, what generally occurred was the opposite — especially at the local government level.[21] To some, this expansion in the size and scope of local government may have been desirable; to others, undesirable. Regardless, any analysis of the present-day concept of service shedding must be evaluated in the context of the actual outcome.

For this reason, an analysis was done of several studies of U.S. urban history, focusing on the development of urban service delivery.[22] Based on a limited review, three hypotheses can explain why local governments gradually began to provide more and more urban services.

Historical Outgrowth

In the Anglo-American tradition, local streets have been publicly owned and operated. Hence, a number of services related to the streets tended to be provided by government. These include street lights and sewers, and various forms of urban transit. Many local governments initially franchised urban transit to private providers. Transportation economists now generally agree that the politization of franchise regulation, such as price and entry restrictions and operational mandates to achieve social-welfare objectives, caused the demise of urban transit.[23]

Interest Groups

A group of people would organize to pressure government into providing urban services in order to socialize the cost of the service they themselves wanted. Businessmen, through chambers of commerce, for example, sought to spread the cost of public-works infrastructure (transit, roads, bridges, etc.) from which they would disproportionately benefit, to all taxpayers, including laborers and farmers who may not have desired or proportionately benefited from such facilities.[24] Thus, laborers and farmers were denied the opportunity to invest their resources to further their own personal objectives. Civic groups promoted the provision of middle-class amenities such as parks, libraries and even public high schools in which middle-class children who could afford to stay out of the workforce longer, could enhance their skills.[25] Professional groups such as civil engineers and landscape architects viewed local government as an excellent place to establish employment.

Ideological

As the natural rights/limited government philosophy was replaced by a kind of public-interest utilitarianism, people accepted as proper the expansion of the role of government in providing a wide variety of urban services.[26] Many people, for instance, felt that no one should make a profit from supplying vital necessities such as water, and later this was extended to such services as electricity.[27] Many also felt that government had a responsibility to socialize people different from themselves, thus leading government to provide various forms of "cultural" stimulation such as taxpayer-provided or subsidized symphony orchestras, patriotic assemblies, libraries, and public schools. Such activities were intended to inculcate the dominant cultural values into new immigrants and various religious and ethnic minority groups.

With the exceptions as stated above, there appears to be no inherent reason why many of the urban services that have come to be provided by government cannot now be shed to the private sector. First, dominant ideologies can change over time. In recent years, for example, the apparent resurgence of conservatism, libertarianism (or classical liberalism), and free-market ideas (especially among economists) encourages a more serious consideration of turning over public services to the marketplace.

Second, while interest groups will no doubt continue to seek to socialize the cost of services that disproportionately benefit them, and liberal (and conservative) reformers will probably persist in pressuring government to socialize those with other cultural backgrounds using taxpayer-provided services, more and more social scientists and economists are questioning the legitimacy of these efforts.

Finally, in regard to the outgrowth of many urban services due to government ownership and operation of local streets, the fact that local roads were publicly owned and operated is no longer a sufficient justification for public provision or regulation of related services such as transportation. It should be noted that even the monopoly provision of roads by government is being questioned.[28]

Privatization and Service Shedding

The initial (and now classic) major work on privatization was Robert Poole's *Cutting Back City Hall*. In providing hundreds of real-world examples where the private sector was already providing many public services, Poole first identified a phenomenon — privatization.[29]

The next major work was by Professor E.S. Savas in his seminal book, *Privatizing the Public Sector*. Savas makes an excellent case for the proposition that "public services can be provided through a broad range of mechanisms, most of which involve government in more limited roles than conventional thinking allows." In support of this thesis, Savas develops an innovative theoretical framework for the analysis of various goods and services, dividing them into private goods, toll goods, common-pool goods, and collective goods. Through a careful analysis of goods and services now commonly provided by government, Savas demonstrates that many of these goods and services are in fact not the "public goods" that many economists assert can be provided only by government (what Savas refers to as "collective goods").[30] Essentially, Savas narrows down considerably the range of what has been considered "public" or collective goods.

With regard to service shedding (or what he refers to as "load" shedding), Savas suggests that service shedding could be applied to day care, recreation, education, and a variety of public works and public-safety services.[31]

Much of Savas' theory was based on his insightful observations of innovative service-delivery techniques developed by financially pressed American state and local governments in the mid- to late 1970s. But substantial privatization efforts were also to occur in Britain under the Thatcher administration beginning in 1978. The Adam Smith Institute (ASI), a public-policy think tank in London, provided much of the impetus for these privatization efforts. After several years of study, ASI scholars had delineated a theoretical basis for early ad-hoc privatization efforts. This theoretical analysis is the substance of a recent new book, *Dismantling the State: The Theory and Practice of Privatization,* by Dr. Madsen Pirie. Pirie is President of the ASI and one of the leading architects of the

Thatcher government's top-to-bottom efforts to shrink the size and scope of government.[32]

Some of Pirie's major theoretical insights are his ideas on the *inherent* deficiency of government service-delivery, or what others have termed "political failure."[33] Pirie argues that public-sector supply of most services is deficient, and that reforms to improve efficiency in government are temporary at best, and ultimately doomed to failure.[34]

Pirie provides the first in-depth articulation of the strategic sophistication of privatization. His analysis of privatization strategy constitutes a convincing assessment of the potential for the success of this approach. Privatization, unlike simple calls for "government to get out of the ____ business," seeks to construct a scenario, based on a realistic assessment of interest-group dynamics, to shed a given function in such a way as to lessen the concerns of entrenched opposition groups. This would include the use of incentives to neutralize their opposition or actually gain their support.[35]

Pirie believes that privatization, properly implemented, will entail the creation of a ratchet-like, anti-statist mechanism to replace the apparently irreversible Fabian socialism engulfing Western countries for many decades.[36]

In addition to Pirie's theoretical breakthroughs, he itemizes no less than 22 separate privatization methods, each of which has been successfully applied by either national or local government. These 22 methods may be grouped into eight broad privatization categories: service shedding, diluting the public sector, contracting-out, deregulation, incentives, counteracting interest groups, user charges, and vouchers.[37]

Pirie classifies the service-shedding methods successfully employed in Britain as "selling the whole," "selling complete parts of the whole," "selling a proportion of the whole," "selling to the workforce," "giving to the workforce," "giving to the public," "selling off ownership assets," "applying liquidation procedures," and "withdrawal from activity." Particularly relevant to local government are the sale of ferry services and government lands/buildings; giving the provision of hovercraft services over to the workforce; liquidating unneeded hospitals; and eliminating unnecessary public bodies.[38]

Among the areas to which service shedding could be applied by local governments in the U.S. are turning over garbage collection to the private sector by auctioning off trucks and equipment (as did Wichita in 1979)[39]; selling off municipal auditoriums or convention centers[40]; giving title of some residential streets to adjoining property owners (as in St. Louis and other cities)[41]; and at least some withdrawal from land use and building-regulation activities (as in Houston or its surrounding suburbs in Harris County, Texas).[42]

Major media attention to privatization in Britain has focused on the activities of the national government — e.g. the sale of British Telecom — rather than local-services privatization. Policy analysts are beginning to affix privatization concepts to the federal government. The first major effort in this vein was the Grace Commission's Task Force on Privatization. The Commission recommended several forms of service shedding, in addition to contracting-out federal services. For example, the Commission recommended sale of electrical utility assets, phasing out construction of veterans hospitals, and selling federally owned airports. As of 1986, few of the Grace Commission's privatization recommendations have been acted on.

A more comprehensive study of the application of privatization to the U.S. government is Dr. Stuart Butler of the Heritage Foundation in his recent book, *Privatizing Federal Spending.* Butler substantially concurs with Pirie's analysis and proposes privatization as the only realistic means of significantly reducing the size of government in the United States. He fleshes out and further extends Pirie's ideas with the specific intent of applying privatization to major federal domestic problems, including housing, transportation, public lands, welfare, postal service and social security.[43]

Another significant addition to privatization theory is the work of Steve Hanke of Johns Hopkins University. Hanke observes that the essential difference between private and public service delivery is the property rights arrangements that underlie each approach. He argues that private property ownership entails incentives that give private providers an almost inherent superiority over public providers. He buttresses his theory with a comprehensive review of empirical evidence.[44]

Examples of Service Shedding

There are few case studies of service shedding. This is due in part to a lack of documentation as to where service shedding is actually occurring. One major journalistic account focused on an example in Wichita, Kansas, where the city government completely eliminated municipal solid-waste collection services. The precipitating factor was a long and difficult strike of city refuse workers. After the decision was made to terminate city collection, an exclusive franchise system was considered, with the city to be divided into exclusive franchise areas. But the city later rejected the franchising alternative and terminated municipal collection, except for provisions to ensure service for the poor, auctioning off all its trucks and equipment. This function was shed to a marketplace with numerous pre-existing providers who were already serving parts of Wichita and surrounding areas. After the dust had settled, some consumers had higher prices than before (possibly those in lower-density areas that were more costly to serve) and some lower prices (possibly lower-income customers in higher-density areas). But all consumers had a greater choice regarding the type of service they desired (e.g., number of collections per week, and backyard versus curb pickup).[45]

Another example of service shedding was Buffalo's (New York) transfer of its zoo to a non-profit association—the Buffalo Zoological Society. The city did, however, commit to financing a portion of any future operating deficits, thereby partially adulterating the service-shedding concept.[46]

Urban Institute researcher Harry Hatry observes that hospital care is one of the few areas in which service shedding has been relatively extensive. He notes that one company, Hospital Corporation of America, owns or leases 25 hospitals formerly operated by municipalities. Sale and lease conditions in such situations may include provisions for future care of the indigent. This is a problem that has to be addressed in shedding hospital services. Some jurisdictions resolve this problem by directly paying private hospitals to provide indigent care.[47]

Perhaps the most cited examples of service shedding are in reference to the results of Massachusetts' Proposition 2½. The city of Everett, for instance, eliminated emergency ambulance service in January 1982. The service was consequently taken over by private ambulances. Other Massachusetts cities discontinued such activities as driveway widening and unplugging sewer back-ups.[48]

Profile of Service Shedding by U.S. Local Governments

The Local Government Center (a project of the Reason Foundation, Santa Barbara, California) recently computerized data from the 1982 International City Management Association (ICMA) alternative service-delivery nationwide survey, compiled by the U.S. Department of Housing and Urban Development (HUD). The data were structured so as to permit the identification of local governments by the specific local service privatized, including by means of the service-shedding method.[49]

Table 1 shows how many local governments (of those surveyed) have engaged in service shedding. A surprisingly large number (23.9 percent) have resorted to service shedding one or more times. A slightly higher percentage of cities (25.3 percent) than counties (19.5 percent) have implemented service shedding in one or more cases.

As shown in Table 2, most service shedding has been to for-profit and non-profit organizations (56.3 percent), rather than discontinued with no provisions. This percentage is even higher (and may take on more significance) if one particular service—meter maintenance/installation—is excluded from consideration. With this omission, the amount of service shed-

Table 1

U.S. Local Governments Shedding Services in One or More Activity Areas

Jurisdictions	N	% of Total Jurisdictions Surveyed
Cities	346	25.3
Counties	81	19.5
Totals	427	23.9

SOURCE: Privatization Database (ICMA data), Local Government Center

Table 2

Recipients of Service Shedding

Recipient	All Local Governments — N	% of Total
For-Profit	303	39.9
Non-Profit	125	16.4
Discontinue	332	43.7

SOURCE: Privatization Database (ICMA data), Local Government Center

ding to for-profit and non-profit organizations is significantly higher (68.7 percent). Thus, over *two-thirds* of the service-shedding examples identified in the ICMA survey (omitting the aforementioned category) have been turned over to for-profit and non-profit organizations in lieu of straight discontinuance.

In Table 3, the ten highest states are ranked according to instances of service shedding by local governments within their boundaries. It may be of significance that the top three states (on the periphery of the Sunbelt) contain local governments accounting for over one-fifth of the service shedding examples; the first four states (all with large populations) for over one-quarter. In gross terms, one should not be surprised that large-population states would have more examples of service shedding. Further analysis is needed before other conclusions about this data can be made.

The jurisdictions with the most instances of service shedding are ranked in Table 4. The top three local governments in service-shedding activity are counties. It is of interest to note that all three are comparatively low-population counties and that the cities on the list also share this characteristic (with populations of 22,000 or less).

The functional area in which most instances of service shedding has occurred is in public works/transportation (50.8 percent), as shown on Table 5. This is followed by health and human services (19.6 percent) and public safety (13.3 percent). Not unexpectedly, a significant percentage of parks and recreation/cultural arts functions, health and human services, and public-safety activities have been shed to nonprofit agencies (51.6 percent,

Table 3

Ranking of States by Instances of Local Government Service Shedding

State	N	% of Service Shedding
Texas	63	7.8
Florida	52	6.8
California	49	6.6
Pennsylvania	44	5.8
Michigan	41	5.4
Georgia	33	4.3
Ohio	32	4.2
Montana	32	4.2
North Carolina	29	3.8
Kansas	24	3.2
Total	399	52.10

SOURCE: Privatization Database (ICMA data), Local Government Center

Table 4

Ranking of Jurisdictions by Instances of Service Shedding

Name	N	Type of Jurisdiction
Wilbaux, Montana	17	county
Monroe, Georgia	11	county
Highlands, Florida	10	county
Laurel, Montana	8	city
Prattville, Alabama	7	city
Texarkana, Arkansas	6	city
Clearwater, Kansas	6	city
Willimantic, Connecticut	6	city
Dublin, Georgia	6	city
Newport, Kentucky	6	city
Berwick, Pennsylvania	6	city
North Wales, Pennsylvania	6	city

SOURCE: Privatization Database (ICMA data), Local Government Center

32.2 percent, and 26.7 percent, respectively). The percentage of public works/transportation services "discontinued" is also of note (59.6 percent), except that if meter maintenance/ installation is once again omitted, the percentage drops dramatically (37.3 percent). So when meter maintenance/installation is dropped, more than half (56.5 percent) of public works/transportation activities shed are turned over to for-profit firms (in contrast to the 36.1 percent shown in Table 5).

Table 5
Service Shedding by Functional Category

Functional Area	N	% of Functional Area	For-Profit		Non-Profit		Discontinue	
			N	%	N	%	N	%
Public works/transportation	386	50.8	141	36.5	15	3.9	230	59.6
Public Utilities	20	2.6	18	90.0	1	5.0	1	5.0
Public Safety	101	13.3	60	58.4	27	26.7	14	13.9
Health and Human Services	148	19.6	51	34.2	48	32.2	50	35.6
Parks and Recreation/Cultural Arts	62	8.2	5	8.1	32	51.6	25	40.3
Support Functions	42	5.5	28	66.7	2	4.8	12	28.6

SOURCE: Privatization Database (ICMA data). Local Government Center

Table 6
Ranking of Services Shed Most Frequently by U.S. Local Governments

Service	For-Profit	Non-Profit	Discontinue
Meter maintenance/installation	1		138
Commercial solid waste collection	48		6
Solid waste disposal	39		5
Ambulance service	23	10	3
Bus system operation/maintenance	6	3	26
Operation/management of hospitals	12	10	10
Vehicle towing and storage	24		4
Animal shelter operation	8	14	6
Paratransit system operation/maintenance	3	6	14
Residential solid waste collection	21		1

SOURCE: Privatization Database (ICMA data). Local Government Center

Six of the ten most frequently shed services, as shown on Table 6, are within the public works/transportation category: meter maintenance/installation (138); commercial solid-waste collection (54); solid waste disposal (44); bus system operation/maintenance (35); and residential solid-waste collection (22). The fact that solid-waste collection and disposal activities constitute three categories within the top ten is consistent with the observation of some economists that the area is the least like a "public good" and most amenable to private provision.[50]

Summary and Conclusion

This paper has reviewed a number of the complexities involved in service shedding. It has identified the types of evidence and considerations that should be taken into account, and has profiled in a preliminary way the extent of service shedding by local government in the U.S. Over one-fifth of local governments surveyed have engaged in service shedding to one extent or another. Perhaps much of this was in response to financial constraints in the late 1970s and early 1980s (tax revolts, federal cutbacks, and recession). If so, it was most likely done on an ad-hoc basis with relatively little analysis and planning. (Although, in a surprisingly high percentage of examples, services were explicitly turned over to non-profit and for-profit organizations — especially if one service, meter maintenance/installation, is omitted from consideration.)

A great amount of service shedding (22 percent) occurred in three large population states on the periphery of the Sunbelt (containing about 22 percent of the U.S. population). And over half of the service-shedding activity identified in the survey occurred in the public works/transportation area of local government operations (even if frequently shed meter-maintenance/ installation activities are omitted — public works/transportation still has the largest plurality of services shed in comparison to the other functional categories). Solid-waste management and disposal constituted a major subfunction of activities subjected to service shedding (120).

Service shedding is the most controversial and purest form of privatization (e.g., in comparison to contracting-out) and undoubtedly the most radical response to resource constraint. But it also has the most potential for reducing expenditures. Local government policymakers are obliged for this and several other reasons to give careful thought and consideration to service shedding.

5. Public Services and the Private Sector

Terry Peters

Should "public" services be produced by government — or by the private sector?

This issue is generating growing interest nationwide among states and local government officials, especially in the cities. In the wake of taxpayer revolts and retrenchment at the federal level, many municipalities have faced a fiscal crunch. They have begun searching for alternative ways of delivering services, and one of the most popular alternatives is privatization.

Privatization is a new word that means transferring the production of a service — and sometimes other aspects as well — to the private sector.

Forms of Privatization

The most common form of privatization is contracting, in which a government contracts out the production of a service to a private firm while retaining the responsibility for planning and financing the service. The most radical form is full privatization, in which a government ends or phases out its provision of a service entirely, leaving the field open to private firms, non-profit corporations or civic groups.

Other forms of privatization, involving the use of franchises, subsidies and vouchers, fall somewhere between contracting and complete privatization in their degree of reliance on the private sector for service provision.

Government contracting with private companies is not a new practice, but it appears to be growing in popularity. More and more services are being considered for privatization.

Terry Peters, "Public Services and the Private Sector." Reprinted with permission from Texas City and Town, *Vol. LXXI, No. 11, November, 1984. Published by the Texas Municipal League, Austin Texas.*

ICMA Survey

The International City Management Association in Washington, D.C., surveyed 1,780 local governments nationwide (1,433 cities and 347 counties) between March and June 1982 to find out how many were employing alternative means of delivering services, i.e., means other than the exclusive use of government employees.

In a special report on the survey titled *Rethinking Local Services: Examining Alternative Delivery Approaches,* the ICMA defined seven alternatives: contracts, franchises, subsidies, vouchers, volunteers, self-help, and regulatory and tax incentives.

The report, the most comprehensive survey of privatization available, includes separate chapters on the various service delivery alternatives and 32 case studies illustrating examples of those alternatives in cities and counties nationwide.

Contracting

The ICMA survey revealed the services most commonly contracted out to private firms were: vehicle towing and storage, legal services, solid waste collection, street light operation, fleet management and vehicle maintenance, tree trimming and planting, street repair,traffic signal installation and maintenance, labor relations, solid waste disposal, data processing, building and grounds maintenance, and ambulance services.

More than 1,000 of the cities and counties surveyed reported that the above services were being provided in their jurisdictions, and at least 20 percent of the reporting jurisdictions said they were contracting for the services with a private firm. (The highest proportion, 80 percent, was reported for vehicle towing and storage.)

Many cities and counties to not provide some of the services listed in the survey. Of the services offered by fewer than 1,000 of the jurisdictions, five were being contracted to private firms by 20 percent or more of the reporting governments: operation of day care facilities, hospital management, airport operation, and the operation or maintenance of bus and paratransit systems.

Nonprofit Organizations

Contracts with nonprofit organizations were also reported by many cities and counties. Contracts with nonprofit organizations were more common in the areas of health and human services and parks and recreation than in other service classifications.

Twenty percent or more of the reporting governments indicated that they were contracting with nonprofit organizations for operation of day care facilities, child welfare programs, programs for the elderly, hospital management, public health programs, drug and alcohol treatment programs, operation of mental health and mental retardation programs or facilities, operation of cultural programs, museum operation, and operation or maintenance of paratransit systems.

The ICMA survey also included a special classification for contracts with neighborhood groups. Five percent or more of the reporting governments said they had such contracts for crime prevention or patrol, operation of day care facilities, recreation services, and cultural programs.

Franchises

Franchises, the second alternative, are arrangements whereby local governments authorize private organizations to provide a service in a certain geographical area. The governments often regulate the service level or quality, and sometimes the price, but the users pay the service providers directly.

Franchise agreements are not commonly used for a wide variety of services. In the ICMA survey they were in effect in five percent or more of reporting governments for only ten services: residential and commercial solid waste collection, solid waste disposal, bus system operation or maintenance, airport operation, utility billing and meter reading, street light operation, vehicle towing and storage, and operation or maintenance of recreation facilities.

One reason for the limited use of franchises is that they can be employed only for services received by identifiable individuals, since the provider must charge consumers directly. It is easy to identify the users in the case of solid waste collection for example, but not in the case of street repair.

Subsidies and Vouchers

Subsidies are sometimes used by local governments to encourage private organizations to provide a service. They are used most frequently in connection with health and human services, and with bus and paratransit system operation, ambulance service, and the operation of museums and cultural programs, according to the ICMA survey.

Vouchers, the fourth alternative in the ICMA survey, are used even less frequently than franchises and subsidies. Under a voucher system, individuals are issued coupons with monetary value that can be redeemed only through the purchase of a particular service. (The food stamp program is a voucher system.) They are, in effect, subsidies to consumers rather than to service providers.

The rationale behind vouchers is that individuals are given access to a service they might not otherwise be able to afford, but they are allowed to choose among a variety of service providers rather than being limited to one (either the government itself or a contracted or franchised private provider). In this respect, a voucher system resembles a free market.

For only 11 services listed in the survey did even one percent of the responding governments report the use of vouchers. Those services were paratransit system operation, fire prevention and suppression, operation of day care facilities, child welfare programs, programs for the elderly, hospital management, public health programs, drug and alcohol treatment programs, operation of mental health and mental retardation facilities, recreation services, and cultural programs.

Volunteers

Volunteers, as defined by the ICMA survey, are individuals who work without pay for a local government. Although the use of volunteers in recreation programs, libraries and social services — and as firefighters — is not a recent innovation, governments have begun to recruit them for a wider range of services.

The survey results show that public safety, human services, and recreation are the service classifications with the most widespread use of volunteers. Although volunteers may help a local government provide a higher level of service without an additional tax burden, they generally do not contribute to the development of private alternatives to government services.

Self-Help

Self-help is a variation of the use of volunteers in which the volunteer workers are the beneficiaries of their own efforts. Neighborhood watch groups are examples of self-help organizations. Four services were named by five percent or more of the reporting governments as having at least a self-help component in their jurisdictions: crime prevention and patrol, programs for the elderly, recreation services, and cultural programs.

Regulatory and Tax Incentives

The seventh alternative in the ICMA survey is the use of regulatory and tax incentives. By changing the cost of a service these techniques can reduce the demand for the service or encourage the private sector to provide it.

Even less common than vouchers, regulatory and tax incentives were reported to be in use by one percent or more of the responding governments for only 11 services: residential solid waste collection, bus system operation or maintenance, ambulance service, insect or rodent control, operation of day care facilities, programs for the elderly, operation or management of public housing, hospital management, drug and alcohol treatment programs, operation of mental health and mental retardation facilities, and operation of convention centers or auditoriums.

Proposition 13

A significant factor in the recent growth of interest in privatization was California's passage in 1978 of Proposition 13, which slashed property taxes and forced local governments to cut services, raise other revenues, or become more efficient (or some combination of the three).

One result was an increase in government contracting with the private sector in California. A survey on the practice by the California Tax Foundation indicated that the most common reason given for contracting out services was anticipated cost savings.

The advantages of contracting most commonly cited by the survey participants — 92 California cities, counties, school districts and special districts — were availability of special equipment and skilled personnel, reduced cost of labor and material, and avoidance of start-up costs. The disadvantages most commonly cited were difficulty in monitoring contracts, and unreliability of contractors.

Urban Institute Study

Similar views of the virtues and drawbacks of privatization were expressed in a 1973-74 study by the Urban Institute based in Washington, D.C. An updated version of the study, titled *Private Provision of Public Resources: An Overview,* was published in May 1978.

The study recommended that local governments review services on a periodic basis to determine whether some form of private provision might be the most efficient way to provide them. It concluded that the evidence was mixed on whether private contracting was more economical than provision by government employees.

The Case *For* Contracting

A variety of arguments have been made for and against private contracting. The following list summarizes the advantages asserted by its proponents:

- Competition arising from contracting leads to reduced service cost or improved service quality, or both;
- The growth of government, or at least of governmental employment, is limited;
- Persons with specialized skills can be obtained as needed, and without the constraints imposed by salary limitations or civil service restrictions;
- New projects can be undertaken without large initial capital outlays, thus facilitating experimentation with new services;
- The size of a program can be adjusted without employee layoffs or negotiations:
- The full cost of a service becomes more visible, providing a yardstick for comparison;
- Economies of scale can be realized;
- Government managers can devote their attention to planning and monitoring rather than administering day-to-day operations, thus promoting better management and greater objectivity in evaluating current operations;
- The consequences of managerial decisions are borne more directly by the decision maker, since profits are at stake and costs can't be automatically passed on to the taxpayers;
- The need to clearly define services and monitor performance produces management information that is often otherwise unavailable.

The Case *Against* Contracting

Critics of private contracting have raised the following objections to the practice:

- The contractor's profit and the cost of contract monitoring may make services more expensive rather than less so;
- The profit motive leads to cost-cutting practices that reduce the quality of the service;
- The desire to obtain contracts leads some contractors to engage in bribery, kickbacks and payoffs;
- Services may be disrupted if a company declares bankruptcy, goes out of business, or is hit by a strike or work slowdown;

- Public employees may become demoralized and may engage in job actions or bring costly legal challenges against contracting;
- Contracts that clearly define desired services are difficult to write in many service areas, and often have cost-plus-fixed-fee provisions that give no incentive for efficiency;
- Governmental accountability and control is reduced;
- Public policy objectives such as equal opportunity employment or veterans' preference in hiring may be undermined;
- Competition may not exist in a particular service area, and once a company is awarded a contract it may be renewed almost automatically, thus limiting competition;
- Responding quickly to emergencies or major changes in service needs may be difficult because of contract constraints;
- Close monitoring of the contractor's activities is needed to ensure contract compliance;
- Contractors may acquire undue political power;
- Contracting may co-opt nonprofit social service agencies and cause them to downplay their role as a social conscience.

Conclusions

Except in the case of solid waste collection, no systematic comparisons of government service delivery with private service delivery have been reported. There is a great deal of favorable anecdotal evidence on privatization, and evidence of benefits in particular cases, but given the current state of research it would be difficult to prove or disprove the above assertions.

In its discussion of the contracting alternative the ICMA report concluded that local governments are apparently contracting a growing number of services with the private sector. But it said the surveys done so far are not definitive enough to declare it a major trend.

The services that appear to be the best candidates for contracting, the report said, are new services (such as day care), services for which outputs can be specified clearly (solid waste collection), services that require specialized skills (legal) or specialized equipment (sewer cleaning), seasonal services (snow plowing), and services with a large number of providers (solid waste collection).

The other forms of privatization are less widely practiced than contracting and, like contracting, have not been the subject of intensive research.

6. Privatization May Be Good for Your Government

Thomas B. Darr

The anecdotes are endless, and each has its own seemingly unequivocal conclusion. Privatization of public services is either the greatest innovation in government management since Benjamin Franklin's first American fire company or an insidious means of destroying the public work force. For instance:

- Fairfield, California, sought schedule changes and more flexible job descriptions from its unionized firefighters. When negotiations failed, the city of 70,000 northeast of San Francisco contracted for firefighters with a private company. While the new workers only augmented the existing staff, they were willing to work shorter shifts than union members and agreed to perform non-firefighting duties during time spent on neither emergency calls nor training.
- Maricopa County, Arizona, contracted with a private firm in 1982 for computer services after a study by the same firm indicated that the county's own computer operation was too expensive. Four years, many problems and millions of dollars later, Maricopa cancelled the contract and returned to in-house computer operations, with savings estimated by one county supervisor at more than $1 million per year.

Those experiences illustrate one certainty when governments contemplate turning the performance of public services over to the private sector: Nothing about the process is either certain or clear-cut. What works one place or in one circumstance doesn't necessarily work somewhere else. Cost savings can be real or elusive, and problems caused by privatization —

Thomas B. Darr, "Pondering Privatization May Be Good for Your Government." Reprinted with permission from Governing, Vol. 1, No. 2, November, 1987. Published by Congressional Quarterly, Inc., Washington, D.C.

including its impact on public employees — can make its achievement as an alternative means of delivering public services difficult.

"You can't write a textbook to say that one way of delivering public services is better than another," says H. Edward Wesemann, former township manager of the Pittsburgh suburb of Mount Lebanon and the author of a how-to book entitled *Contracting for City Services* (Pittsburgh: Innovations Press, 1982). "All you can do is look at individual circumstances to see what works."

Advocates — including would-be contractors, some academics, some city managers, and politicians looking to save a buck and earn a vote — say privatization saves tax dollars and increases public-sector productivity. Opponents — including labor unions, other academics, some city managers, and politicians looking to save jobs and earn a vote — argue that privatization raises serious issues of accountability, quality, flexibility and integrity.

Despite those reservations, it's clear that more and more functions traditionally performed by public employees are increasingly being turned over to the private sector. "There is not a single city service that is not being contracted out to a private firm somewhere in the United States," said a report issued recently by the National Center for Policy Analysis, a Dallas-based think tank with a free market orientation.

Nearly 80 percent of local government officials responding to a recent survey by Touche Ross & Co., an international accounting and consulting firm, believe that privatization will be a primary tool to provide local government services or facilities in the coming decade. That survey, sponsored jointly by Touche Ross, the Privatization Council and the International City Management Association, found that nearly 60 percent of the respondents contract out their solid waste collection or disposal and 45 percent contract out vehicle towing and storage. Nearly 45 percent contract for building and grounds maintenance, 36 percent obtain administrative services by contract and 31 percent contract data-processing services.

While not directly comparable to similar statistics gathered by ICMA in 1982, the Touche Ross study does seem to indicate growth in most areas of privatized public services. The New York-based Privatization Council, a group of providers and consultants that promotes privatization efforts, estimates that the practice now accounts for more than $100 billion of government services a year, compared to a Council of State Governments estimate of $27 billion in 1975.

The governmental practice of contracting with private firms to deliver public services is not a new concept. In the late 19th century and the first decade or two of this century, transit systems, waterworks and other services usually thought of today as being provided solely by municipal governments often were private enterprises holding public franchises. But cronyism in the award of those franchises and other forms of corruption led to demands for reform. These reforms spawned more professional public management, greater public accountability in the delivery of services, and a decline in the private sector's role in their delivery.

Sustained economic expansion for more than two decades following World War II financed the public's demand for broader services by state and local governments, but fiscal pressures at all levels of government beginning in the 1970s brought this expansive era to a close. In California, Proposition 13 signaled tough times and fewer dollars for state and local governments. At the federal level, continuous deficits forecast a similar message that Ronald Reagan's 1980 election reinforced. What followed were cuts in federal support for state and local government, forcing rethinking of the public sector's role in service delivery. Officials across the country began to look at contracting as a solution — even, perhaps, as a panacea — for their newfound problems.

Rather than being a panacea, privatization may prove to be more of a management tool. Of itself, it may save tax dollars, but in many cases privatization is more likely to save money by forcing detailed government cost and management analyses and by creating external competition for the existing service providers: the public employees.

"Often one of the best results of privatization is that it forces government to reconsider the nature of the service, the rationale for providing it and the means by which it's provided," says Mark Menchik, a senior analyst for the Advisory Commission on Intergovernmental Relations.

Citing the Reagan administration's enthusiasm for privatization at all levels of government, Dan Malachuk, who supervised internal management in the Carter White House and now consults on privatization projects as an Arthur Young & Co. partner, echoes Menchik's comment: "Good things have come from President Reagan's approach, to the extent that it's forced governments to think in more self-sufficient terms."

Cleveland, which earlier this year completed its long fight back from the brink of financial ruin, serves as a good illustration. "We think privatization works in some cases and not in others," says Deputy Mayor Ed Richard. "If properly prescribed, privatization can cut both ways. It can provide cost savings from the private sector and it helps to motivate public-sector people to work more efficiently."

Richard, who founded and ran a manufacturing business for 20 years before joining the administration of Mayor George Voinovich, cites an example from his days as Cleveland's public works director. "We had 11,000 clogged catch basins which we contracted to have cleaned at $42 per basin. Subsequently, our union came to us and said they could do it cheaper. They got the cost down to $19 per basin, and now we don't contract out that service."

Richard and other government officials point to three broad factors —

accurate cost accounting, sensitive labor relations and skillful management — as essential to successful privatization efforts.

Savannah, Georgia, uses industrial engineering methods to routinely examine whether and how it can improve productivity. If the analysis indicates that the regular city work force can be cost-effective, changes are made accordingly. But if contracted services seem to make more sense, city manager Don Mendonsa says he's not at all reluctant to privatize.

A 25-square-mile area Savannah annexed years ago illustrates the disparate results that can occur. The city analyzed service delivery in two critical areas: fire protection and solid-waste collection. Its analysis showed that it would be more cost-effective to contract with the area's existing firefighting force, consisting of both paid and volunteer firefighters, rather than to extend its own municipal force. Mendonsa says fire-insurance ratings in the annexed area remain the same as those in the city, an indication that the quality of service in both areas is similar.

Garbage collection was a different story. The annexed area had been served by private contractor, but Savannah officials suspected that the city might be able to do the work more cheaply. They calculated the city's cost to extend municipal service to the annexed area, then requested bids from private contractors. Mendonsa says most bids were nearly twice the city's estimates of its own costs, and one bid was almost three times as large. The city is now collecting garbage in the annexed area.

"If you're managing the way you should be managing, then you look at the alternatives and determine what's most productive," Mendonsa says. He is quick to point out, however, that Savannah's system emphasizes performance improvements through more effective management, rather than simply branding rank-and-file city employees as unproductive.

While contracting out public services clearly can be cheaper in many instances, the revival of privatization is widely criticized on many grounds other than cost.

Public-employee unions probably have the longest lists. The American Federation of State, County and Municipal Employees, for example, publishes at least a half-dozen booklets detailing the drawbacks it sees to contracting out public services. AFSCME asserts that privatization:

- Masks hidden costs to government, including the expenses of contract preparation and monitoring of contractor performance.
- Emphasizes the profit motive, making contracted services neither cheaper than publicly provided services nor of comparable quality.
- Locks public officials into inflexible contracts that prevent responses to unforeseen circumstances.
- Increases opportunities for corruption.
- Diminishes government accountability to citizens.

Perhaps the one issue that encompasses many of labor's concerns about privatization is that of accountability. Who is in control? Who must answer for shortcomings and failures when government delegates provision of services to private contractors? Does privatization effectively disenfranchise those for whom government was established — the citizens themselves?

"Absolutely," says Abby Haight, a research associate with Local 660 of the Service Employees International Union in Los Angeles. "We found that having a contractor creates a problem with accountability."

Haight says the problem is evident at county-owned golf courses, many of which are now managed by contractors. "It used to be that if there was a problem, there was a county employee at the course for golfers to complain to," she says. "Now we're getting complaints from golfers that the contract employees just don't care. [The contractors have] got the long-term contract and all they want to do is make the profit."

Not that labor is against profit, says Chuck Richards, the AFL-CIO's public-employee department field director. The problem, he says, "is that profit-makers sometimes ignore the original role of government."

"What makes government government?" Richards asks. "Does it have any responsibility any longer to do anything?"

Some observers of privatization argue that efforts to contract out services reflect an abrogation of responsibility based on the inability of municipalities to manage their own services.

Among those observers is Donald Harney, the purchasing agent for Arlington County, Va., who also has worked extensively in the private sector. Harney believes the reasons for the success of privatization of government services are threefold.

First is the ability of private contractors to complete jobs faster and with fewer employees. Harney believes this advantage is the primary consideration in explaining lower private-sector payroll costs, as opposed to suggestions that private-sector wages and benefit levels are typically lower than those of the public sector.

Second, Harney believes that the private sector obtains cost advantages by purchasing more effective equipment better suited to performing specific tasks. Public agencies, Harney says, "purchase equipment to match the budget," while private firms buy equipment "to match the task."

Finally, Harney says the private-sector managers use cost-management techniques more effectively and with greater frequency than do public-sector managers. It's this factor that leads to Harney's main criticism of government and its willingness to privatize services.

"If public officials decide that privatization of a service is best for their community, I submit that the principal reason for the decision is that their organizations don't have the qualifications or expertise to economically manage their own service delivery," he recently told the Northern Virginia annual conference of the American Society for Public Administration. Harney attributes this failure to manage service delivery effectively to two factors: public managers who lack appropriate training and intransigent bureaucracies that hinder the application of innovative cost- and task-management techniques.

Harney's view, repeated by AFSCME Research Director Linda Lampkin in recent testimony before a U.S. House Small Business subcommittee, is that the growth of privatization may ultimately lead to a shift from public-service monopolies to private-service monopolies. The former, Harney says, are controllable, while the latter are considerably less so. In this scenario, Harney believes a limited number of public-service contractors will end up dictating expenditure levels for the delivery of public services.

An example of how privatization might lead to that sort of development occurred in Massachusetts, following the deinstitutionalization in the 1970s of many people who had previously been treated in state hospitals and similar facilities.

Susanne Tompkins, vice president of the Massachusetts Taxpayers Foundation Inc., says the state chose to buy services for people who had been released from institutions rather than provide them directly. The state's goal, she says, was to free itself of the bureaucracy. "We drifted into that policy without thinking about it. The idea was that it would give us competition and the ability to change vendors quickly if there were problems. Frankly, it just hasn't worked that way.

"In many cases the service providers were created in response to the state's need for services. They were private, but not really private because their only client was the commonwealth. That doesn't create competition if the state is the sole service purchaser."

The practical effect of Massachusetts' lack of control of human-service providers has been an overemphasis by both the state and the providers on administrative issues — primarily developing budgets and negotiating providers' rates — and too little emphasis on provider performance, says B.J. Rudman, an assistant secretary in the state's Office of Administration and Finance.

Not that Massachusetts' experience in privatizing public services is all bad. Tompkins of the Taxpayers Foundation says, "I don't mean to suggest that private services haven't worked in many instances, and we continue to do it. I think the decision making could have been more sophisticated, though."

More sophisticated decision making may be part of the impetus for the creation of a separate office within the Massachusetts agency that focuses solely on contract management. Peter Nessen, who heads the office, says its goals include the simplification of administrative systems and the determination of how contract and state employees can be used more efficiently. Or as Nessen puts it, "My first job is to review the contract system to make sure it's the right system to deliver the services."

An AFL-CIO booklet designed to counter the spread of privatization succinctly states labor's case for the retention of government-provided public services: "We must insist that, in a democratic society, government perform and not simply provide certain services and functions.... The bottom line of our social accounting system must differ from that of commercial business."

Labor acknowledges "that there are areas where efficiency can be improved," says the AFL-CIO's Chuck Richards. "We're saying before services are privatized, it's about time that labor and management decide that there doesn't have to be an adversarial relationship 365 days a year. Quite apart from the normal bargaining process, let's just sit down and problem-solve."

AFSCME labor economist Mike Messina says fiscal pressures on local governments, Reagan administration advocacy and the perception that the public sector offers lucrative new markets for American industry combine to cast privatization efforts in a far more positive light than they deserve. But AFSCME's arguments frequently rely on case histories of individual privatization failures rather than on persuasive analysis that the failures themselves constitute a negative trend.

While privatization advocates also rely on the case study approach in efforts to garner support, they bolster their position with more convincing research findings.

One study, conducted by Connecticut-based Ecodata Inc. for the U.S. Department of Housing and Urban Development, compared public- and private-sector costs for eight services, including street sweeping, waste collection and payroll administration, in 20 cities around Los Angeles. Half of the cities contracted out each of the services, while the rest relied on traditional, government-provided public services. The results showed that in seven of the eight areas surveyed, private contractors were able to perform public services an average of 54 percent more cheaply than their public counterparts could. Perhaps more important for those favoring privatization was Ecodata's finding of no essential difference in quality between services provided by contractors and governments.

Not even the AFL-CIO is able to shake the findings of the Ecodata report, although the union contends that HUD was seeking a proprivatization conclusion when it commissioned the study.

"I frankly believe that we probably lose the argument on the cost alone," says the AFL-CIO's Richards. Rather, he points out that the Ecodata study says that neither the public nor the private sector is able to provide services more effectively than the other.

"Repeatedly they talk about no statistical difference in effectiveness [between contracted and municipal services]," says Richards. "We don't make the claim that it's more effective to stay public, but they have consistently tried to make the claim that it's more effective to privatize."

Privatization advocates say the cost savings described in studies like that performed by Ecodata result primarily from productivity gains in the private sector. Opponents argue that public employees can easily match private-sector productivity. They say lower private-sector wages and benefits account for privatization's cost advantage.

Not only do the savings exist, but they can be substantial. The Touche Ross/Privatization Council/ICMA survey of contracted services by local governments reports that 10 percent of those surveyed say they were able to save 40 percent or more by contracting. Forty percent reported savings of 20 percent or more, while 80 percent saved 10 percent or more.

Los Angeles County, with 183 contracts for service in force worth about $44 million annually, offers specific proof of the point. Annual savings amount to $25 million a year, according to Harriet Pope, an L.A. County senior administrative analyst. Among the dozens of contracted services: golf-course operation, embalming, inmate medical services, claims management, equipment maintenance and large-scale records management.

Los Angeles County's employee unions, which represent the majority of county employees, oppose the practice of contracting services. Among their primary points of opposition are suggestions that contracting reflects an ideological predisposition against government (a localized version of the Reagan agenda) and has a disproportionate impact on women and minorities.

According to a 1985 study by the Washington-based Joint Center for Political Studies, a research organization that studies the impact of government policies on minorities, the latter occurs because women and minorities are better represented in the public work force at both ends of the wage scale than they are in the private sector. Thus, public-sector layoffs resulting from privatization tend to erase affirmative action gains of the past two decades.

But Pope points out that of more than 2,800 L.A. County positions cut since contracting began in 1982, only 34 workers have been laid off. Employees whose jobs were targeted for elimination were matched to other county jobs created by attrition, she says.

Guarding against employee layoffs is only part of an extensive analytical process by which the county determines whether privatizing services makes sense. That process, developed by the Arthur Young & Co. government services group, trains county managers to make "step-by-step, apple-to-apple comparisons," says Arthur Young partner Dan Malachuk.

Arthur Young found that much of the financial analysis done by L.A. County managers failed to consider the full cost of publicly provided services, including overhead and employee benefits. With training, however, managers can more clearly make the crucial comparisons to judge whether service delivery should remain in-house or be contracted out.

The decision is made to contract out a particular service based on favorable cost analysis (a by no means universal assumption). Arthur Young also has shown managers precisely how to structure bid requests and contracts and how to prescribe performance measures to ensure that the county gets the kind of services that it has decided it wants.

To protect a municipality from contractor failure and to ensure maximum competition, Malachuk offers several suggestions for governments that have reached the bidding stage. First, request bids from both private firms and from whatever in-house group is currently performing the service.

Second, make sure to preserve some in-house service capacity and never sole-source a contract for all of the required services. Without some form of planned backup, a municipality can easily find itself frantically searching for a garbage collector and being forced to accept unfavorable rates.

Third, be sure to consider service quality and not just price. The lowest bid may offer neither the best quality nor the quality to which citizens are accustomed, causing especially tricky political problems down the road.

Letting the private sector perform public services is a growth industry with a number of skeptics. Often that skepticism is centered in the East and reflects political concern for the interests of a variety of constituencies. Yet the majority of experts would appear to agree that real financial savings are frequently possible, although they are neither automatic nor easily achieved.

"You can almost follow municipal innovation by charting a course from east to west," says Ed Wesemann, the former township manager from Pittsburgh. He adds, however, that while contracting can be a political risk, particularly in the East, the greater risk may be failure to respond to public pressure for municipal services at reasonable costs.

Malachuk of Arthur Young agrees, noting that some of local government's first severe fiscal problems occurred in places like California. But when those problems migrated eastward, the solutions, including widespread efforts at privatization, didn't necessarily follow.

"I see an attitude of some people who won't ever think about privatization," he says. "They'll say they need a different funding source, a wage and hiring freeze, layoffs, or they'll do without before they will consider privatizing.

"The best managers don't look at it as a threat, but rather as another tool to manage productivity. They're aware of the pitfalls, but proceed in a way to minimize the risk. My own sense is that cities get what they deserve."

7. Status of Local Privatization

Philip E. Fixler, Jr., and Robert W. Poole, Jr.

State and local governments in the United States, more than anywhere else in the world, are serving as laboratories for privatization. Virtually every type of service provided by governments — ranging from ambulances to zoning — is being provided privately in one form or another somewhere in the United States. For many "public services," such as residential garbage collection, vehicle towing, and day-care centers, private provision is probably more common than government provision. And the extent of privatization appears to be growing rapidly.

State and local privatization began rather quietly with the contracting out of "housekeeping" and support services — janitorial services in government buildings, vehicle maintenance, computer-center operation, and so on. Since government itself was the customer, it was less controversial to engage in a "make-or-buy" decision for these routine sorts of services. But the cost savings and sometimes greater accountability of private service provision soon led to an expanded scope for privatization. Moreover, because state and local governments were hit by the tax revolt of the late 1970s and the leveling off in federal aid of the early 1980s, they began to look more favorably on shedding certain services to private enterprise, like ambulance service, garbage collection and disposal, and hospitals, or at least contracting them out. The 1981 tax law changes (especially the new, shorter depreciation lifetimes) also contributed to an expansion of

Philip E. Fixler, Jr., and Robert W. Poole, Jr., "Status of State and Local Privatization."
Reprinted from Prospects for Privatization, *The Proceedings of the Academy of Political Science, Vol. 36, No. 3, 1987. Published by The Academy of Political Science, New York, New York.*

privatization, with "turnkey" projects to finance, design, build, and operate costly infrastructure projects.

What has been learned about privatization from the ongoing experiments in the 50 states over the past decade? How likely is the continuation of the privatization revolution?

Growth and Cost Savings

There is considerable evidence to support impressionistic signs that privatization has grown tremendously in the United States since the early 1970s. Probably the best evidence is provided by a National Center for Policy Analysis (NCPA) comparison of the 1973 survey by the Advisory Commission on Intergovernmental Relations (ACIR) and the 1982 survey by the International City Management Association (ICMA).[1] Although the surveys differed in several respects, including sample size, service definitions, and number of respondents, NCPA's analysis of 17 services covered in both surveys indicates significant growth in at least one privatization method—contracting out with for-profit firms. The NCPA analysis indicated that from 1973 to 1982 "the percentage growth ranged from 43 percent for refuse collection to 3,644 percent for data processing (record keeping)."[2]

Other indicators for specific services also support the proposition that there has been significant growth in privatization. A survey conducted by the Michigan Road Builders Association, for example, found that the state and local contracting out of road repair and other highway services grew by 10 percent in the last three years. A comparison of the value of bonds sold to finance wastewater-treatment privatization projects in 1984 and 1985 shows a 400 percent increse. And an analysis of landfill surveys reported in 1975 and 1984 indicates an approximate 129 percent increase in contracting out for solid-waste disposal in landfills.

The 1982 ICMA survey also indicates that certain privatization methods are used more frequently in particular functional areas. For example, the predominant privatization method in public works-transportation, public safety, and support services is contracting out to for-profit firms. The three most frequently used methods for the private provision of health and human services are contracting out with for-profit firms and nonprofit organizations and relying on volunteers. The four most frequently used methods for private delivery of services for recreation, parks, and cultural arts are contracting with for-profit, nonprofit, and neighborhood organizations and enlisting volunteers. With regard to public utilities, franchising and contracting out to for-profit firms are the predominant methods.

One of the major factors leading to the growth of privatization has undoubtedly been the increasing number of state and local governments that have discovered the significant cost-savings potential of privatization. Almost every single quantitative, empirical study has confirmed this phenomenon, including a 1975–76 study of solid-waste collection sponsored by the National Science Foundation, a 1977 study of fire-protection services conducted by the Institute for Local Self Government, a 1983 study of solid-waste collection in Canada by researchers at the University of Victoria, a 1984 study of school bus transportation in Indiana by researchers at Ball State University and elsewhere, and a 1984 study of Federal support services in the Department of Defense as reported by the Office of Federal Procurement.

A 1986 study of urban bus transportation by researchers at the University of California, Irvine, found that privately owned systems were more efficiently operated and required less in subsidies than publicly owned systems.[3] However, the study also found that there was no significant difference in costs when publicly owned systems contracted out the *management* function for urban bus transportation. However, the authors of the study suggested that this exception to the findings of other studies of contracting out could be due to the high number of fixed-cost or percentage-of-revenue contracts and the fact that the management function is a small, nonlabor-intensive portion of a larger service function. This latter point is supported by the fact that there is some evidence that contracting out the *entire* transit function leads to cost savings of about 50 percent.

The most comprehensive study of contracting out was conducted by Ecodata, Inc., for the U.S. Department of Housing and Urban Development.[4] The 1984 Ecodata study compared government versus contractor delivery of eight public services by cities in the Southern California area. The study compared 20 different cities for each service, 10 providing the service in-house and 10 using contractors. For 7 of 8 services, direct government provision was 37 to 96 percent more costly than when provided by contractors. The one exception was payroll processing. But, as with the transit study, the researchers suggested that there could be special causes. Payroll processing, in contrast to other services, is not so much a separate, distinct service because the cities themselves provide and process the raw data and distribute the checks. Thus, as with transit, the anomaly could be explained by the fact that the contractors were handling only a portion of a larger function and had no real comparative advantage. In sum, there is moderately strong quantitative evidence that privatization has grown dramatically and that it has yielded significant cost savings for a variety of services.

Review by Functional Area

As indicated above, routine support services are among the first areas to which privatization and partial privatization have been applied. Nineteen percent of the cities and counties responding to the ICMA's 1982 survey indicated, for instance, that they contract out for building and grounds maintenance with for-profit firms. There are many examples of cost savings from contracting out building and grounds maintenance. At the local level, Little Rock, Arkansas, contracted out its city hall janitorial services in 1977, cutting its total costs for this work by almost 50 percent;[5] Cypress, California, saved 20 percent, and Phoenix, Arizona, 57 percent. At the state level, Oregon State University, contracting out building maintenance to a for-profit firm, saved about 21 percent. California and Pennsylvania contract out for the cleaning of some state buildings.

Data processing is another support service often contracted out at the local level. A comparison of responses to the 1973 ACIR and 1982 ICMA surveys indicates that the rate of increase in contracting out for this service has been nothing short of phenomenal — 3,600 percent. One of the first areas in this trend was Orange County, California. After contracting out its data-processing function in 1973, the county saved about 33 percent, according to one estimate.

Fleet maintenance and management is yet another housekeeping service that has been contracted out. In the 1982 ICMA survey, 28 percent of the reporting cities and counties contracted out with for-profit firms for fleet management and vehicle repair. An even higher number contracted out for maintenance of specialized vehicles: 30 percent for emergency vehicles and 31 percent for heavy vehicles. Gainesville, Florida, began contracting out its vehicle repair work several years ago, with an estimated savings of 20 percent.[6]

The provision of food service in public facilities is another partially privatized support service. Many city and county cafeterias are franchised or contracted out, but perhaps more significant is the contracting out of food service in public institutions, such as schools, correctional facilities, and hospitals. One special district, the Evergreen School District near Vancouver, Washington, began contracting out for food service as far back as 1976, after many years of in-house provision. In contrast to the years of deficits under in-house provision, contract provision allowed Evergreen to operate in the black after the first year. In Oregon, Multnomah County contracts out food service at its correctional facility.

In recent years, after the success that many jurisdictions have had contracting out routine housekeeping services, some jurisdictions are beginning to apply this privatization method to higher-level support services, including those traditionally provided by professional-level personnel, such as attorneys and accountants. Probably the most frequently contracted-out support function is that of legal services. A comparison of responses to the 1973 ACIR survey and the 1982 ICMA survey indicates a 421 percent increase in the contracting out of legal survices. According to the 1982 ICMA survey, 48 percent of the reporting cities and counties contracted out for legal services. Many small towns and cities traditionally contract out with local law firms to obtain legal representation and even a city attorney. But now larger jurisdictions are finding it advantageous to contract out public legal services normally provided in-house. For instance, Los Angeles County contracts out for some of its public-defender services. Shasta County, California, turned over its entire public-defender function to a local law firm after a study indicated that the cost of providing the service in-house was about one-third more than contract service. And in Washington state, at least seven local governments contract out for some public defender services.

Tax collection is also a professional-level support function that is frequently contracted out. The 1982 ICMA survey reported that tax bill processing was contracted out by 10 percent of cities and counties, assessing by 27 percent, and delinquent tax collection by 18 percent. For property-tax assessment, an explicit industry has developed in many states. And "although some states forbid cities or counties to contract out for this service, Ohio actually requires contracting."[7]

Recreation and parks is another major functional area of state and local activity to which privatization and partial privatization have been applied. According to the 1982 ICMA survey, 19 percent of the reporting cities and counties used volunteers to provide recreation services and 12 percent contracted out with non-profit organizations. For the operation and maintenance of recreation facilities, however, the predominant privatization methods were different: 9 percent contracted with nonprofit firms, 8 percent with for-profit organizations, and only 4 percent relied on volunteers. A comparison of responses to the 1973 ACIR and the 1982 ICMA surveys indicates that contracting out for recreation facilities increased by a dramatic 1,757 percent.

A major impetus for the contracting out of recreation services and the operation and maintenance of recreational facilities in California was Proposition 13. Most of the contracting out of recreation services has traditionally been to non-profit organizations. The Hesperia Recreation and Park District, for instance, cut its budget by 37 percent by contracting out with the local YMCA for the provision of recreation services. But several California jurisdictions contract out with *for-profit* organizations for recreation and parks services. La Mirada, California, for example, began contracting out its recreation and park services to a for-profit firm in 1980, after the revenues of the independent park district previously supplying the service were cut by 50 percent.

Public utilities constitute another major functional area to which some type of privatization has been applied. There has been some contracting out of utility support-services, such as utility billing and meter reading to for-profit firms. Again, comparing responses to the 1973 ACIR and 1982 ICMA surveys, the contracting out of utility billing to for-profit firms increased by some 65 percent over that period. The 1982 ICMA survey indicates that 12 percent of reporting jurisdictions contracted with for-profit firms for this service, 8 percent had franchises providing service, and 1 percent contracted with nonprofit organizations. Lake Oswego, Oregon, contracts out utility meter reading to a private for-profit firm that uses innovative methods, such as requiring its readers to use motorcycles and to make tape recordings for later transcription.

Another major application of privatization to utility service is that of contracting out the operation and maintenance of water-supply or treatment to for-profit companies. In Pennsylvania, for example, a number of municipalities that took over regulated water companies supplying their area continued to contract out for water-system operation and maintenance. As a matter of fact, the Pennsylvania-based American Water Works Company manages government-owned water and sewer facilities for more than 95 communities and serves over 500,000 people in Pennsylvania.

Recently, according to representatives of the American Water Works Association, several jurisdictions in other states have begun to contract out for the operation and maintenance of water supply or wastewater-treatment facilities, including Chandler and Scottsdale, Arizona; Decatur, Illinois; and Pampa, Texas. Several states have passed enabling legislation for wastewater-treatment privatization projects, including Alabama, Arizona, Arkansas, California, Colorado, Georgia, Louisiana, New Jersey, New York, Tennessee, and Utah.[8]

Public works and transportation are probably the general functions to which privatization techniques have been applied the most. Unquestionably, solid-waste collection and disposal is one of the earliest and most basic public-works services contracted out to the private sector. The most comprehensive United States study on the subject, sponsored by the National Science Foundation, indicates that as of 1976–77, about 62 percent of United States cities relied on some form of private provision of residential solid-waste collection (e.g., contract, franchise, private-competitive), although municipal agencies served 61 percent of the United States population. Major urban areas relying, at least in part, on some form of private collection include Atlanta, Houston, Los Angeles County, San Francisco, and Wichita.

As indicated earlier, there has also been a significant increase in contracting out for the operation and maintenance of landfills. A survey conducted by the Association of State and Territorial Waste Management Officials (ASTWMO) and *Waste Age* magazine in 1985 indicates that 444, or 6.4 percent, of publicly owned landfills are contracted out.

Contracting out has also been extensively applied to a variety of other basic public-works services. According to the 1982 ICMA survey, reporting cities and counties contract out 30 percent of their tree trimming, 26 percent of their street repair, and 9 percent of their street cleaning to for-profit firms. At the state level, there is also evidence of increased contracting of highway sweeping and repair. The state of Washington, for example, contracts out for some highway sweeping. And North Carolina has recently initiated a pilot program for the routine mowing of highway strips, cleaning up rest areas, and operating some drawbridges.

In the last few years there has been a significant increase in the use of another form of privatization for certain public works — wastewater-treatment, resource recovery, and water supply. Essentially, this form of privatization involves a significantly greater role for the private sector, beyond mere operation and maintenance of existing facilities. It means the provision of "full services" on a "turnkey" basis, that is, financing, design, construction, operation and maintenance, and sometimes even ownership. A number of factors brought this about, including increasingly stringent environmental regulation, tax incentives for private infrastructure development, and a decline in federal funding for these types of projects.

For these reasons, local jurisdictions across the country have initiated infrastructure privatization projects. Chandler, Arizona, began the first major wastewater privatization project when it entered into a service contract with a large engineering firm to purchase treatment-reclamation services from a $23 million, 5-million-gallons-per-day treatment plant to be constructed. At least fifteen jurisdictions have begun steps toward similar privatization projects since that time, including Auburn, Alabama; Baltimore, Maryland; Baton Rouge, Louisiana; Downington, Pennsylvania; East Aurora, New York; Gilbert, Arizona; Greenville, South Carolina; Hubbard, Ohio; Jefferson Parish, Louisiana; Oklahoma City, Oklahoma; San Luis Obispo, California; Smithville, Utah; Snyderville, Utah; and Springboro, Ohio.

Transit is another major service area to which privatization and contracting out have been extensively applied. Some of the principal reasons include the increasing perception of the failure of local bus and fixed-rail systems, deregulation of smaller forms of transit like minibuses and taxicabs, and the discovery of the cost effectiveness of contracting out for some transit services.

The factor that characterizes all types of government-operated or -regulated transit services is probably increasing costs. Largely because of increasing costs, many jurisdictions decided to contract out for special transit services to meet low-volume demand, such as service on Sunday or at night and service to the elderly and the handicapped. Phoenix, Arizona, for instance, replaced costly, subsidized Sunday bus service with dial-a-ride service provided by a private taxi company in 1981. The city subsidy for this service has been reduced by an estimated 500 percent because of this switchover.[9]

Many cities' transit districts have become dissatisfied with the cost of municipal bus service, and several have begun contracting out or sponsoring peak-hour commuter service, including Houston, Los Angeles, and San Francisco. The Dallas transit district, however, leads the country. It contracts with Trailways for extensive suburban bus service involving hundreds of buses. And private (subscription, subsidized, or unsubsidized) commuter-bus service exists or has recently begun in Boston, Chicago, Los Angeles, and New York.

Westchester County, New York, contracts with 16 bus companies to provide countywide service. The cost of operating Westchester County's contract buses is about 50 percent less than that of comparable New York City transit district buses.

Another major method of fostering the private provision of urban transit is deregulation. Transit deregulation is a growing trend. The Federal Trade Commission (FTC), for example, reported on a study indicating that from 1977 through 1982, 16 of 103 cities surveyed reduced entry controls, while only 3 increased them; 17 deregulated fares and 13 eliminated controls over fares; and 4 changed from mandatory to maximum fares. Cities deregulating entry or price included Berkeley, Sacramento, and San Diego, California; Charlotte, North Carolina; Phoenix and Tucson, Arizona; and Seattle, Washington.

Privatization is also being increasingly applied to another major functional area—health and human services. Nonprofit organizations seem to be providing more and more of these services. Recently there has been increasing interest in expanding the role of for-profit organizations in providing them. One manifestation of this trend is the willingness of nonprofit organizations to set up for-profit subsidiaries.

One of the first services that many local governments contracted out or otherwise privatized was hospitals. A comparison of responses to the 1973 ACIR and 1982 ICMA surveys indicates that the contracting out of hospital management and operation to for-profit firms increased some 53 percent. According to the 1982 ICMA survey, 25 percent of the reporting cities and counties contracted with for-profit firms; 24 percent contracted with nonprofit organizations; and 4 percent subsidized private hospitals. Several California counties, for example, contract out the management and operation of their hospitals to private organizations. Sonoma County, for instance, reduced its subsidy by more than 50 percent in the first year after turning over the operation of its county hospital to a for-profit chain.

In some cases, local public hospitals have been converted into private, nonprofit entities. At least eight major government-owned hospitals have been converted into private, nonprofit hospitals since 1980. Others have awarded management contracts to for-profit firms. And in a few cases, local governments — for example, York County, South Carolina, and Detroit, Michigan — have turned over their hospitals almost completely to for-profit companies.

A recent trend is for some local governments and state universities to lease or otherwise contract out their teaching hospitals to the private sector. The most notable example is the University of Louisville, which leases its hospital to the Humana Corporation, renowned for its implantation of artificial hearts.

Several states also contract out for the management and operation of specialized state hospitals or health facilities. Florida, for example, contracts out the management and operation of its South Florida State Hospital, and Kentucky contracts out to a for-profit firm the management and operation of one of its four facilities for the mentally retarded.[10]

Other specialized health services in which there is increasing private interest include community mental-health services and alcohol-drug rehabilitation. According to the 1982 ICMA survey, 38 percent of reporting cities and counties contracted out for the operation of mental health and retardation programs or facilities to nonprofit organizations; 15 percent subsidized private organizations; and 6 percent contracted with for-profit firms. For drug-alcohol treatment programs, 38 percent contracted with nonprofit organizations, 12 percent subsidized private organizations, and 6 percent contracted with for-profit firms.

Public safety is the last, and probably most controversial, major function to which privatization is being applied. Fire protection is one example. Of course, essentially private volunteer organizations protect thousands of small towns and rural settlements. But the private provision of fire protection by for-profit firms is increasingly controversial. Today, even though the cost-savings potential is high, out of a total of 36 public agencies that contract out for private fire protection, only a few jurisdictions actually contract out for *general* (residential and commercial) fire protection, including Scottsdale, Arizona; Elk Grove, Illinois; and Hall County, Georgia. This, of course, is due to the intense political opposition to private fire protection. As a result, the latest trend is to contract out for specialized services, such as fire protection at airports. Five jurisdictions currently rely on private firms to protect their airports, including Sioux City, Iowa; Kansas City, Kansas; Manchester, New Hampshire; Reno, Nevada; and Dane County, Wisconsin.

Corrections is another controversial service for the application of privatization. At least three local governments now contract out for the management and operation of local jails to for-profit firms, including Hamilton County, Tennessee; Butler County, Pennsylvania; and Bay County, Florida. Ramsey County, Minnesota, contracts out for the operation of its local women's prison to a nonprofit organization.

Several states, including New Jersey and Rhode Island, already contract out for the management and operation of juvenile corrections centers. Other states are interested in privatizing their prisons. Three Western states — Montana, New Mexico, and Texas — have passed enabling legislation to allow their cities and counties to contract out the operation of local jails. The governor of North Carolina has proposed a minimum-security prison for adult males. And Kentucky has gone as far as issuing an official request-for-proposal for a private, maximum-security prison. California's Corrections Department, however, has taken the lead. It recently contracted out the management and operation of several minimum-security, return-to-custody facilities for parole violators to for-profit firms.

Finally, police services are undoubtedly the most controversial public-safety application of privatization. Yet about one-fourth of the country's large and medium-sized police departments already deputize or give special police powers to private-security personnel. In Oregon, North Carolina, and Maryland, the governor can designate private-security personnel as "special policemen" under certain circumstances. In one recent survey, 44 percent of public law-enforcement executives reported that local or state governments in their jurisdictions contract out with private agencies for the protection of public property, including schools, libraries, hospitals, parks, and government buildings. Private for-profit firms provide security for public buildings and facilities in Denver, Houston, Los Angeles County, New York, San Francisco, and Seattle.

Jurisdictions that have contracted out for the patrol of their public parks or housing authorities include San Diego and Norwalk, California; Saint Petersburg, Florida; and Lexington, Kentucky. Other jurisdictions contract out for traffic control or parking-lot enforcement, including Arizona Department of Transportation, the University of Hawaii at Hilo, and the Eastern Idaho Regional Medical Center. Finally, there is some degree of contracting out for prisoner transport. For example, Santa Barbara County, California, contracts with private firms to transport some prisoners from faraway jurisdictions.

While there are no United States jurisdictions now contracting out for general police service, some have successfully done so in the past.[11] Currently, the only truly private police in the United States are in San Francisco, where the police commission licenses private individuals trained at the police academy to provide police-patrol services along certain "beats."

The private police licensees, who are uniformed and armed, are hired by merchants in their patrol areas.

Overcoming Privatization Problems

While the dramatic growth in privatization has been quantitatively demonstrated and innumerable success stories published, a review of some privatization failures is certainly appropriate in any broad survey of the subject. Criticisms of privatization by the American Federation of State, County and Municipal Employees (AFSCME), for example, have focused on a number of problem areas, including unrealized cost-savings, low quality, corruption, lack of control and accountability, and reduced services to the poor.[12]

Unquestionably, as AFSCME and other critics have observed, contractors may on occasion bid too low to obtain a government contract and subsequently try to raise the price to make up for initial losses. AFSCME refers to this as "low-balling." If unable to recover initial losses, contractors may default on the contract, thus requiring the governments that depended on them to expand additional reserves in restarting public departments or in obtaining new contractors.

The city of Garden Grove, California, encountered such a situation. The city began contracting out its street-sweeping service in about 1977. After the city awarded a five-year contract, the contractor requested renegotiation because of substantial increases in the cost of labor and fuel. It was also clear that the contractor might default on the contract. The city knew it could not quickly bring the service in-house or obtain a contractor who could provide all of the service needed by the city. City officials feared significant price increases in the future.

But Garden Grove resolved the problem by dividing the city into two districts and rebidding the service. By doing so, the city was able to generate greater competition, because smaller bidders were capable of handling the service when the contract area was reduced in size. Moreover, the city reduced its dependence on a single contractor. The city public-works director was satisfied that the city had met its objective of increasing competition and reducing its vulnerability to price increases and service defaults.

Another potential problem is that of reduced quality of service. One approach to dealing with this problem is, of course, to develop detailed specifications and performance standards. In some cases, however, the contractor may be unable to comply with these requirements. Cypress, California, faced such a problem in contracting out janitorial service. After terminating one contractor, the city determined that it should modify its bidding process so that the bid would be awarded to the lowest, qualified bidder and not necessarily just the lowest bidder. Although there were minor losses in flexibility because of contracting out, the city was generally satisfied with the quality of service, and it estimated a cost savings of 20 percent.

The lack of accountability and control are other potential problems with privatization. These problems, of course, can occur in public as well as private organizations. The civil-service system, for instance, may prevent policy-makers and public executives from imposing accountability and exerting control over a work force delivering a service. If a contract is badly drawn, similar problems could occur with contractors providing a service. But various jurisdictions have developed techniques that could help ensure accountability and control. Cypress, California, for instance, has the right to ask its custodial-services contractor to remove unsatisfactory employees and to deduct the cost of doing incomplete work from the contractor's fee. Gainesville, Florida, built incentives and penalties into its vehicle-maintenance contract. Hall County, Georgia, requires its contract fire chief to report to the city manager to discuss and resolve management problems and issues. La Mirada, California, requires its recreation-services contractor to take part in city staff meetings. Loma Linda, California, can adjust the contract price downward if its landscape maintenance contractor fails to perform the specified work. And Pasadena, California, requires its landscape-maintenance contractors to submit daily work schedules to city monitors. These are just a few of the techniques developed by United States local governments to enhance accountability and control.

Corruption can also be a problem when contracting out a service. AFSCME, for example, cites dozens of cases where the contracting out process was corrupted by payoffs, bid-rigging, price-fixing, and kickbacks. Such incidents have occurred in some of the country's largest cities, including Chicago, New York, and Philadelphia. Yet one must remember that there are tens of thousands and perhaps hundreds of thousands of contracts awarded each year by state and local governments. An in-depth, systematic analysis would likely indicate that although corruption is a problem, it is not a major one.

One example of corruption cited by AFSCME was the award of Union City, New Jersey, contracts to businesses owned by the mayor. But this obvious conflict-of-interest could have been easily avoided by requiring bidders to have no connection with current city employees or officials.

Corruption and many other problems are often due to flaws in the bidding or contracting-out process itself and are easily correctable. "The basic answer to the potential-corruption problem is to make use of rigorous, open-bidding procedures. Such procedures include a clearly defined Request for Proposal, spelling out the specific service requirements, written evaluation criteria, public access to all meetings and hearings, and written records dealing with the selection process."[13] An excellent source of workable procedures is *Contracting Municipal Services,* edited by John Tepper Marlin.[14]

A final problem that might arise in connection with the use of privatization is that of ensuring service to the poor. This is not so much a problem when government contracts out a service, because the service remains a tax-financed activity. However, when a privatization method that entails financing by service users is implemented (e.g., user fees, franchises, service shedding), a problem could arise—the same problem that faces many local governments that transfer their public hospitals to the private sector. One frequent strategy to cope with this problem is to reserve a portion of the proceeds from the sale to finance services to the poor. The state of Michigan used another approach in regard to patients treated at the Detroit General Hospital after that city turned over the hospital to a private organization. Michigan "agreed to reimburse the hospital for the costs of treating indigent patients not covered by federal Medicaid."[15] The use of vouchers is another possible method of dealing with this problem.

Barriers to Privatization

There are several potential obstacles to the continued growth of privatization. Two of these are in the hands of Congress. federal tax laws greatly accelerated the move toward private development of infrastructure projects during the past few years. But critics have attacked the use of tax-exempt bond financing, investment tax credits, and short depreciation schedules that have helped make these projects attractive to private firms. The 1986 tax-reform legislation limits the extent of tax-exempt revenue bonds, repeals the investment tax credit, and increases depreciation periods. Some projects that would have worked out under the old laws will no longer do so, and hence, will not be built by private enterprise. Instead, being built by municipalities, they will remain off the tax rolls, generating neither corporate income taxes nor local property taxes. In the name of reducing "tax expenditures," the federal government will actually lose revenue to the extent that the changes succeed in discouraging privatization.

Another potential barrier is Congress's circumvention of the Gramm-Rudman-Hollings Act of 1985. In spite of this spending-reduction measure, state and local governments could continue to receive significant revenues from the Federal government. Cushioned by these funds, they will be under less pressure to seek out more cost-effective means of service delivery, like privatization. For example, the Reagan administration has sought to terminate subsidies to local transit systems via the Urban Mass Transportation

Administration. The loss of such subsidies would lead to drastic changes in local transit systems, with significant replacement of costly centralized service by lower-cost, flexible private providers. Continuation of the subsidies, however, will probably prolong the existence of today's bureaucratic-centralized systems.

Actual barriers to privatization exist in many states, generally embedded in state statutes or local-government charters. These barriers include outright bans on shedding or contracting out certain services, limits on the application of user fees and vouchers, laws requiring private contractors to pay employees as much as public employees receive, and laws imposing other onerous requirements on private firms. During the past few years a number of states have enacted privatization enabling legislation, usually to authorize privatization in a specific field (e.g., corrections, wastewater treatment) but sometimes to authorize general contracting-out. The Privatization Council published a compendium of state laws on privatization in April 1986.[16]

One of the major barriers to privatization continues to be employee opposition, which is often translated into political decisions not to privatize. Public employees fear that privatization will mean either the loss of their jobs altogether or at least a reduction in pay and fringe benefits. While either of these consequences may occur, public-sector managers in many jurisdictions have developed a number of techniques for reducing negative impacts on employees and thereby reducing or defusing their opposition.

There are three basic approaches: assisting those who go to the private sector, helping those who stay in the public sector, and easing the personal-adjustment process. One of the most important examples of the first approach is for the governmental unit that is contracting out a service to require the contractor to give the current government employees the right of first refusal for most or all of the jobs under the contract (generally excluding management positions). There are a number of variations of this provision; some governments require only that jobs be offered to current employees; others require that they be hired, at least for an initial period.

A newer technique is to assist public employees in forming companies to take over work previously performed in-house. One example would be to make the initial contract award on a sole-source basis to the former work force organized as a private enterprise. In subsequent rebidding of the contract, the new firm would have to compete against commercial bidders. The city of South Lake Tahoe, California, contracted out the provision of bus service to a company formed by two former city employees who engineered a buyout and designed an employee stock ownership plan. National Freight Corp. and Hovercraft Services are examples of successful British privatization that involved employee and management buyouts, sometimes for nominal sums.[17]

Another important way of reducing employee fear and opposition is to adopt a no-layoff policy. In such cases, the city government may decide that any net reductions in staffing levels due to privatization will be dealt with via attrition and transfers to other departments, rather than via layoffs. Both Los Angeles County (a leading practitioner of contracting out) and the federal government have formal no-layoff policies. Attrition is especially useful if only a portion of a department's services are contracted out at one time, so that fewer people are affected at once. If attrition and transfer opportunities are too limited, a jurisdiction can at least adopt a "rehire" policy giving preference to those laid off.

Other options include using some of the money saved during the first year of privatization, either for one-time redundancy payments to the displaced employees or to pay for their retraining for other jobs. Another possibility is to provide incentives for early retirement. In Canada, for example, the government offered early retirement to older custodial personnel as part of its program of contracting out public-works cleaning services. Displaced workers may also be allowed to retain certain fringe benefits, at least for a while. When the federal government transferred its Alaska Railway to the state of Alaska, the former federal employees were allowed to remain in the federal pension system.

Techniques for overcoming or defusing employee opposition have been spelled out in several recent publications. A detailed catalog of such methods is provided in *Employee Incentives for Privatization,* developed by the federal government's Privatization Concerns Task Group and published by the U.S. Office of Personnel Management (OPM), and the OPM's "FED CO-OP: An Alternative Contracting Out Approach."[18] The issue is also addressed in the Council on Municipal Performance's excellent handbook, *Contracting Municipal Services.*

Conclusion

As should be clear from this overview, privatization has grown rapidly at the state and local levels in the United States. From the contracting out of mundane housekeeping services to the provision of such sensitive functions as fire protection, jails, and even police patrols and the provision of large-scale infrastructure, privatization has become an important new way for public-sector managers to provide needed public services.

What accounts for the popularity of privatization in the face of strong status-quo opposition? One very important factor has been the growing cost-revenue squeeze on government. Beginning with the tax revolts in the 1970s and continuing through the Reagan efforts to slow the growth of federal spending, the era of big-spending government appears to be over — or at least suspended. Fiscal pressures have thus forced most governments to seek more for their money, usually through privatization.

Another factor is that the intellectual climate supports a turn away from government programs and toward private enterprise. Several decades of scholarly work under the headings of "law and economics" and "public choice theory" have applied the insights of economics to the political and bureaucratic realms. As a result, scholars, writers, and commentators today take a much less naive view of government administrators and public employees. They can now be seen objectively as people seeking to advance their own interests, like everyone else in society, rather than as textbook figures pursuing an idealized public interest. Moreover, several decades of empirical studies of government versus private provision of services have demonstrated the general superiority of profit incentives over bureaucratic incentives.

This intellectual shift is reflected in popular attitudes, which have grown increasingly skeptical of big government over the past two decades. Moreover, entrepreneurs have become the United States's new culture heroes. Thus it is hardly surprising that substituting competitive, entrepreneurial private enterprise for big-government bureaucracies would prove to be a popular program, when presented in those terms.

Finally, one would do well to appreciate the decentralized American federal system. It is precisely the fifty-state, thousand-city system that has allowed the freedom to experiment with various forms of private service delivery. It has, moreover, given the economists and political scientists the diversity of examples and multiplicity of data points needed to draw empirical conclusions. And those empirical conclusions again and again point to the superior flexibility, responsiveness, and cost-effectiveness of privatization.

Part Two: The Process

8. Contracting as an Approach to Public Management

Ted Kolderie and Jody Hauer

City managers continue to try to extricate themselves from the bind of limited or declining resources and the constant or increasing demand for services. Of the various ways to do this one of the most common, according to an International City Management Association report, is the purchase of services arrangement: Cities make the buying decision, but purchase the production of the service, either from another unit of government or from private organizations. This concept of contracting is not new. But there are different ways it can be used which make it a much more flexible and useful strategy than traditionally thought.

In this article we explore the *variations* of contracting for services. Cities can purchase a service, or they can break the service down into its different components and buy certain elements of it: pieces of the work itself, support services for the work, the supervision of the work or of the support services, or the equipment and facilities needed for the work. We also look at how the "purchase of service" arrangement creates incentives for improved program *management*. With the option to renew contracts, a city has a mechanism for holding the producers accountable for their performance.

Variations on the "Contract" Model

The "base line" from which we begin in thinking about the public sector is the classic administrative bureau, in which the entire service is

Ted Kolderie and Jody Hauer, "Contracting as an Approach to Public Management." Reprinted with permission from Municipal Management, *Vol. 6, No. 4, Spring, 1984. Published by the Department of Public Administration, Barney School of Business and Public Administration, University of Hartford, West Hartford, Connecticut.*

produced with people the governmental organization hires directly, and with equipment and in facilities which it owns. There may be no "pure" case of this. The United States Postal Service comes fairly close. But even here some operations are contracted out to private parties (some rural delivery routes, and some postal stations); and of course it buys space in the commercial airline system for its Express Mail since it does not own its own planes.

But the concept of a consolidated organization gives us a place to start, at least, in looking at the variations on it.

1. Buying the Entire Service

At the other extreme, a governmental agency can sign a single contract with a single organization to produce the complete service required. In Denmark, for example, about half the cities contract with a nominally private but effectively non-profit organization for fire suppression and rescue services.

In a case of this sort the contractor becomes responsible for setting up the entire operation. The contractor may then hire all of the employees required, or may secure certain of the needed services, facilities and equipment through one or more sub-contracts. In either case, from the point of view of the government, the entire service is effectively "bought."

For the duration of the contract such an arrangement is non-competitive. The buyer will be able to protect its interest, in this potentially dangerous situation, to the extent it can keep the contractor aware that (a) the term of the contract is limited and that (b) at the end of the term the buyer has a real option to get a different contractor to take the work back to administer directly.

Buying the Entire Service in Multiple Contracts

The governmental body responsible for providing the service can also contract-out the entire service *but to two or more competing producers*. The Department of Transportation does not let the state's entire road-construction program as a single contract.

Buying the Entire Service; Owning the Capital

At times, as a way of making it possible for a wider variety of competing producers to bid, the governmental body will itself own the facilities and or equipment, contracting only for the personal service. The City of Minneapolis, for example, owns the impoundment lots for the vehicle-towing service, so that a company wanting to bid for the work need only supply its own tow trucks. The Metropolitan Sports Facilities Commission installed and owns the equipment at the concession stands, contracting only for their staffing.

Buying the Capital; *Owning the Service*

A governmental body, like a private organization, can hire all of the employees required (both the administrators and the people in direct-service-delivery) and contract for (that is, lease and rent) its equipment and buildings. This is quite common, of course.

Buying Through a Performance Contract

Incentives can be built into contracts, often with interesting results. Anxious to get the road into service at the earliest possible date, the Minnesota Department of Transportation built an incentive payment (so much per day) into the contract for the construction of I-94 in North Minneapolis. The contractor got the work done *a year* ahead of schedule (and made an extra million dollars).

2. Buying a *Part* of the Service; Owning a Part

Not infrequently, in a conscious effort to maintain a more competitive arrangement, a local public body will handle a part of a service with its own employees and, at the same time, buy a part of the service from some other organization (a private firm or another government, as the case may be). There are several variations, in turn, of this approach.

A city may organize a particular service in such a way that city crews and the contractor operate side by side. Phoenix, Arizona, does this with refuse collection; half the city is handled by public employees and half by contract.

Or a city may organize the two different elements (so to speak) end to end. If we think more broadly in terms of refuse collection *and disposal,* this arrangement is visible in a city where city crews collect the refuse but where the transfer stations and the trucks to the landfills and the landfill disposal itself are secured (as they are in Minneapolis) through contract. (Actually, Minneapolis also operates a part-city, part-contract collection system.)

3. Buying the *Support* Services Only

Commonly, an agency will own and run its main-line service directly and contract for the various support services required: accounting, printing, transportation, legal services, public relations, etc. In most communities there is a considerable industry prepared to produce and sell these services on an out-of-house basis.

Governments in the Twin Cities area do a fair amount of this kind of contracting. Central cities tend to have their own attorneys (suburbs, to retain theirs on contract). Many public schools produce their own school lunches, but state universities contract for food service. About half the school districts own and run their own fleet of buses; about half contract for pupil transportation.

The most curious case we encountered is surely in San Francisco, where the city has contracted for the service of budget preparation. This would seem a peculiar service for a city council to buy on contract; and in truth it was a very special situation. As we understand it, the city's budget director (then on a traditional employment arrangement) approached the city council, saying he would like to operate as a business, so that he could begin to build a group that could work for other cities as well as for San Francisco. The city agreed.

4. Buying the *Management* Only

Another variation in the contracting arrangement is for the public agency to buy not the whole service but simply *the management of it*.

Locally, the best-known example is almost certainly the Metropolitan Transit Commission, which from its inception has bought the management of bus operations from American Transit Enterprises, a company headquartered in Cincinnati, Ohio, which has similar contracts in more than 50 American cities and in Saudi Arabia. ATE Management and Service Company was founded in 1969. In addition to the operating management of transit systems (involving about 10,000 vehicles) it sells consulting, data and other services to transit systems which hire their own management.

In the local arrangement the drivers are hired by the MTC, the buses are owned by the MTC and the garages belong to the MTC. It is simply the management that is brought in on contract.

The MTC's use of contract management was broadened even further in the late 1970s when, after the retirement of Camille Andre, the ATE executive then managing the bus operations was given responsibility also for Andre's duties as executive director of the commission.

Contract management is also coming into hospitals, here as elsewhere in the country. Mount Sinai Hospital in Minneapolis is now managed by Hospital Corporation of America, which has supplied an executive and a financial control officer; the other employees remain the employees of the hospital itself. At Divine Redeemer Hospital in South St. Paul, similarly, the building is owned by a Catholic order and the employees are employees of the hospital, but the management is supplied through a contract with American Healthcare Management Inc. of Dallas, Texas.

5. Buying the Management Only
of the Support Services Only

One of the most intriguing variations in contracting is the model represented best by the activities of a company in Downers Grove, Illinois, ServiceMaster Industries Inc. In contrast to ATE or to HCA, Service-Master says, in effect: "You concentrate on your main business (the bus service or the health care). Let us manage your support departments."

It has been a growing business, to say the least. It appeared early after World War II as an in-home carpet-cleaning business, as carpets began to replace the rugs traditionally sent out to the "rug laundry." This (franchise) operation remains today, and many people know the company only by the gold-and-blue panel trucks used in this part of its business.

In the 1960s, as executives tell the story, ServiceMaster was approached by some Catholic sisters who pointed out that hospitals have a cleaning problem and inquired whether the company would consider that line of work. It decided it would enter that market, and began to grow rapidly with the growth of hospitals and of professional hospital administration. Over the 12 years 1971 to 1982 the volume of services under its management grew from $54 million to $594 million. In 1982 it also entered the hospital field in Sweden, Canada and Japan. From hospitals, ServiceMaster is now broadening into education (both public school districts and colleges), into major industrial plants and, most recently, into home health care in the Chicago area.

In hospitals it began by managing simply the cleaning operation; then moved on to the management of the mechanical plant, to the management of inventories, to the management of the maintenance of clinical equipment, to the management of the laundry and linen service, and to the management of hospital food service (through the acquisition in 1981 of a company called Service Direction Inc., based in Pentagon park in Edina, which manages the food service in, among other hospitals, Hennepin County Medical Center). Throughout, the object is to find ways to improve both quality and cost-effectiveness in the operation of these support departments of an organization.

Its arrangement with a hospital (or other institution) begins with a survey of the existing situation which usually shows, one executive says, "a group of dedicated and frustrated employees along with some number of incompetents and goof-offs." After a survey of the operation the company gives the hospital the cost at which it finds the service can be produced, and contracts to operate at that defined cost plus a management fee.

The hospital sets the specifications for the service; the company installs the system it has developed for doing the work, and makes the decisions about the amount of materials and the hours of labor to be used. The cleaning staff remain employees of the hospital. Essentially, ServiceMaster subcontracts the labor back from the hospital, working with whatever wage rates the hospital pays and with a union if one is present.

The resident manager is essentially a contract department head for the hospital administrator or school superintendent. The idea is to become an indistinguishable part of the management group. This is in contrast to some of its competitors whose managers wear distinguishing emblems or clothing.

The company emphasizes the ethical and religious character reflected in its name: Service to the Master. It sees this set of values, which includes a strong orientation to the growth and development of the individual employee, as one of its major assets, setting it apart from its competitors.

It has about 5,000 employees of its own, about 3,000 of whom are managers. About two-thirds of its new managers are referred by its existing people. In total, they now supervise almost 60,000 employees in the facilities that are under contract.

We talked with an official of the Lakeview school district near Battle Creek, Michigan, one of ServiceMaster's early contracts in school maintenance. It has 3,565 students in six schools. Under a $456,000 annual contract the company has taken on the responsibility for all custodial salaries, substitutes and overtime, and for all supplies and equipment.

Essentially, the approach has been to convert maintenance away from an individual-building basis. It has developed the employees into a district-wide maintenance team, able to perform for themselves many of the repairs which the district formerly had to buy, at considerable cost, from outside plumbing, electrical and other suppliers. ("Broken windows," the district official says, "can eat you up.") Candidly, he says there were some difficulties between the custodians and the first resident manager. ServiceMaster sent in another manager August 9. The two-year contract will probably be renewed by the school board, at a price estimated to be roughly $117,000 below what the district would have been spending had it continued under its previous system. The district does not buy its food service from ServiceMaster. It gets that from Service Systems, a company formerly based in Minneapolis, now a subsidiary of Del Monte.

Interestingly, resistance to the contract arrangement came not from the former manager (who retired as ServiceMaster came in) but from the principals of the district's schools. Under the old arrangement they had been the immediate supervisors of the school custodians. Now, the custodians work for the director of buildings and grounds in the district office, who is the ServiceMaster resident manager. The principals are to supervise the teaching and learning.

Augsburg College in Minneapolis went to contract management for housekeeping and physical-plant operation in 1982. Wayne Peterson, the vice president for finance and management, reports a considerable improvement in performance over the previous system as the maintenance jobs are upgraded (and as supervisors are now willing to "get their hands dirty," rather than taking the conventional view that a manager's job is to work only with paper). The difference that makes the difference, he says, is that retaining an organization brings to bear a much greater skill in working with people and a greater resource of technical skills than does the hiring of an individual buildings and grounds superintendent.

Contracting, Management and Administration

Even this brief a look at the variations in the contracting model, and the different combinations that are possible, raises some interesting questions about the whole definition of management, especially in the public sector.

What it suggests can best be described by saying that the object of the verb "to manage" is not the word "organization." Clearly, the public officials involved in the examples of contracting cited above are simply not in charge of the organizations that are actually doing the work. What they *are* in charge of is the *program*. So the definition of "management" that is appealing, that helps explain what we see when we look at the way many of these services are actually coming to be organized, is one that has at its core the concept of *reaching objectives*. The program and its objectives may be contained within a single organization; but they may also extend beyond the organization, as we have seen, through contract arrangements. This definition illuminates in a useful way the key distinction between "management" and "administration." It is not that "management" somehow includes "administration," or is found at higher levels in the organization. Rather, it is that "management" is oriented toward objectives, given limited resources; while "administration" is not. (In this sense "management by objectives" is a redundancy; the concept of reaching objectives being inherent in the concept of management.)

This distinction (offered to us by a local hospital executive) helps us see, too, that at the heart of public service redesign—that is, the need to break away from the traditional idea that the level of service produced is affected only by the volume of financial resources coming in, and the need to see that it is possible to do "more" by doing things differently—is precisely this shift from *administration* in the public sector to *management* in the public sector. "Up to now hospitals have been administered," the hospital executive said. "From here on, and especially with the coming limitations on Medicare reimbursement, they will have to be managed."

Put another way: What is centrally involved is the shift from maximizing income to maximizing effectiveness.

Issues for Discussion and Research

These other thoughts, hypotheses, and questions occur, about the relationship between contracting and management, and with policy-making, in the public sector.

Additional Variations

There may be even more ways to arrange the use of the "purchase" option that we have suggested above. One question, for example, is whether a public body might buy the management (only) of a service from two or more different suppliers. This is roughly what the boards responsible for pension programs have done, for example, for the management of their investments.

Structural Changes and Appropriate Incentives

The contracting arrangement would seem to contain, inherently, a number of incentives that would encourage management (as we have been defining that term here).

In the administrative arrangement typical of the public sector the board and its principal executive do play double roles: as policy-maker, and as operator. On the one hand they are buyers who think about the interests of the taxpayers and consumers. On the other they are sellers who think about the interests of their employees and about their own pride in the organization and the facilities they have built and run. And this can sometimes lead to problems. It brings to mind the complaint of one county commissioner that the rising expenditures for health care were forcing the county board to reduce its program for general assistance during the recession, and what she said when it was pointed out to her that the board could secure medical and hospital care elsewhere in the area for significantly less than it was spending in the county medical center. She said: "But it's our hospital!"

The "purchase of service" arrangement does separate these functions and thereby reduce this conflict. By its nature, too, the contract arrangement would seem to force on the buyer the requirement to be clear about its objectives, and on the seller the requirement to be clear about its performance, and on both the requirement to establish a mechanism for accountability that addresses the question so often left hanging in the traditional arrangement. This is the question: "Or else, what?" If there is no answer to that question, and therefore no sanction for non-performance, there is no effective accountability.

The Difficult Question of "Control"

Quite often the elected officials and top professionals in the public sector do not perceive the sense in which they are playing a double role as provider (buyer) and as producer; or, if they do perceive it, they do not admit it as a conflict of interest.

To the extent the dual role and the conflict are perceived and admitted, they are usually vigorously defended (especially by elected officials) with the argument that "We can control the operation better if we own and run it directly."

This assertion absolutely staggers contractors, who are so acutely conscious of the way they are always "at risk." They get their work a project at a time. They believe they live by delivering the service the agency wants. If they do not perform they do not return. They contrast their own vulnerability with the permanence of the public agency and the job-security of its civil service employees; and when they hear elected officials talk about having better control over a public agency they literally cannot believe what they are hearing.

Probably it is a mixed issue. On small things the elected official may well be right. If a piece of street work requires parking to be banned and traffic to be re-routed, and a merchant along the street calls a member of the city council and complains that, "My business is down by 50 percent!" the councilman in a city that hires its own work-crews may be able to call the director of public works and to persuade him to tell the foreman to leave a lane of traffic or parking open even if it does disrupt the progress of the repair. A contractor in truth might not be so responsive.

The question is whether the administrative system will be equally responsive on the really large questions, where the changes requested by the elected officials would impact adversely on the employees themselves.

This is not a particularly important question in a stable period when everyone is satisfied with the way things are working and where there is plenty of money to continue the operation in the traditional ways. That is, when programs can simply be administered.

It becomes a *very* important question in a period like the present, when many people are *not* satisfied with the way things are working and when there are *not* the resources to continue all the services in all the usual ways. When, as we have said, programs need to be *managed*. The use of the contract model may, then, be a far superior arrangement to secure the change that is required.

The question of "cost savings." Quite commonly the justification offered for switching to a contract arrangement is that it "will be cheaper." The interesting questions are: When *is* it cheaper? When is a contract worth doing? When it is *not* cheaper? And: How can a public body tell whether it is cheaper or not?

Presumably, the cost of contracting will be compared with the cost of "doing it yourself." But *what is* that cost of doing it yourself? Are all the costs included? More basic: Are all the real numbers known? If over the years a public agency has been simply administered, rather than managed, what reason is there to think that it will know its real costs?

Is it possible that one of the by-products of a contracting arrangement is the management information it will produce (or force the agency to produce) about the real costs of delivering the service?

Finally: How should a contract arrangement by valued if it ends up costing as much or more than the traditional arrangement, but succeeds in accomplishing an important management improvement in the operation of an agency which the administrative system had proved unable to accomplish at all?

Or how should it be valued if one of its effects is to leverage the alternative producers (whether the public agency itself or other, competing contractors) into improving *their* price and performance?

Opportunities for New Producers

It is striking how often "contracting" is studied and discussed primarily for its benefits to the buyer side. Our discussion in this article has in fact been considering contracting from this point of view: as a strategy which those on the policy/buyer side can use to leverage some kind of program improvement they could not secure their own administrative bureau.

A second and important benefit, however, runs (or can run) to the producer/seller side. The pressure which the contract relationship will stimulate for better management and for creative approaches can become a major opportunity for innovative and creative persons now working in public agencies to expand their roles (and to be rewarded, both professionally and financially) well beyond what would ever be possible were they to remain simply as employees of the organization.

9. A Means to Achieve "More with Less"

John R. Miller and Christopher R. Tufts

America's industrial leaders have come to realize that to be competitive in the global economy they must demonstrate to the buying public that their products represent the best value. Such mode of economics-based decision making is now being applied by taxpayers to the goods and services produced by government. Taxpayers and consumers alike are demanding the best quality and value for their hard-earned dollars.

Companies realize that in order to win in the marketplace and make a profit, they must "accomplish more with less" — fewer people, less money, less time, less space and fewer resources in general. To be competitive and profitable, many companies are adopting "downsizing" business strategics. Key components of downsizing include productivity and quality improve ment programs, mergers, streamlining operations, and divestiture of businesses in which they are not competitive. These strategies must be balanced by more creative management.

Government has a comparable challenge. Faced with public demand for increased or improved services in a period of diminishing resources and a changing pattern of accountability, government officials must also develop innovative solutions to win public confidence. This article discusses the concept of downsizing government and specifically focuses on privatization of service delivery as one alternative.

John R. Miller and Christopher R. Tufts, "Privatization Is a Means to 'More with Less'."
Reprinted with permission from National Civic Review, *Vol. 77, No. 2, March-April, 1988.*
Published by the National Civic League Press, Denver, Colorado.

Downsizing

Government downsizing is the selective application of a broad range of management and cost reduction techniques to streamline operations and eliminate unnecessary costs. These same techniques can be applied to the development of expansion of government service, as well as to maintaining service levels, improving quality, and reducing existing government service cost. In all cases the objective is the same: Identify practical solutions and implementation plans that best serve the public through more effective management and delivery of government services, while saving or avoiding unnecessary costs.

Downsizing alternatives can be grouped into five major categories:

- Productivity and quality improvement programs;
- Consolidation (intra- and inter-government cooperation);
- Privatization;
- Program reduction;
- Program abandonment.

The objective of "accomplishing more for less" is most frequently achieved by exercising a combination of downsizing alternatives. For example, a government may initiate a productivity and quality improvement program in its health services; consolidate, through a multijurisdictional agreement, to provide shock trauma medical treatment; contract with the private sector to provide drug prevention programs; attempt to reduce the demand for service through the imposition of user fees for ambulance service; and eliminate minor injury treatment services at government hospitals. Each potential opportunity for downsizing must be approached creatively to ensure the public still receives the best service at the lowest possible cost.

Privatization as a Downsizing Choice

As many corporate leaders are retrenching to do better what they do best, so too must government be willing to do the same. Peter Drucker, in his book *The Age of Discontinuity,* called for "reprivatization" of many government functions, saying "The purpose of government is to make fundamental decisions and to make them effectively. The purpose of government is to focus the political energies of society. It is to dramatize issues. It is to present fundamental choices. The purpose of government, in other words, is to govern. This, as we have learned in other institutions is incompatible with 'doing.' Any attempt to combine governing with 'doing' on a large scale paralyzes government's decision-making capacity."

One downsizing alternative for government to consider is to competitively engage the private sector to produce goods and services that are readily available from many commercial sources. Although the current impetus for privatization is largely pragmatic, the guiding political philosophy behind it is as old as the nation itself. Americans have long alternated between the Jeffersonian and Hamiltonian philosophies of government. However, the new momentum for privatization transcends political and ideological boundaries, and is rooted in the determination of creative government managers to develop innovative solutions to serve the public interest.

Today a broad and growing consensus recognizes that privatization, properly implemented, is a viable and legitimate response to a wide range of philosophical and practical concerns. Experience is showing that the private sector can indeed provide many services rendered by government with equal or greater effectiveness, and at lower cost. Consequently, privatization is likely to exert a powerful influence over the shape of political and economic institutions in coming years.

What Is Privatization?

George W. Wilson, Distinguished Professor of Business and Economics at the Indiana University School of Business, defines privatization on a philosophical plane. He writes, "The broader and more relevant meaning of privatization must refer to nothing more or less than greater reliance upon market forces to generate production of particular goods and services."

In practical terms, privatization is a process by which government engages the private sector to provide capital or otherwise finance government programs, purchase government assets, and or operate government programs through various types of contractual arrangements.

As privatization usually occurs in combination with other downsizing initiatives, so too do many privatization transaction[s] involve a combination of methods. For example, private sector capital financing, using such vehicles as leveraged leasing, lease purchases, and turnkey contracts, is frequently accompanied by operation of government programs through one of four types of arrangements: franchises, grants, vouchers, or contracts.

Privatization is nothing new. It can be traced to the first Bank of the United States which served as the federal government's fiscal agency and principal depository of the treasury and was owned by private shareholders. When the federal government wanted to deliver mail to its citizens west of the Mississippi, it contracted with 80 horseback riders and spawned the Pony Express. The Homestead Act gave settlers government-owned land for a small fee if they would cultivate soil for a fixed period.

In the last decade, privatization has expanded from capital construction and professional service contracts to traditionally in-house administrative and public service programs. The majority of governments now contract for at least some legal, medical, engineering, technical and other professional services. Indeed, state and local government spending for public services performed by the private sector rose from $27.4 billion in 1975 to well over $100 billion in 1985. The trend toward privatization will continue to grow even though the growth rate for state and local governments appears to be slowing.

State governments, though less active than local governments with privatization, are experimenting in many areas. The state of California alone in 1985 wrote 7,000 contracts, worth over $2 billion, to carry out administrative or public service functions, including mental health, corrections, and a full range of administrative services.

Objectives of Privatization

What are the primary objectives of privatization? They are:

- To improve the use of scarce resources by reducing the costs of providing public services, particularly where private enterprise is strong and government is assured of more effective services at lower costs;
- To modify the role of government from that of a primary producer of goods and services to that of governing;
- To enable government to meet responsibilities that might otherwise be abandoned because they are too costly;
- To reduce the debt burden;
- To limit tax rates.

Privatization of government services should be considered:

- When government's operations are unrelated to the central function of governance. Examples of governance are legislative, judicial, and certain financial activities (e.g., rate setting, debt issuance, revenue policy);
- When current government service is in direct competition with services operated by the private sector;
- When the cost of an existing government-provided service exceeds the available or projected resources;
- When current government operations are inefficient and or service is of poor quality and all remedial actions have resulted in insufficient improvement.

Privatization Successes

As already noted, privatization transactions cover a wide range of services. The following are examples of applications of various types of privatization.

Fire Protection

Rural/Metro Fire Department Corporation, a privately owned company, serves half a million people in Arizona (one-fifth of the state's population), and 100,000 more in Tennessee. Rural/Metro Corp.'s $4.3 million contract with Scottsdale, Arizona, for 1987–88 averages out to $36 per capita per year, compared with an average of $50 for public fire departments in similar cities. Scottsdale's fire insurance rates are average.

Ambulance Service

Newton, Massachusetts, estimates saving nearly $500,000 by privatizing its ambulance service while at the same time increasing ambulance availability and coverage.

Street Light Maintenance

The City of New York is divided into eight service areas for the provision of street light maintenance. All eight are competitively bid. No single company can "win" more than two service areas.

Legal

In Los Angeles County, Rolling Hills Estates broke off a contract it had with the County Prosecutor to handle all its cases, mostly involving violations of building and other town codes. Rolling Hills Estates now pays a private law firm to act as Town Prosecutor.

Grounds Maintenance

The school district of Rye, New York, recently contracted for grounds maintenance with a private company at an estimated savings of $34,000.

Prisons

The Dade County Jail is run by the Corrections Corp. of America, which runs several correction facilities throughout the United States, including two for the United States Immigration and Naturalization Service in Texas. Some interesting questions arise in privatizing corrections. Who chases escapees? Who is liable for the prisoners and their actions? Is prisoner rehabilitation compatible with profit? (Court decisions so far indicate that *both* the government and private contractor are liable for the actions of private guards.)

Fleet Maintenance

The city of Philadelphia contracts for the repair, maintenance and replacement of its motor vehicle fleet at an estimated savings of more than $4 million over the past four years.

Health Care

In Corsicana, Texas, the Navarro County Hospital was old, losing money, and about to lose its accreditation. To put it in shape, $12 million was needed. The county turned it over to the Hospital Corporation of America, which built a new hospital right next to the old one. The former hospital cost taxpayers $50,000 a year to operate. The new one is paying taxes of over $300,000 a year. In a similar vein, in 1983 the city of Louisville, Kentucky, turned over the operation of a teaching hospital at the University of Louisville to the Humana Corporation. This hospital now benefits from the advantages of mass purchasing, gained by being part of Humana's 85-hospital chain.

Public Defender Services

Shasta County, California, reported a $100,000 per year savings in indigent-defense court costs by contracting its entire public defender program to a private firm run by a former member of the district attorney's staff in an association with six full-time lawyers, three secretaries and a part-time investigator. The switchover was prompted by a study that showed Shasta's in-house Public Defender's Office was about one-third more costly than contract services would be.

Data Processing

Orange County, California, whose population has doubled to over 2 million since 1973, estimates that it has saved more than $3 million over the past 12 years by hiring a private firm to run its computer center. "Without automation and the professional know-how to use the computers efficiently," said Howard Dix, manager of the center's operations, "the county would have faced an explosive growth in costs for personnel and facilities."

Privatization Failures

Let us now look at some failures in privatization, and the pitfalls they illustrate.

Two towns in Ohio hired a private security firm to provide police protection. The equipment provided was totally unacceptable. Both towns fired the private company and hired the guards to be public police officers.

In another case, a city contracted for trash pickup at one cent per household per month less than the city could provide the service. The company could not work that cheaply. Within months, the company was raising cash by selling equipment given it by the city. At Thanksgiving and Christmas, garbage piled up faster than the company could collect it. A new company took over the contract. Said the mayor of the city, this "case makes me a lot more cautious. It was false economy to take a bid that was low by one cent per household per month."

New York City's Parking Violations Bureau scandal is a sore reminder of what can happen in contracting for services. Several public officials and business people pled guilty to, or were convicted of, serious crimes involving contract corruption. Two contracting corporations, without admitting any guilt concerning the alleged bribes, reached an out-of-court settlement with the city wherein the companies paid $600,000 in damages.

In a New Jersey city, private trash haulers bill residents directly. As local landfills close, the haulers' costs rise dramatically, and they in turn raise the rates they charge. Complaints to the haulers have been unavailing, and the reaction of some residents is to cancel service and dump their own garbage illegally in any open space. This has precipitated a limited health emergency. City officials are now considering eliminating use of the franchised haulers and instituting municipal trash collection, even though it will require raising property taxes.

How to Accomplish Privatization Transactions

To avoid the pitfalls of the failure examples, a careful process should be followed. The process should begin with analysis of privatization alternatives (franchises, grants, vouchers, and contracts) relative to the current delivery methods practiced. This analysis should examine implementation feasibility, technical performance, and costs. Its objectives are to determine which services may be privatized, select the most appropriate privatization method, and develop a scheduled work plan for implementation of the privatization transaction.

In order to meet these objectives, a multi-disciplined team approach should be followed. At minimum, this team should consist of personnel with technical experience in the function under review; legal, personnel, fiscal, and contracts staff; and political advisory and independent review support. The team approach provides the appropriate balance of expertise to ensure that all issues are identified and practical solutions are formulated. In addition, the use of political and independent review advisory support will assist in building the necessary consensus and commitment to change among all constituent groups. Most important, the team approach provides appropriate balance between program, fiscal, and political considerations.

Implementation Feasibility Analysis

Implementation feasibility analysis is the study of the political, legal, market, government operations, and other factors of each privatization option relative to the status quo, to anticipate the difficulties in accomplishing each option. The team approach provides the appropriate expertise to identify issues and barriers and develop solutions to minimize the impact of the issues and eliminate the barriers. The objective of the implementation feasibility study is to develop action plans identifying the specific objectives, scope, process, responsibilities, and timing for implementation of each service delivery option. The implementation feasibility study must address:

Political Barriers

Are the current coalitions of beneficiaries, near beneficiaries, service providers, government administrators, officials, political activists, unions and general populace amenable to change? How do you build the coalitions necessary to support the change process?

Legal Issues

What are the statutory, regulatory and tax law barriers, incentives, and or requirements for privatization? What modifications to union agreements or ongoing contracts are required? What is the impact on liability?

Market

Is the private sector market mature or developing? Has the private sector shown interest through unsolicited proposals, industry studies, or research by industry experts? How capable is the private sector of providing quality goods or services? Is there a sufficient number of qualified bidders to ensure competition and provide the government a favorable risk/reward ratio? Does the private sector perceive a favorable risk/reward ratio? What is the private sector track record in government contract performance?

Government Operations

Will privatizing selected functions disrupt continuity of operations? How will the affected employee be treated? What effect will privatization have on accountability? Who will monitor the private sector? How, and with what frequency will the private sector be monitored? What performance measures will be used to determine whether performance standards have been met? How will the government control the quality, timing and cost of delivery of services to be privatized? What are appropriate penalties (or incentives) to ensure compliance with performance standards and service requirements?

Other Factors

Who will have control over the staff, equipment, and facilities? Are the resources available to do the necessary analysis, conduct the planning, preparation, and execution of privatization transactions?

Technical Performance Analysis

Once a government has examined the implementation feasibility of the privatization options, it needs to compare the overall implementation difficulties anticipated against the total benefits to be derived. Each option must be evaluated in terms of technical performance criteria including — but not necessarily limited to — availability, quality and effectiveness, risks, and program impacts. Through review of historic experience within and outside the jurisdiction, demographic and geographic studies, and or the performance of pilot programs, analysis can be performed to evaluate each option. Criteria should be weighed and each alternative scored to determine the optimal anticipated technical performance option. At a minimum the criteria should include:

Availability and Costs to Citizens

Will individual consumers obtain improved choices of supply and service levels? Will all customers including disadvantaged groups or geographically remote regions be served? If user fees are charged, will disadvantaged users be able to afford the level of service they need? Will the service cost to all consumers be fairly distributed? Will the overall cost to citizens increase?

Quality and Effectiveness

Will government objectives be achieved more effectively? Will the quality of service improve?

Risks

Will service disruptions be more likely? What contingencies will be required? A risk analysis that quantifies the technical, implementation, and cost risks associated with each of the alternative delivery options provides a comprehensive and disciplined approach towards reducing uncertainty and focuses the attention of the team on the most critical issues.

Program Impacts

What synergies or benefits will be derived? Will the government benefit from new technology? What impact will there by on the operations of other departments, especially if the program or service is for internal government use?

Cost Analysis

Since privatization is heavily influenced by cost, a thorough costing, economic, and pricing analysis must be performed for each option. The purpose of this analysis is to estimate potential savings, assess the economic impact, determine specific costs, and establish pricing requirements. The three types of studies most frequently performed are:

Financial Feasibility Studies

A determination of the current and future gross and net costs or savings of the planned privatization transaction in relation to the costs of the current method of operation.

Cost Benefit Analyses

A determination of the costs of new methods of providing services or doing business, compared against the benefits of the alternatives, to identify the methods that are the most cost-responsive.

Cost and Pricing Studies

An identification and examination of the direct, indirect, fixed, variable, opportunity, and oversight costs associated with a privatization transaction for different levels of service; a definition of what will happen to total costs as the service levels change; and the recommendation of pricing strategies and or prices to achieve desired utilizations, cash throw-offs, and or rates of return.

For each study the first step should be to determine what constitutes cost, where the data should be obtained, how costs should be calculated, and how costs should be projected for future years. For a cost comparison between government service performance and a service contract between government and a private vendor, the major cost elements to examine include:

Government Performance Costs

- Personnel costs: basic pay (salaries or wages), other entitlements (e.g., night differential, hazardous duty differential), fringe benefits (e.g., FICA, pension, workers' compensation), other (e.g., overtime, uniform and meal allowances);
- Materials and supplies costs: costs of raw materials, replacement parts, repairs, office supplies, and equipment, necessary to provide a product or perform a service;
- Overhead costs: operations overhead (e.g., supervision) and general administrative overhead (e.g., personnel, data processing, legal);
- Other specifically attributable costs, such as rent, utilities, maintenance and repairs, insurance, depreciation or use charges, travel;
- Additional costs, unusual or specific circumstances that occur only under government operation or don't fit other categories.

Contractor Performance Cost

- *Realistic* contract price: the contractor must be able to deliver the service at the quantity and quality desired at the bid price, and still make a reasonable profit, for a contract price to be realistic;

- Start-up costs (e.g., learning curve);
- Contract administration costs, including execution of quality assurance monitoring, payment processing, negotiation of change orders, and contract close-up;
- Conversion costs (e.g., disposing of expendable items, retraining, severance pay, lease termination penalties, conducting the privatization transaction);
- Additional costs (e.g., lost volume discounts).

Cost Advantage Based on the Above Costs

The cost advantage is defined as the difference between the total government performance cost and the total contractor performance cost, adjusted for additional or lost tax revenues. Because of the risks involved in implementing such a change, public managers should generally look for a major cost advantage before shifting to new modes of service delivery, to avoid being caught short like the city that changed to contracted trash pickup for only a one cent per household cost differential.

Selection and Implementation

Having completed implementation feasibility, technical performance, and cost analyses, a government manager can select the preferred method of service delivery. Privatization can be one of several downsizing alternatives available to government managers. It is not a panacea for challenges facing government managers. If analysis shows that government provides a service more efficiently and effectively than the private sector, it should continue to do so. Privatization offers an opportunity to introduce the cost-saving, creative, service-generating aspect of competition into the public arena. It is important that public managers retain both decision-making and ultimate responsibility for public services. It is they who must decide what services will be privatized and who will provide them.

Not all methods of privatizing will benefit all parties or work in all situations. The concept works best when public managers carefully examine public assets and services to determine which could be replaced by private functions, thoroughly evaluate private sector competition, assemble representatives from all affected parties to agree on alternatives and solutions, and analyze the combination of tactics to satisfy a broad range of constituents. The key is to develop a workable mix of program and fiscal alternatives.

Privatization is an appealing concept because it offers governments flexibility in meeting their public responsibilities and, at the same time, presents entrepreneurs with a new set of challenges. Entrepreneurs, as George Gilder notes in his book *The Spirit of Enterprise,* are "engineers of change." The challenge to public managers today is to identify and manage change.

10. Making the Decision

Larry J. Scully and *Lisa A. Cole*

As competition for federal, state and local funds increases, local decision makers are turning to innovative techniques to finance the construction and maintenance of their infrastructure and services. The involvement of private companies in the design, construction, operation, ownership and financing of facilities (commonly referred to as privatization) is one innovative technique that can provide a cost-effective solution for certain projects.

Privatization can take many forms, ranging from private operation of a small project to a service contract where a private company designs, constructs, owns, operates and finances a major facility. There are literally hundreds of privatization options for each project. Selecting the most effective privatization option requires an "apples-to-apples" comparison of the costs and risks associated with full municipal development, full privatization and several partial privatization options.

This article presents a strategy for making an "apples-to-apples" comparison for a privatization decision. The strategy uses a decision matrix to array the critical cost, management, and risk elements of each privatization option. The analysis reduces each option to a "common denominator" to clarify the relative annual cost to the municipality.

An overview of the steps in the analysis is discussed first, followed by a review of the ownership/financing options. The last section presents an illustration of privatization analysis using a decision matrix.

Larry J. Scully and Lisa A. Cole, "Privatization—Making the Decision." Reprinted with permission from The Privatization Review, *Vol. 2, No. 2, Spring, 1986. Published by The Privatization Council, Washington, D.C. (Printed by Maxco Publications, Inc., Little Falls, New Jersey.)*

Steps in the Analysis

The analysis for making the privatization decision consists of five steps:

- Define Project Scope,
- Develop Options,
- Define Engineering and Financing Assumptions,
- Estimate Costs, and
- Analyze Management and Risk Factors.

Define Project Scope

In the first step, a clear description of the purpose and scope of the project is developed. The basis for this description normally is found in the capital improvements plan. But often, as a project is placed under the spotlight, the true purpose and scope may need clarification or alternation to meet changing needs of the community. For example, a sludge disposal project may need to be modified to help solve a solid-waste disposal problem. A combined resource recovery and sludge disposal facility may be the best solution. These "global" issues need attention early in the project development cycle to avoid wasted effort or having to backtrack once detailed analysis begins.

Develop Options

As mentioned earlier, there are a myriad of options for private involvement in a municipal project. To provide some order to the option analysis a decision matrix is developed (see Exhibit A). The matrix arrays the ownership, financing, design, construction and operation options and, thus, provides a framework for highlighting differences and the relative cost of each option.

Since the major impetus for private involvement normally comes from the inability or unwillingness of a community to finance a project using conventional techniques, the first step is a review of the financing and ownership options available for the project.

As shown in Exhibit B, the financing and ownership options generally can be broken down into two polar approaches: public ownership/financing (options 1 and 2) and private ownership/financing (option 3).

Turning to the public ownership/financing options first, public ownership offers the municipality traditional security in having a long-term ownership interest in the project and control of the assets of the project. The finance options for a publicly owned facility vary from traditional to creative and can include:

Exhibit A

Privatization: Making The Decision
Overview Of Decision Matrix

Ownership Options	#1 Public			#2 Public			#3 Private (Full Service Contract)	
Financing Options	General Obligation Bond	Revenue Bond	Tax-Exempt Lease	General Obligation Bonds	Revenue Bond	Tax-Exempt Lease	Industrial Development Bonds	Commercial Financing
Design, Construction and Operation Options	Conventional 3 Step Approach Municipality Responsible for Design, Construction, and Operation			Private Firm or Joint Venture Responsible for Design, Construction, and Operation			Private Firm or Joint Venture Responsible for Design, Construction, and Operation	
Financing and Engineering Assumptions	• Size of Facility • Construction Costs • Operating Costs • Interest Rate • Term of Finance • Buyout Provision							
Cost to City	• Total Annual Cost • Cost Per Unit							
Management and Risk Analysis	• Use of Debt Capacity • Total Time for Project • Performance Risk • Legal Complexity • Labor Compatibility							

Exhibit B
Define Options

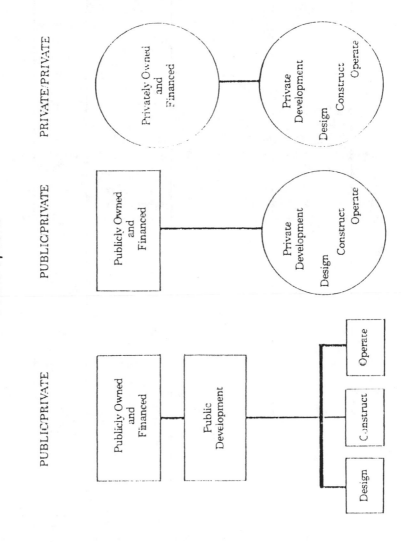

PUBLIC/PRIVATE

PUBLIC/PRIVATE

PRIVATE/PRIVATE

Publicly Owned and Financed

Public Development

Design

Construct

Operate

Publicly Owned and Financed

Private Development

Design

Construct

Operate

Privately Owned and Financed

Private Development

Design

Construct

Operate

Decision Matrix

	#1 Public	#2 Public	#3 Private
Ownership and Financing	Public	Public	Private
Project Development — Design — Construction — Operation	Public	Private	Private
Engineering and Financing Assumptions			
Cost Comparison			
Management and Risk Analysis			

- partial federal or state grants,
- current revenues,
- carry-over fund balances,
- low-interest loans,
- general obligation bonds,
- revenue bonds, and
- tax-exempt leases.

Within each of these financing techniques, there are a number of suboptions (i.e., variable rates, tender options, and insurance) which need analysis on a case-by-case basis. The objective is to select the best option for a particular project under given market conditions.[1] This article will focus on projects that are candidates for privatization. This normally would preclude projects funded with federal and state grants. To simplify the presentation, we will direct our attention to three major forms of public finance: general obligation bonds, revenue bonds, and tax-exempt bonds.

It should be noted that with public ownership/financing, involvement of private firms in the design, construction and operation of the project is not precluded.

Under the private ownership option there are again a number of institutional arrangements and financing strategies which can be employed. The most common type of private proposal would be a full service contract. In a full service contract, a private firm or consortium of firms enters into an agreement with the municipality to design, construct, own, operate and finance a project and provide a service, such as wastewater treatment, to the municipality. The Tax Reform Act of 1984 expressly allows special classes of service contracts for solid-waste disposal, energy, and water and treatment facilities. Under this structure a private firm owns the facility, provides a service to the municipality, and qualifies for investment tax credits and depreciation.

The capital assets used in the full service contract can be financed with conventional commercial financing or industrial development bonds. Industrial development bonds (IDBs) are issued at tax-exempt rates and provide attractive financing for the debt component of a private project. Constraints on IDB financing are discussed in the next section.

The second step in the analysis is the review of design, construction and operation options. Here again, the role of private firms can vary from no involvement in a conventional development to complete control in a full service contract, with a number of options in between.

In many cases the municipality follows a conventional three-step project development cycle shown as option #1 in Exhibit A. An independent engineering firm is hired to design the facility, and a second firm is hired to construct it. After construction and acceptance, the operation of the facility is then taken over by the municipality.

For certain municipal projects, it may be more efficient for a single private firm to take responsibility for the design, construction and operation of the facility. Since a single firm is responsible for design and construction, the total time for design and construction can be reduced, which reduces interest costs during construction. Also, since a single firm both designs and operates the facility, efforts to reduce operating costs are integrated into the design process. A private firm can take responsibility for the design, construction and operation of the facility either under public financing (option #2) or private financing (option #3).

In option #2, there is public ownership and financing, with private development of the project. Here, a municipality using one of the public financing techniques discussed above enters into a master contract with a developer to design, construct, and operate a municipal facility. This option offers the municipality the advantages of maintaining ownership and control of the facility as well as tax-exempt public financing. This structure allows the government to capture the most widely discussed advantages of private involvement in a municipal project, which are:

- reduced time for design and construction,
- reduced interest during construction,
- reduced administrative costs due to single company responsibility,
- vendor discounts,
- reduced operating and maintenance costs since the operations and maintenance concerns are more closely integrated into the design process, and
- design of the facility to meet current needs and fiscal capacity of the municipality.

Of course, the existence and magnitude of such advantages are subject to documentation in the case of any particular project. In option #3, private development of the facility is linked with private ownership and financing in a full service contract. This option gives the private firm full responsibility for the project's performance and allows investment tax credits and depreciation tax benefits to be passed to equity investors. Once the ownership, financing, and development options are reviewed, the analysis turns to the engineering and financing assumptions associated with each option.

Define Engineering and Financing Assumptions

For each option the following engineering and financing assumptions must be defined:

- size of the facility,
- construction costs,

- annual operating cost,
- interest rate for construction and long-term financing, term of financing,
- debt covenants, and
- buyout provision.

The clear statement of the value of each parameter in the decision matrix clarifies for the municipality the size, cost and product that it would have if that option were selected.

Estimated Cost

For the options identified above, the municipality develops a cost estimate for a complete project. For example, as shown in Exhibit A, a municipality may develop its own cost estimate for option #1 which is public ownership with conventional development, and then request proposals from private entities for options #2 and #3. The request for proposal sent to private developers defines the purpose and scope of the project. These cost estimates should include the cost to the city to buy the facility from a private developer if a fair market buyout provision is included in the private proposal. The request for proposals should also specify the input and output requirements of the facility and ensure that lower cost estimates are not for a scaled-down project.

In the resource recovery and waste-to-energy field this procedure has been refined, and a municipality can now describe its project needs, request bids from private developers, and compare those overall costs to the cost for conventional development and public ownership of the facility.

The city's request for information and its own development of cost estimates should establish a common denominator formula for comparing the city's cost over the life of a project. The common denominator attempts to fairly estimate cost over a specified project life, such as 20 years. For some projects these costs can be expressed as the total annual cost to the city or as a cost per unit, such as an annual cost per gallon of wastewater treated or a cost per ton of solid waste handled.

One option for a common denomination is a levelized cost per year. A levelized cost is calculated by first estimating the cost to the municipality for each of the 20 years of the project's life, then taking the present value of those different annual costs and finally calculating a levelized annual payment that equates to that present value. Once this annual cost is calculated, it can be divided by the tons of water handled or gallons of water treated to obtain a cost per ton or per gallon.

Analyze Management and Risk Factors

Having developed comparable cost estimates for public and private development of the facility, the municipality can then array that information against the administrative, management and legal issues and complexities associated with each option to select the best option for the project. Typical issues include:

- use of debt capacity,
- total time for project,
- performance risk,
- legal complexities, and
- labor/union concerns.

In general, the municipality is evaluating the cost/reduction advantages and the legal and management advantages and disadvantages of private development. The key criterion for the municipality is determination of the level of private involvement that best equates with cost reduction and risk minimization by the city while at the same time allowing the city to play an active role in the development and control of the project.

We will return to an illustration of the decision matrix for a wastewater treatment plant, after reviewing financing/ownership options.

Ownership/Financing Options

The ownership/financing options available to a public entity that has decided to construct a major project — be it a wastewater or resource recovery facility, or any other capital asset — are many and their characteristics have similarities as well as differences.

Public Option

In the public option, the municipality retains control of the project and provides the financing. This option is often appropriate when certain powers and authorities of the city are necessary to move the project forward. For example, the construction of a water main or sewer which would require extensive use of right of way and eminent domain powers would lend itself to a municipal ownership structure.

There are three financing options for public ownership — general obligation bonds, revenue bonds, and tax-exempt leasing — that can be classified as public approaches because they involve public financing and ownership of a facility. For each of these three alternatives, facility design, construction, and operation can either be by the public entity or contracted to the private sector.

For each option, common questions occur that must be answered in order to evaluate them fully. In addition to the structural, legal and administrative issues that obviously influence their cost, it is extremely important that their treatment under the federal tax laws be understood. As the 1984 Tax Reform Act has proved and as the current tax proposals threaten, the financing options are volatile and subject to significant change or elimination by Congress.

Private Option

Private ownership of municipal utility projects has taken several forms in the past. The Tax Reform Act of 1984 has modified the attractiveness of some of those options and eliminated others. What has emerged as a viable private ownership option for municipal projects is the full service contract. As mentioned earlier, under this arrangement, a private firm or consortium of firms contracts with a municipality to provide a service. At a minimum, service contracts have to meet the following six tests specified in the legislation in order not to be considered a lease and subject to new federal restrictions governing the use of accelerated depreciation and investment tax credits:

1. The governmental entity must not be in possession of the property,
2. The entity must not control the property,
3. The entity must not have significant possessory or economic interest in the property,
4. The owner or service provider must bear the risk of substantially diminished receipts or increased expenditures if there is nonperformance under the contract,
5. The owner or service provider must use the property to provide service to its unrelated entities, and
6. The contract price must substantially exceed the rental value of the property for the contract period.

However, certain solid-waste disposal facilities, energy facilities and water treatment facilities are exempted from federal restrictions and may continue to be financed using the service contract approach, provided that the service recipient does not:

- operate the facility,
- bear significant financial risk if there is non-performance,
- benefit from lower than anticipated operating costs, or
- have a fixed or determinable purchase price.[2]

Financing options for service contracts include industrial development bonds and commercial financing.

Industrial Development Bonds. Industrial development bonds provide low-cost financing to private owners and, in the full service contract being discussed, ownership stays with the private investor. An IDB may be issued by a public or quasi-public agency for projects to be owned and operated by private investors who provide the service to a government.

The key disadvantage to IDBs is that they have come under public scrutiny and have received negative publicity. As a result, the 1984 Tax Reform Act established the requirement that caps be set that limit the volume of IDBs that can be sold on a state-by-state basis. And, while the ink is barely dry on the 1984 legislation, new proposals have emerged that would abolish the tax-exempt interest on IDBs with nongovernmental purpose. As a result, while IDBs offered opportunities in 1984 and earlier and provide limited opportunities in 1985, their future availability is highly questionable.

However, since they currently are an option, it is important to understand the tax benefits that accrue to the private investors involved in full service contracts for wastewater and solid waste facilities. The 1984 Tax Reform Act specifically allows the structuring of full service contracts for such facilities and allows the investors to borrow at the tax-exempt interest rates and be eligible for investment tax credits and depreciation benefits. The 1984 act does limit the extent of the depreciation for solid waste and water treatment projects funded with IDBs — straight-line Accelerated Cost Recovery System (ACRS) must now be used for these projects.

Commercial Financing. Full service contracts can also be financed with taxable debt and funds from equity investors. The financing can be structured as a lease, a partnership or be provided by the major vendor of equipment for the project.[3] The debt would be at commercial rates, and the equity investors' return would consist of cash flow and depreciation and investment, and in some cases, energy tax credits. Equity investors require a 20 to 30 percent return on their investment and normally provide from 20 to 30 percent of the funds for the project. The required return depends on the risk of the project and the current market conditions for alternative investment opportunities.

The equity investors also share in any residual value that the project may have at the end of the contract. The facility is normally sold to the municipality at the end of the contract (at fair market value) or the contract can be renewed and the equity investors can maintain an interest in future proceeds. Commercial financing carries a higher interest rate than the tax-exempt options but requires less long-term debt to fund the project.

Summary

The analysis is intended to illustrate the key issues facing a municipality in the decision to involve private firms in the financing, design, construction and operation of a public facility or service. The most cost-effective option for other projects may evolve quite differently for each city. The decision matrix approach establishes an "apples-to-apples" cost analysis for the options and arrays the data in a format that clarifies the cost components of the different options. From that point on, the analysis moves to the examination of risk and management issues and brings the municipality to a privatization decision based on a clear understanding of the costs and risks of the project.

11. Contracting for Services

Edward C. Hayes

Contracting for services provides cities with a method for injecting marketplace competition into service delivery. You will save yourself time and grief if you take a systematic approach; even the best of ideas needs a workable format to succeed. The following steps are used by many cities and are presented to help you organize your thinking and action.

Step I—What Are the Alternatives to Contracting-Out?

You may be able to improve your program operation without contracting-out. Ask yourself the real reason for thinking about contracting. Is it excessive problems with personnel? Costs running up too quickly? Contracting surely does address these problems, but so do other approaches, and you will be doing yourself a favor to compare contracting with other options. They are:

- Service reduction. If you simply need to reduce costs, this is done the most simply by reducing service levels. Reduce the hours of the city pool, library, recreation center, or even city hall.
- "Load shedding." To really cut costs, just stop providing the service. Sell the city's landfill or golf course to the private sector; get the county to take over operations of the library; simply discontinue providing recreation services. This may cause a backlash from citizens—and it may not.
- Employee motivation. Personnel problems can be handled in several ways other than contracting. It may be time for someone to take early retirement. An employee recognition program might help. Asking em-

Edward C. Hayes, "Contracting for Services—The Basic Steps." Reprinted with permission from The Privatization Review, *Vol. 2, No. 1, Winter, 1986. Published by The Privatization Council, Washington, D.C. (Printed by Maxco Publications, Inc., Little Falls, New Jersey.)*

ployees for suggestions on improving program effectiveness and efficiency can restore a sense of importance to "neglected" employees.

- Co-production. Get volunteers to take over at least part of the job. San Diego County has an office for volunteers, funneling all recruits into the appropriate departments. Any city can obtain thousands of hours of free labor time in this way and screen volunteers for future paying jobs.

Step II — Preliminary Comparison of Public v. Private Service Delivery

If you have decided that contracting is the way to go, you now need to compare your department with several private (profit or non-profit) suppliers. First you need to determine if there is *any* supplier who can deliver the service. To find this out, try the Yellow Pages, the Local Government Center database, or the Privatization Council.

The Local Government Center, in Santa Barbara, California, has a large database of service providers in all service areas in all states. The Privatization Council has many useful contacts to help you.

If all else fails, consider spinning off the whole department as an independent non-profit corporation (as San Francisco did with its Accounting Department, now The Accountancy of Harvey Rose Inc., and as San Diego did with its Data Processing department).

Try to locate more than one possible service provider, and do some preliminary checking as to their qualifications. Experienced contractors will tell you: *quality service delivery is more important than simple low-bidding.* Find out about the track records of your short list of potential contractors. Ask them for a list of clients; then call those clients. Go to the state Better Business Bureau, the local chamber of commerce. If you stick yourself with a shoddy contractor you have only yourself to blame.

Preliminary Costing

In your preliminary comparison, get a really clear picture of what your own costs are for service delivery. In fact, I recommend you take a year to set up a system for measuring exactly your own service costs, month by month, including direct/indirect costs and overhead. Once you have your own costs, ask your short list of suppliers for a tentative price. Try to get your own costs into a "production unit" basis; thus, "$200 to maintain Elm Street Park," or "$2.00 per garbage-can pick-up," and ask your potential suppliers to give you an equivalent cost.

You can ask for this in writing, but be sure that you state in your letter requesting this information that your letter does not constitute a solicitation of bids and their reply will not be considered an offer.

You can also ask them if they will pick up your employees (right of first refusal). Orange County even gives bonus points to contractors who will offer a certain wage/benefit package in operating their data processing center.

Then get all this down on one piece of paper (see "Preliminary Data Sheet").

Do or Buy List

This list includes costs, and all other factors necessary to deciding correctly whether to contract-out ("Buy") or keep the service in-house ("Do"). This list includes:

- Is contracting-out less expensive?
- Is contracting legal under state and local law?
- Do labor contracts prohibit contracting-out?
- Will my elective body support the change?
- Will the change have an adverse effect on other services? (If you contract-out the paramedic program, will the fire department be left with nothing to do?)
- Are there enough service suppliers?
- Is corruption possible or likely?
- Would service interruption be catastrophic?
- Can I be sure of getting the same or higher levels of service quality?

The Question of Legality

Contracting can run afoul of several bodies of law: civil service may prohibit it; union contracts may prohibit it; and it may be found a violation of federal or state anti-monopoly laws. If you sign a contract with a single provider for all of Elmtown's garbage collection, you may be creating a monopoly, and the bidder who lost out might be only too happy to sue on this basis. Keep your lawyer involved fully.

Step III — Program Design and Avoidable Costs

Let's look at "avoidable costs." This is the real cost that you want to use to compare with the private service cost.

"Avoidable cost," as used by Los Angeles County, is defined as "that cost you can avoid by contracting-out." It rarely amounts to the actual cost of in-house delivery. Why? Because by contracting-out, you will not "shed" all, or even most, of the indirect costs and fixed costs associated with your service delivery. Indirect costs include the costs of the city manager, accounting, data processing, etc. — departments that form a part of your

Preliminary Data Sheet

Personnel

Total Affected_____ # Layoffs_____ Attrition_____

First Refusal? _____

Available Contractors

1. Name_____ Comment_____

2. Name_____ Comment_____

3. Name_____ Comment_____

Current Program Operating Costs_____ Equipt. Salvage____

Other Savings_____ Net Avoidable Costs_____

Contractor Costs (Rough)

Contractor 1_____ Amt. Saved_____

Contractor 2_____ Amt. Saved_____

Contractor 3_____ Amt. Saved_____

Political Factors

Union_____ Elective Body_____ Public_____

Contractor Reliability

_____

_____

Resume City Service if Contractor Fails? _____

©1984 Metro Associates

service costs. Fixed costs are building and equipment depreciation and maintenance.

You may contract-out parks maintenance; but you cannot get rid of the fleet yard, where parks equipment is stored, and you can't reduce the amount of work of the city manager. These are unavoidable costs.

If you contract out a lot, you may be able to free up a lot of city management time, and this should be counted as a cost saving.

Make a "Cost Analysis Tree" to estimate exactly what you spend on each function of your potentially contracted program.

Program Design

After all of the above, you still have the choice of deciding how much you will contract-out: will it be full service? Or just management? For example, ATE Inc. of Cincinnati will handle labor negotiations and fleet repair for your bus system; or they will run and manage the whole system. ARA will buy out your fleet and take over the whole operation. In Los Angeles County, the sheriff's department is hiring a consultant to work with its department to fully understand the new dispatching system — not to operate it, just to understand it, in case physical illness should incapacitate someone in the sheriff's department and leave this multi-million-dollar program with no leadership.

Bronson, Michigan, contracts with an engineer to run and upgrade its sewage treatment plant; Chandler, Arizona, and Auburn, Alabama, have contracted with major engineering firms to build, own, and operate sewage treatment plants. (See Fall 1985 issue of *The Privatization Review*.)

In "Program Design" you have several choices to make:

- Contract-out or franchise?
- Service delivery or facility ownership?
- For-profit or non-profit contractor?

Step IV — Writing Objectives & Performance Indicators

To get the best from your contractor, you should write out what you expect of him in measurable terms.

Take park maintenance as an example. It probably has several tasks: 1) cut grass, trim trees & shrubs; 2) maintain golf course; 3) clean park restrooms. Here I will just focus on the first task.

To insure the best results, you must write this task as an objective, in quantifiable (measurable) terms; thus:

Metro Associates
Program Cost Analysis Tree
(Program Level)

Resources / Personnel	Admin.	Support	Supervision	Delivery	Training	Resource Total	Percent of Total Cost
Functions							
Manager	1				37		
Clerical/support		9			38		
Staff 1		10					
Staff 2			19		39		
Staff 3				28			
Consumables							
Office supply	2	11	20	29	40		
Field supply		12	21	30			
Equipment, Facilities							
Office equipment	3	13	22	31	41		
Vehicles	4	14	23	32			
"In lieu" rent	5	15	24	33			
Utilities	6	16	25	34			
Miscellaneous							
Special projects	7	17	26	35	42		
Training	8	18	27	36	43		
Function Total						Grand Total _____	
Percent of Total Cost							

NOTE: All cost data (except totals) are entered in cells 1–43

"Cut grass to 2″ height, twice monthly"
"Maintain shrubs at 4′ height and 2′ width on park borders"
"Maintain conical evergreens at maximum 12′ height, between 8′ and 10′ at base"

One city in Los Angeles County has a diagram of each shrub and tree in its parks, by type and location, with size specifications drawn right on the diagram. That gives the contractor clear guidance, and the city a clear standard to enforce.

Performance indicators are of two kinds: 1) Quantitative (workload) and 2) all others — primarily quality, efficiency, responsiveness, and cost. Quality indicators refer to the quality of the job done. This can be measured by customer/user complaints, by visual scales, or by citing standard quality guides (such as a construction standards manual). Thus:

"Contractor will pick up from 100% of residences [workload] with 5 or less complaints per month [quality] and fewer than 5 monitored spills per month [quality]."

Efficiency indicators refer to the amount of time taken to perform any task. Thus:

"Contractor will replace 25 curb center noses a month [workload] in 2.5 hours per curb nose [efficiency]."

Responsiveness indicators refer to how quickly a crew or team gets to a job and finishes it. Thus:

"Contractor will replace all broken signal lights within 1 hour of reported complaint."

Cost is either total cost, or cost per production unit. Thus:

"Contractor will replace 25 curb center noses per month at a cost of $100 per curb nose."

Step V — Deciding Penalties & Incentives

Next, in writing the contract, you will want to do several things: decide who is responsible for contract monitoring, who will furnish which materials/equipment, a plan for monitoring the contractor, a list of information/data that you want the contractor to furnish to you (such as monthly production levels and customer complaints).

You would be wise to write in a page which defines exact penalties for failure to meet performance standards.

Suppose, for example, you have contracted with a company to replace all your broken street signal lights within 1 hour of reported breakage; and suppose you have monitored the contractor and know he is only replacing about 50 percent that quickly and the rest at up to 6 to 12 hours.

Your contract should write out a schedule of penalties stating exactly what 50 percent compliance means (it might mean withholding all payment that month; or withholding half).

You should also give your contractor a chance to excel and win a bonus. Suppose he corrects all broken lights in 45 minutes. Fantastic! Give him a $500 bonus that month, and write the exact schedule of incentives into the contract.

Step VI — Soliciting Bids/Writing the Contract

First you must write a Request for Proposals (RFP) for a major service, or an Invitation to Bid (ITB) for a standardized service. In this document you will lay out a proposed Statement of Work, the basic scope/services required by the contract. Having already written out your Performance Indicators, you have done the most difficult part of the Statement of Work. In the RFP or ITB you will outline exactly what work you want done, how you want it done, penalties and incentives, and what you want in a contractor.

Try to get at least three bidders. Pre-qualify them by checking into their reputation; visit their offices; ask for a balance sheet; verify that they can provide the service at the price they are asking (no "low balling").

Many criteria are possible in evaluating proposals. Here are some very common ones:

Proposal Evaluation Criteria	*Points for each*
Proposal Responsiveness to RFP	_____
Contractor capacity (staff, fiscal, facilities)	_____
Experience, reputation	_____
Total cost; cost per unit	_____
Pick up city employees	_____

You can use or discard these criteria, or develop new ones more suited to your situation. You may weight the criteria or give them all the same number of points.

If you are preparing a standard bid, the bid sheets filled out by the contractor can be used as the contract itself. If you plan to save yourself work that way, note that fact on the ITB.

Step VII — Administering the Contract: Monitoring

Your monitoring plan will list all the ways you are going to keep track of your contractor. These could include, for Parks Maintenance, 1) a weekly contractor report showing contract completion; 2) city field monitor reports; 3) vehicle maintenance report (if contractor is using city machinery); and 4) a citizen complaint log.

You should draw up a formal monitoring plan which will show you 1) exactly which parks you will monitor and on which days; 2) the Performance Indicators, and how much (if any) slippage from stated standards you will allow; and 3) a checklist of all required reports (items 1 through 4 in preceding paragraph).

Your plan could also include in it a penalty/incentive arrangement. From this, your field monitor can know exactly what to look for, and how much of a penalty/bonus should be given out.

The Monitoring Plan should also include a "Monitoring Results Sheet," with the exact findings of your field inspectors; a Contractor Blue Sheet, outlining how the contractor has failed in service delivery, and giving the contractor himself space to write in acknowledgment of the failure. That puts him on record as being notified; that protects you. He gets a Blue Sheet and you keep one. So many Blue Sheets and he gets penalized; or, you can have a formal "Cure Notice" notifying him and warning him.

The contract should note that, after so many Blue Sheets or Cure Notices, the contract will be terminated.

Step VIII — Contract Closeout or Renewal

If you have written a clear contract with measurable performance indicators, and if you have monitored carefully, the decision whether to terminate or renew should be easy.

If a contractor has done an unusually good job, you can consider diminishing some of the reporting requirements. This saves his time and yours. You can write a contract that provides for semi-automatic renewal for one year, provided standards have been met; this saves long bidding procedures. You can grant up to a five-year contract, with or without some evaluation on a yearly basis. Every contractor, being human, requires a little incentive to do a good job year-round; if you have built quarterly incentives into the contract, you're likely to find he's done a better job.

Summary

Contracting has its pitfalls! The greatest of these is a service provider who does a shoddy job, or who raises prices halfway through the contract. You can all but eliminate these problems by writing into the contract measurable performance indicators. And one final tip: don't contract out 100 percent of your capacity, e.g., all of your garbage trucks. Keep 50 percent or more the first time out; that way if the contractor really messes up you're ready to pick up the slack. Moreover, a contractor who knows you can step back into service delivery is very unlikely to horse you around with demands for money, or to ignore citizen complaints.

12. The Politics of Advocacy

Frances E. Winslow

In this era of central-city revenue decline, suburbanization, taxpayer revolts, and business tax incentives from the federal government, a new trend — privatization — is arising in the delivery of municipal services. Municipalities are reexamining the services they provide to ascertain which should or may be privatized. The motivations for this movement toward privatization vary.

Decreasing Revenues, Increasing Choices

Declining tax revenues continue to plague many municipalities, including industrial cities which have experienced vacancies in obsolete industrial buildings. Recycling of these buildings as small shops or loft apartments generally results in a lower assessment than that placed on the former industrial use. Older residential areas are decayed, blighted, condemned, or demolished, erasing other ratables from the tax rolls. Sizable net loss of tax revenues, in many older cities, force governments to seek ways of cutting expenditures. Cutting back or eliminating city services is one way of handling the problem. Privatizing the services offers a creative alternative.

On occasion, specific municipal services "fall from grace" politically. Services that are perceived as favoring one element of the community over others or using tax money to benefit the wealthier citizens more than the poor are eliminated to release funds for projects aimed at more timely or fashionable concerns. The municipality's governing body may prefer to privatize a service rather than eliminate it. In this way the clients of current

Frances E. Winslow, "Privatization — The Politics of Advocacy." Reprinted with permission from Urban Resources, Vol. 2, No. 4, Summer, 1985. Published by the Division of Metropolitan Services, University of Cincinnati, Cincinnati, Ohio.

programs will continue to find providers of services while new priorities may be set for tax money expenditures.

Privatization may solve problems of obsolescence, technological innovation, and capital-intensive development. At times city services require a major investment in new capital equipment to remain efficient and cost-effective. Capital funds may be lacking or insufficient to cover costs. In cases like municipal refuse collection, privatization may yield higher-quality service at similar costs to the citizen. Recycling, tax incentives, and capital markets may all work to attract private capital investment beyond the means of the municipal government.

From time to time citizens protest against "big government." They rebel against the idea of a large standing bureaucracy with its attendant fixed labor costs. Citizens pressure their representatives to reduce the size of the municipal budget or the government itself. They may force on administrators choices that can be resolved only by eliminating programs.

Once a political decision has been made to eliminate some government services, privatization may be a useful alternative to dismantling an existing program area. Privatization can save jobs for the employees of the program and possibly provide a buyer for municipal property and equipment used in the program. Resolution of the political pressure through privatization results in maintenance of services while dismantling government bureaucracies.

Planning for Privatization

Planning for privatization is the key to successfully realigning government services. Time spent in developing a thorough plan is a valuable investment and helps to assure its ultimate acceptance. Once defeated, a plan will be hard to revive in any guise and may mitigate against any successful privatization developing under the same leadership.

Begin by carefully assessing why privatization is being proposed. Are there budgetary constraints that it will overcome? Will it improve the quality or level of service? Will it allow for the development of other unprofitable service areas? Then take the time to carefully study each step in the privatization process. Who are the alternative providers? How competent are they? What other municipalities have successfully privatized that service area? Which have failed in a privatization effort, and why?

Enlist the support of professionals in each area of study. Have the budget director prepare fiscal impact assessments with alternative levels of service at various costs. Engage the councilmember associated with that service as soon as possible. Make him or her a major participant in the development of the skeleton proposal. Listen to his understanding of the political impact he foresees, no matter how negative he may be. Remember that he has to answer to the voters at the polls. Seek the counsel of non-governmental professionals in the area. For example, if the plan is to privatize the paramedic service, ask some emergency room doctors for their advice. How would the physicians in the area respond to the suggestion for change? What advantages can the physicians foresee in privatization?

Carefully analyze the current arrangements for the provision of the service being considered for privatization. Could other steps be taken to improve the efficiency/effectiveness of the service without removing it from the government structure? Could a contract be let for some aspects of the service while keeping others within the government structures? (This can be viewed as an intermediate step to privatization in an incremental plan.) Are there other areas of government where economies could be made more easily? Is the desire to privatize based on philosophical, financial, or political concerns? Whose idea is it? What basis of political support would the plan have from that quarter?

Once a commitment is made to a privatization plan, talk with various possible providers in exploratory conversations. Let them know that these conversations are preparatory to outlining a strategy. Encourage them to convince city staff that privatization is going to benefit the citizens. Take a position of "devil's advocate" to push the limits of their expertise and commitment. Solicit any documentation of their success in providing the service to private firms or other public agencies.

Talk with a city manager who has guided a successful privatization campaign in the service area under consideration. Solicit his advice on timetables, consultants, and political issues.

The plan must be concrete, factual, and fiscally sound. It needs to include information on alternative levels of service at various costs, with and without private involvement. Never announce public support for a plan that is not thoroughly acceptable. There is always next year, there is always another consultant, there is always another way around the red ink.

Once an acceptable privatization plan has been developed, the city staff must accept the role of advocate for it. No privatization plan will succeed if its sponsor is vacillating. The force of personal enthusiasm is necessary for success. Alternatively, if the privatization plan has been mandated by city council, allow the politician who advocates it to be known publicly as its sponsor. Political opposition can develop against even the most sensible and fiscally sound plan, so its proponents must be committed to fighting for its passage at whatever levels of effort are required for success.

If the plan loses, anything less than total commitment will look like sabotage, so make any reservations known early in the planning process. If they are not resolved, stand on them privately and allow someone else to handle the campaign with the public and the media. It is better to be a non-supporter than to be blamed for a failure that was half-heartedly supported.

The Politics of Privatization

Often the decision to privatize is made within the ranks of the city's professional staff. Budgetary realities are clear to the career civil servant who must write justifications for the finance committee hearing. With scarce public resources and lessening federal grant programs, the administrator is forced to evaluate the services being provided by the municipality and select areas where funds can be saved.

Privatization offers an alternative to severe cutbacks, elimination, or marked decline in quality of service. The logic of privatization seems compelling to the staff that is forced to balance a municipal budget with decreasing revenue sources, but making this sensible solution obvious and palatable to the politicians who sit on the city council and must publicly cast votes for the change is sometimes difficult. In this situation the city manager, who has always viewed himself as a businessman running a public corporation, must recast his image. He must become a politician.

At some point in the past, the city service that is now being considered for privatization developed from a need or a want somewhere in the consuming community. Its continued existence in the budget is proof that it still has some consumers, some supporters, and they are crucial to the success of the privatization campaign. Do not discount the consumers because they are old, poor, or members of a minority. If they have the means to get to the next city council meeting and pack the hall, they can be a threat to the privatization plan. Also, do not assume political naivete. Some people in the community will be astute enough to see in the privatization issue a new political base for themselves. Some individual or group will use the privatization plan to advance its political goals. Make sure that group is supporting the plan, not opposing it.

Another incorrect assumption is that no one cares about the service being considered for privatization. Someone makes his living providing it, and he has friends, relatives, and neighbors. If the consumers do not care about the service, the providers will. The threat of losing a steady income is a major motivator for most people. Be sure the providers are on your side.

Do not be deluded by the beauty and ingenuity of the privatization plan. Regardless of how well-researched and -written your proposal, how thoroughly documented, and how worthy of citizen support, every privatization plan will require active lobbyists working at the political level to obtain its successful passage. If the service proposed for privatization is politically sensitive, consider starting the process with the least political route available. Start an incremental plan of privatization with small changes that require no legislative approval, that cause minimal change in the status quo.

1. *Change the terms of the existing contract.* The easiest route toward privatization is to change the terms of an existing service contract to place more authority and responsibility in the hands of the provider. Give financial incentives toward cost cutting and evolution toward privatization in the future.

Begin requiring the provider to use his own equipment and personnel exclusively. Phase out old city equipment. A de facto privatization can be accomplished over a few years' time with employee attrition. This method is especially effective in areas where services are supported by a fee schedule that is modified without city council approval and in areas that do not directly affect service to consuming voters. Examples would be professional contracts with accountants, planners, engineers, data processing services, and legal services. Since these providers are not city employees, they will not sustain a change in their income source, having always been self-employed. City support staff can be diverted into new areas of activity. Obsolete city equipment can be discarded and modern equipment leased for the provider or included as a detail item in his contract.

2. *Change the contractor.* Services that are put out to competitive bid are readily amenable to a change in contractor. New bid specifications can be written to decrease city involvement with the activity and move toward privatization. Generally speaking, there will be enough competition to provide the services so that if current providers do not accept the change in terms, a newer or younger firm will pick up the contract for the experience and publicity. Remember, however, that the level of expertise and service a new contractor might be able to provide can become a political issue. Be sure that only qualified bidders are able to compete.

A potentially explosive issue, but one which will not surface until considerable concern has been generated, is the possible political connections of the current contractor. Before attempting this route to privatization, consider whether the current contractor has the position through political connections or influence. If he's the mayor's brother, it probably will not further the goal of privatization to seek another contractor!

3. *Change the public policy.* After the probable political impact has been considered, you may decide to select the political change route from the outset. This will require careful consideration of the factors and groups likely to be impacted by the decision as well as a program design which makes the privatization plan the most politically attractive to the city's politicians.

The Political Route

All successful political plans for privatization have the voter as their base. Support or dissent starts with those who have the power of the vote.

1. *Analyze your community.* Regardless of what service is being proposed for privatization, that service has some actual consumers, and some potential consumers. If the consumers of this service are only city employees, then the change of contract suggested earlier may work well. It is unlikely that city employees will lobby against a new provider of services so long as he is competent.

Assuming that the consumer of the service is the voting public, consider the elements of the community likely to be affected. In designing the rest of the presentation, remember that the goal is to convince the primary consumers that privatization is in their best interest. This will provide the plan with a political power base when city council is approached to make the change. Citizen support will bring more votes in favor of the plan than the best consultant's report ever written.

2. *Present the privatization issue.* Always remember that money is a major motivator for most people. When presenting a privatization program to the voting public, begin with the financial issues involved. State clearly and succinctly how the privatization proposal will affect the city's budget, the individual taxpayer's costs, and the anticipated future costs. Be as specific as possible in all presentations. Generalizations kill! The voter wants to know exactly how much the change is going to cost him, now and next year; how much it is going to save him, now and in five years; and how the city is going to allocate the savings. Will the taxpayer see lower taxes? Will the rise in taxes be significantly smaller as a result of the privatization? Show the cost differential graphically. Emphasize the loss of service that will result from continued government provision. Note the cutbacks that will be required in other service areas if privatization is not successful.

State clearly what levels of service can be expected with and without the privatization plan. Paint as grim a picture as possible if municipal provision of the service is continued. Use the term "socialized" as much as possible in describing government-provided service. Tell voters, for example, that the socialized paramedic service cannot provide the level of service available through the private sector. Use of evocative language can help to make a clearer differentiation between the existing service and the anticipated privatization.

Appeal to voters on the personal level. Be sure to have specific examples of how the change will help individuals. Tell the consuming public how fast the ambulance will arrive at their homes, how often the refuse will be collected, how long the waiting list will be at the child care center. Finally, remember that the privatization must appeal to the majority of voters in your community. Make the change attractive financially and in terms of improved service levels. State that better service will be available, or that service levels will be maintained, or that the loss of effective service will be less under the private provider than with continued socialized services.

3. *Find the interest groups.* Begin by evaluating which groups can be expected to support the privatization effort. Determine which groups are likely to respond, and what kind of response to expect. Generally the business community will approve. They will see privatization as a business opportunity and as an attempt at economy in government. Taxpayer groups will be supportive of efforts to increase efficiency while maintaining service levels. Homeowner associations, the League of Women Voters, PTAs, civic betterment groups, and church groups are all potential supporters. Unions for the private sector business that will benefit from the privatization may offer support as well.

Strengthen the support of these groups, once identified, by providing them with full information on the privatization plan. Offer to send a speaker to one of their meetings. (In fact, this technique can be used to target and create a constituency for privatization that is needed but lacks political support and sponsorship.) Encourage the members of these groups to speak to their neighbors about the plan and offer simple literature that graphically explains it.

Identify powerful citizen groups that will not have an immediate position on the privatization issue. Most interest groups focus only on the area of their own concern. They are most effective politically in that area. However, as an organized bloc of voters, their interest may be raised by the proper presentation of the privatization. Try to find some connection between the privatization and their major concern. For example, the privatization of the paramedic service may be the goal. The Audubon Society is not directly interested in ambulance service. However, point out that by privatizing the ambulance service, the city will require less public funding for medical services and so can make additional funds available for the wildlife preserve, or the zoo, or the public park system. Of course, this privatization will allow for additional funds for any and all other public services, but in talking with each group, target their special area of interest. A split of the related "spoils" can be arranged after privatization has been approved. The funding freed for other uses should be distributed with a nod in the direction of community groups that supported the privatization.

By targeting secondary issues, you can turn neutrals into supporters. These groups can be the difference between success and failure at the council meeting because their support will not look as blatantly motivated by self-interest.

Be sure to identify community groups that are likely to oppose the privatization effort. The primary opponents will be any city employees whose job status will change as a result of the privatization. These people need to be reassured of their position in the transition period. In negotiating for the privatization, you should make every effort to involve city employees in the transition process. Their training and experience should be an asset to a new provider who, as a private employer, can negotiate one- or two-year contacts that would allow him to eliminate inefficient people relatively quickly. Without the limitations of civil service rules, he can negotiate performance-based contracts that protect his profit margin while giving job security to a major power block. Employees about to lose their jobs are a formidable group of opponents who can be defeated only in an emergency situation. Ordinarily, politicians will not risk their reelections by angering such a large segment of voters, for the former employees will have on their opposition team all their friends and relatives. Get the former employees a good transition contract, thereby eliminating any negative impact on them.

The public employees' union will probably be opposed, since the change represents a loss of union members and dues payers for them. It may be possible to neutralize negative reaction from this group by explaining that the privatization of one area of services will prevent the need to cut back services in other areas where the loss of unionized jobs might be greater. This approach will be most effective if those employees losing their city employment through privatization have already been guaranteed other positions with the new provider of services.

If the union remains opposed, it may be possible to neutralize their impact on the city council and the electorate by stating that their concerns are self-centered. Raise the issue of their opposition in talks with other community groups. Explain that although the privatization will benefit the average voter and save other city jobs, the union leadership is interested only in their own dues income.

Some groups will be opposed to the privatization on political or philosophical grounds. Some groups prefer government provision of all services; they are opposed to a profit motive in public services or fear graft. Other groups will foresee the privatization of their special service areas and therefore try to stop all privatization regardless of its validity. Certain people oppose all change on grounds that a known evil is to be preferred to an unknown evil. It may be impossible to win over such groups.

The approach here must be to neutralize the opposition. Attempt to discredit the opposition by pointing to the many benefits to the community at large. Identify the opponents as a "special interest" with only their own concerns in mind. An alternative approach is to turn the opponent's issue against them. Take, as an example, a plan to privatize paramedic service. A senior citizen group has stated that the annual fee to be charged by the provider is too high for them to pay. Attack the issue by showing that there is a provision for payment based on ability to pay. Point out that the $60 annual fee is only $5 per month, less than most smokers spend on cigarettes. Show that the annual fee, which covers unlimited service, is less than the cost of one ride in a private ambulance. Then present an outstanding facet of the plan. By privatizing, ambulance response time can be reduced from twelve minutes to five. The ambulance will have an emergency medical technician who is more highly trained and skilled than the present ambulance attendants; in fact, it will really be a rolling intensive care unit equipped with the latest life-support systems. Raise and destroy the issue of the opposition, then fire the best new information into the debate.

Some opponents may have valid concerns that you cannot refute. Sometimes their opposition will be based on bad experiences at a previous residence or on anticipation of future problems that no one can predict accurately. Raise the issue, then give reasons why these negative expectations are not reasonable. Cite the basis for the proposal and the civic support that has gathered around the issue. Point out that if the private system does fail, there are some safeguards to restore services quickly.

Never ignore opposition. Refusal to discuss it looks like weakness. Opponents will emphasize city staff "fear" to discuss their concerns and suggest that it is because there is no good answer to them. This kind of attack raises doubts in the minds of the undecided.

4. *Involve the media.* Although many services have been privatized routinely over recent years, the issue of privatization is still a newsworthy method of resolving financial difficulties. Use the local print and electronic media to carry the message of community betterment through privatization to the voters. Begin by developing a brief press release and holding a news conference. Involve the local politicians in this effort as much as possible. They have name recognition with the voters, while professional governmental staff are usually unknown. (The politicians always like media exposure and will remember it kindly.)

Develop a media campaign designed to display the myriad advantages of privatization. Have a portfolio of photos of old equipment, inadequate facilities, or unserved constituencies. Photograph an incident where the deficiencies led to loss of life or other disaster. Collect quotable responses from consumers who support the privatization of the service.

Encourage the media to view the event as news by informing them whenever a council meeting or community gathering will deal with the privatization. Create news by formally "announcing" various stages of the privatization, such as the selection of a consultant or the support of a community group or politician. Encourage the comment of state and national representatives.

Write a news-feature for your local editorial page. In it present the most persuasive arguments for the adoption of the privatization plan. This is the best way to get free publicity for the plan. An article by city staff qualifies as expert opinion. Enlist the support of the city newspaper editor. An editorial supporting the privatization effort will encourage the support of the politicians. The print media has the power to make a politician look good to his constituents, or to print his photo only when he falls down. This power to mold public opinion can be turned to your advantage in obtaining support from the city council members.

Develop a "Citizen's Committee for Privatization" to support your realignment of services. As a private group, they can raise funds and lobby more extensively for public support. Encourage them to take out an advertisement in the local paper, or pay for the distribution of flyers through the local paper. Similar support may also be obtained from established interest groups that support the privatization, e.g., senior citizen clubs, PTAs, church groups.

Presenting the Plan to City Council

Videotaped presentations have many advantages. No one can interrupt or disconcert a videotape. The script can be written to cover all the most positive highlights of the privatization issue. It can include statements from residents who support the privatization, graphic portrayals of instances when the provider could have done a better job, and photos of other places where the privatization has resulted in some obvious improvement. For example, if the plan is to privatize the paramedic service, the video could show the inside of an ambulance in a city which has a private provider. Then you could show the inside of an older and more poorly equipped city vehicle. Have one paramedic say to the other, "Pass me the oxygen appliance," as he leans over a patient, and the other replies, "We don't have that equipment in these vehicles." Keep the tape short—10 to 12 minutes is ideal.

After the presentation, have a few prepared remarks to present to the city council to reiterate the points made on the tape. Have any financial figures on a chart or graph that the audience can also see. Make the statements as clear and simple as possible.

Be sure to notify the supporting groups well in advance of the night of the presentation and request their presence. It is crucial that the city council chambers be full of citizens who support the privatization. First of all, it shows the politicians that the people really want this change. With reelection in mind, they will be more sympathetic to the proposal if there is a showing of public support. Secondly, it leaves few seats for possible opponents or hecklers. Emotional demonstrations in the city council chambers can destroy all the good will and intelligent work developed up to that point. The plan has not succeeded until all the votes are counted!

Summary

The American system of government is based on the will of the electorate. Public administrators must avail themselves of the power of the voter to obtain changes of public policy. Privatization is a new issue for many voters and local politicians. It may be met with concern and fear. A solid political strategy can develop a strong base of public support for the program, resulting in a successful realignment of public resources for the good of the community. A politically astute administrator will find that when all the votes are counted, privatization is a winner.

13. Coproduction and Local Governments

Jeffrey L. Brudney

Faced with fiscal pressures to economize and popular sentiments apparently favoring a reduction in the size of government, many local officials have embraced the idea of increased reliance on the private sector for carrying out government's many functions. When contemplating a move toward "privatization," public managers think first and foremost — and some, no doubt, exclusively — of contracting with private firms for the delivery of government services. Writes Ted Kolderie, director of the Public Services Redesign Project in the Humphrey Institute at the University of Minnesota, "privatization ... has become simply a new name for contracting."[1] Kolderie's assessment receives support in a 1982 ICMA survey of city and county governments, which found that contracting is, indeed, the most frequently employed alternative to the delivery of services by public personnel.[2] But the survey makes clear as well that a number of other service approaches merit consideration.

Among these are several arrangements that lessen government involvement in service delivery and correspondingly raise that of private and nonprofit organizations. For example, a city government may grant a franchise to a private firm to operate municipal facilities, such as an airport. By awarding a subsidy to a nonprofit health clinic, a county government can provide for the medical care of indigent residents. A local government may institute a voucher system to give eligible parents a choice of day care facilities. In addition, regulatory and tax incentives can be structured to encourage the private sector to produce services that meet community needs.

Jeffrey L. Brudney, "Coproduction and Local Governments." Reprinted with permission from Public Management, *Vol. 68, No. 12, December, 1986. Published by the International City Management Association, Washington, D.C.*

The interest in alternatives to direct government service delivery, including contracting, franchise subsidy, voucher, and regulatory arrangements, stems from a growing realization on the part of local officials that many services can be conceived as a "business," with potential for gains in efficiency and effectiveness if operated in that manner. This position is not simply a cynical rationale for load-shedding of burdensome obligations by local governments. Instead, it is based on a fundamental distinction between the provision and the production of services. As Valente and Manchester explain, "To provide a service is to decide that a service shall be made available and to arrange for its delivery. This is an integral part of a local government's policymaking process. To deliver a service is to actually produce the service."[3] It follows that while local governments must be involved in the provision of services, production is not inherently a governmental task and can be accomplished through a number of mechanisms, depending on the type of service, the objectives sought, etc.

The alternatives discussed thus far preserve government's role as provider but look to private and nonprofit organizations as the producers of services. This view of the distinctive responsibilities of the public and private sectors is the most common interpretation of privatization and has spawned voluminous research and commentary. Yet another method exists, however, to further privatization that has received much less attention. This option calls for local governments to increase citizen participation in the production of community services.

Coproduction

Service delivery approaches premised on citizen involvement are known as "coproduction," so named for the joint cooperation of residents and public employees in the implementation of services that is the hallmark of the process. Of course, citizens are always involved in governmental activities to some degree, but usually as the relatively passive recipients or targets of policy initiatives. Coproduction, in contrast, requires the active participation of residents in the design and especially the delivery of services. This approach takes two major forms: self-help by citizens and government volunteers.

In self-help programs, individuals or groups, often at the urging of local officials, undertake activities that either lie beyond government budgetary capabilities or extend existing service levels. Those producing the service and those enjoying its benefits belong to the same group. The principal example is the rise of associations composed of homeowners or other groups of residents that provide a variety of services to members. These include increased protection from crime and victimization through citizen patrols and neighborhood or community watch. The ICMA survey shows that cities and counties also rely on self-help efforts for services to the elderly as well as programs in paratransit, day care, recreation, and culture and the arts.[4]

Volunteers are citizens who work without pay for local governments, although they normally receive reimbursement for out-of-pocket expenses. As opposed to self-help, in which citizen activities primarily enhance the level and or quality of services received by participants, voluntarism consists of residents' donations of time and energy to benefit the larger community. Depending on the needs and preferences of local officials, volunteer programs can be organized on a government-wide basis, as evidenced by the experience of Arvada, Colorado,[5] or decentralized within individual city departments.

Local governments utilize volunteers in a variety of capacities. In many communities, citizens sit on planning and review boards instrumental to the design, formulation, and approval of government policies and policy changes. While volunteers have traditionally performed such activities, local governments increasingly seek help from citizens in the actual production of services. Volunteers lend valuable assistance to cities and counties in a number of functional areas, particularly recreation, public safety, and human services.[6] Here, they work not only as support personnel to government employees but also as direct providers of services to other citizens. For instance, volunteers operate and maintain public libraries, museums, and recreational facilities. In addition, cities are beginning to draw on the professional skills of volunteers, soliciting contributions of time from lawyers, accountants, computer programmers, and individuals in other occupations. In sum, the meaning of government volunteers is changing, and the jobs to be performed by them in the future seem limited only by the ingenuity of public managers and the availability and qualifications of civic-minded residents.

Like the other approaches to government services discussed here, the coproduction model recognizes the difference between provision arrangements and production means. The nature of coproduction renders this distinction more subtle, however. In the case of self-help, members of citizen groups or associations typically make cooperative arrangements for the delivery of desired services (provision) and then carry them out through their own efforts (production). With respect to citizen voluntarism, local governments usually make the important provision decisions (for example, where, how, and in what numbers volunteers are to be utilized), while citizens again act as valued producers. Yet it would be a mistake to overlook the roles of residents and public officials in both aspects of the service process in coproduction.

On the provision dimension, together with citizens, local governments play a key role in stimulating and sustaining self-help programs. Local officials meet with civic associations, disseminate information, make equipment and facilities available, and coordinate the activities of diverse groups. The significance of these initiatives is underscored by a study of coproduction in Sherman and Fort Worth, Texas, which found that as these cities withdrew funding, publicity, and other support from self-help programs over time, the level of citizen participation in them declined precipitously.[7] Similarly, although government managers ultimately arrange for the utilization of volunteer personnel, they normally enlist the assistance of citizen auxiliary groups and individual volunteers in designing and implementing these programs.

On the production dimension of services, the shared nature of citizen-government involvement is evident as well. Self-help and citizen volunteers extend and supplement public services, but they are not a substitute for the labor and expertise of regular employees. In fact, the level and types of citizen activity forthcoming — and the overall effectiveness of services — are highly contingent on the quantity and quality of services local governments are able to produce. In sum, coproduction consists of joint participation of citizens and public administrators in the provision and the production of services.

Costs and Benefits

Because coproduction does not require monetary payments from local governments to citizen producers, it is tempting to think of this form of service delivery as costless. But coproduction is not free — either to residents or to public organizations.

For the model to be effective, citizens must commit time and labor to service tasks. Some citizens are better able to afford these investments than others. For example, empirical studies report that wealthier, more educated, and nonminority residents engage in coproduction activities most frequently.[8] This finding has serious implications for the equity of self-help programs, for to the degree that these efforts raise the level and or quality of services received by participants, the distribution of public services in a community could become skewed toward more advantaged neighborhoods. In order to alleviate this problem, local officials may need to consider remedial action, such as special attention to poorer areas of a city to stimulate coproduction.

Coproduction imposes costs on local governments as well. Self-help programs rely on a corps of professional service agents to offer ongoing guidance, consultantion, and support to citizen groups. Local governments will need to publicize these programs and to make available facilities, training, and equipment as required by the service. In large cities, governments may find it essential to create community development and liaison positions in order to encourage citizen participation and coordinate the service activities of public employees and resident organizations. With reference to government utilization of volunteers, these individuals must be screened for competence, given requisite instruction, socialized to public work organizations, and extended liability protection. Training in the effective management of volunteers will likely prove necessary for some public employees, and according to researchers, the expansion in job skills and responsibilities "would suggest more highly paid full-time manpower."[9]

Coproduction also entails more subtle costs for local governments. Accommodating citizen participation in service delivery will likely disrupt established routines and procedures predicated on a highly professional service bureaucracy. Managers and staff of departments that come to depend on volunteers and self-help will have to adjust to working more closely with a formerly external group. The utilization of citizens can lengthen and complicate decision making and add another potentially powerful interest around agency affairs. Public employees may resist these changes, (mis)perceiving them as a threat to their authority, expertise, or job security. As a consequence, if local governments do not devote sufficient attention to the implementation of coproduction programs, resentment can develop.[10]

Two steps seem essential to successful implementation. First, coproduction implies the joint delivery of services by citizens and public employees. Citizens are not a replacement but a supplementary resource to trained service agents. Thus, the jobs of public employees are to be protected in such programs, and this policy should be enforced. Virtually all research on the utilization of citizens in a service delivery capacity highlights this point. In most cases, then, self-help and voluntary programs cannot be expected to result in cost savings for local governments, but they will almost certainly lead to greater cost-efficiency.

A second strategy to facilitate implementation is education or training sessions for public employees. These not only should alert employees to the changes necessitated by citizen participation in service production but should also solicit recommendations regarding how and where the model can best be applied. In addition, education should elucidate the benefits to accrue to local governments and their employees from coproduction of services. The advantages can be quite persuasive.

Of primary interest to employees, increased reliance on residents can enhance their jobs. In self-help and voluntary programs, citizens assume some of their more mundane work responsibilities, augment the level of support provided them, and allow employees increased opportunity to pursue tasks requiring professional expertise. In addition, coproduction contributes to the responsiveness of government agencies to citizen needs, ideas, and preferences, a factor that helps to diminish residents' complaints and misunderstandings. Other benefits realized by cities include an increase in public satisfaction with the environment; more positive attitudes toward government; a decrease in mistrust, apathy, and alienation; and more positive neighboring relationships, such as less vandalism and vacancies. Changes of this kind should result in jobs that are easier and more satisfying for public employees.

Yet the most promising aspect of coproduction of services is the potential for greater cost-efficiency, i.e., an improvement in the quantity and or quality of public services achieved for a given budgetary level. The utilization or citizens extends the capacity of government to produce services. It allows public employees to use their time more productively, and it adds to this labor force a supplementary pool of residents ready to help. The consequent gains in services can be substantial. In the area of fire protection alone, citizens provide services worth more than $4.5 billion to local governments. In law enforcement, where coproduction programs have received at least partial credit for recent reductions in national crime statistics, experts contend that citizen involvement is much more effective in combating crime than sizable increases in the number of police officers or in purchases of technical equipment.[11] Because self-help and voluntarism are based on the combination of public employees and residents, they are unlikely to save money for local governments. Nevertheless, coproduction offers significant benefits that should not be overlooked by officials.

Conclusion

Contemporary discussions of alternative methods for the delivery of government services have been useful in stimulating interest in privatization. It would be unfortunate, however, if consideration of alternatives went no further than contracting or similar devices that increase reliance on the private sector for the production of services. Another option is open to public administrators: local coproduction of services by citizens and government agencies. This option has been linked to the possible enhancement of jobs of public employees as well to increases in the cost-efficiency of service delivery. Equally important, by involving citizens directly in the design and delivery of public services, coproduction has the potential to restore values of citizenship and community. In a period in which fiscal priorities seem paramount, that would be no small achievement.

Part Three: The Application

14. Fire Protection

John A. Turner

A few years ago New York Governor Mario Cuomo said, "It is not government's obligation to provide services, but to see that they're provided." Indeed, had government been obligated to provide services in rural Arizona of 1948, the Rural/Metro Corporation of today would not exist.

Rural/Metro Corporation, headquartered in Scottsdale, Arizona, did not hold a lot of promise when its founder, Lou Witzeman, wrestled with establishing it in an area that is now a part of Phoenix. But today fire protection is but one of a range of emergency services that the company delivers.

Last year the combined revenues of its other operations exceeded those of fire operations for the first time. Nevertheless, fire protection remains a significant element of the company's success, and Rural/Metro remains the nation's leader in private fire service. Last year Rural/Metro had gross revenues of over $35 million from a range of emergency services provided to 50 communities in five states.

Rural/Metro—The Early Years

In February 1948 founder Lou Witzeman's thoughts on the future of Rural/Metro did not extend beyond the next ninety days. At that time he was primarily trying to fill a potential crisis in his life and his home—no fire protection. "There was no master plan in forming the company, I simply needed fire protection and was determined to get it," Witzeman said.

John A. Turner, "Privatizing Fire Protection Since 1948—The Rural/Metro Experience." Reprinted with permission from The Privatization Review, Vol. 3, No. 1, Spring, 1987. Published by The Privatization Council, Washington, D.C. (Printed by Maxco Publications, Inc., Little Falls, New Jersey.)

Armed with promises from his neighbors to pay him $10.00 a month for fire protection, Witzeman invested his last $900 in a fire truck only to find that the promises did not convert to cash and he was stuck with a fire truck. "I learned something that every 21-year-old in this world should know," Witzeman recalled. "I couldn't count on my neighbors. When I went to collect, no one paid." This left Witzeman with two choices: either go into business or go bankrupt. He decided to tough it out, and with one fire truck, four men and a modest budget, he began a subscription fire service. Applying brains, hard work and a little luck the business grossed $30,000 the first year.

In 1951 the company landed its first major municipal contract with the newly incorporated Scottsdale, Arizona. Witzeman attributes that contract as the key to the success of the company. "Scottsdale encouraged innovative thinking," Witzeman said. "In order to succeed, we had to be better than the traditional public fire departments. We had to be more than just good firefighters; we had to be good businessmen as well."

The firm began by breaking with tradition, applying innovative concepts and operations to the delivery of fire protection, while emphasizing fire prevention. Underlying the company's success is its ability to deliver cost-effective fire protection in combination with increased productivity. Witzeman's early philosophy of matching the manpower to the fire load remains with the company's 25 fire departments. This concept has been met with both awe and disdain among the segments of the population who cling to the notion that fire departments are an ingredient of government.

Objectives of Private Fire Service

The Rural/Metro system employs full-time firefighters backed up by paid on-call reserves. By not staffing up for the worst case scenario—as traditional fire protection delivery often does—a more productive, cost-effective system results, tailored to meet the requirements of its contracting communities.

Rural/Metro has never been "fired" from a contract, nor compromised quality service in favor of profit. Rural/Metro is not an experiment in privatization, it's a proven concept that has delivered responsive, cost-effective service for almost 40 years. As a demonstration of the company's integrity, they are willing to provide needed emergency services at a loss to some emerging but fiscally strapped communities, nursing them along until they are able to stand alone. Rural/Metro is proud of its flexibility and ability to challenge tradition with innovative cost-effective alternatives.

Critics, particularly the International Association of Fire Fighters, like to argue that because private firms like Rural/Metro must make a profit, somehow that profit is deducted from the level of service. This assumes that municipal fire departments are operating as cost-effectively as possible and that any more cost-effectiveness will result in their providing a lower level of service. This time-worn myth is still a favorite theme of those who fear the advances of the private sector.

Case History—Florida, 1985

A recent case history involving Rural/Metro dramatizes the fear of privatization typically exhibited by union fire departments.

In late 1985 Rural/Metro was contacted by a Northwest Florida gulf-coast community of about 25,000, following the failure of protracted negotiations with the city's unionized fire department. In the view of the mayor, city manager and some members of the city council, the 30-man fire department's continued efforts to negotiate for more money and benefits had divided the two parties, resulting in a breakdown in negotiations and leaving the union without a contract.

In this climate the city considered privatizing its fire department. Members of the city staff came to Scottsdale, Arizona, to look at Rural/Metro as an alternative. The three-member city contingent, which included the city manager, were impressed with what they saw and stated so publicly after returning to their city.

The city firefighters' union response was swift, frenzied and—based on previous experience—predictable. They began by erecting mobile signs on a pickup truck denouncing privatization, and launched a door-to-door petition drive to amend the city charter to require the city to staff their police and fire departments with city employees.

The mayor responded by stating that the city would not be intimidated and would continue to look at privatizing the fire department. To demonstrate their resolve, the city manager ordered the firefighters to remove their sign from in front of city hall where it served as a focal point for picketing and media attention. The firefighters responded by suing the city council for allegedly infringing upon their constitutional rights of freedom of speech.

The unions then implemented new techniques to defeat privatization. Strategies, in addition to the continued picketing, included paid newspaper advertising with an emotional appeal designed to instill fear, statements to news media at the picket lines and door-to-door distribution of a brochure describing what the people could allegedly expect if a private fire department took over. The brochure stated:

- Private companies provide cheaper service by passing their overhead onto the budgets of other city departments.

- Fire losses increase under private companies by 300 to 400 percent.
- Additional services such as rescue, fire safety inspections, hydrant maintenance, etc., would cost extra.
- Privatization of emergency services is dangerous and a threat to public safety.
- Private companies use lesser trained and less experienced people who could strike.

Much of the criticism of privatization came as no surprise to Rural/Metro. It was an old refrain that sought to convince people that the communities which contract with the private sector lose control of the service that is privatized. Rural/Metro responded that private companies under contract to a municipality would not retain their contracts if the service provided were not as cost-effective and as responsive as public sector fire protection. Loss of control simply does not occur. Indeed, controls are stricter in many cases. Performance and equipment standards, staffing levels, contract reviews and renewals pose an ever-present threat to the poor performer. Contracts can be easily revoked for poor performance by the contracting municipality.

In late October 1985, Rural/Metro decided to establish a presence in the city to provide a balance to the biased information being provided to the public by the union. The company sent a representative to the city to monitor events and to inform and educate the public on privatization and Rural/Metro. In mid–November the company contracted with an advertising agency and commissioned a public opinion survey to ascertain views on privatization. The company's representative began interviewing members of the city council one-on-one to determine the extent of their support for privatizing the fire department. Of particular interest was when Rural/Metro could reasonably expect to see a Request for Proposal (RFP). Reaction from the council was mixed but encouraging — while some members were noncommittal, none categorically opposed the concept.

The survey of the population revealed that the public knew very little about privatization beyond the misinformation they had received — and nothing about Rural/Metro. The company set out to change that.

A press conference was called on December 10 that attracted media within a 100-mile radius of the city. The privatization issue had become a media event, and certainly the biggest political issue in recent memory for this small community. Charges and counter-charges between the union and the city were making daily headlines while the union continued its picketing activities. This, together with the mobile anti-privatization sign, continued to be the focal point around which media activity galvanized. Frequent city edicts that the union "cease and desist" seemed to play into the hands of the union and whet the appetite of the media.

The Rural/Metro news conference was held across the street from city hall on the same day as a scheduled evening city council meeting. At the same time, the union beefed up its picket line in front of city hall, and that evening presented the city council with citizens' petitions calling for a referendum on the privatization issue.

A Rural/Metro spokesman told a packed press conference that privatization was essentially an economic issue and that the company's concept of operations provided a more cost-effective and productive alternative to traditional fire protection delivery.

On balance, the reporting of the press conference was fair, although some media bias in favor of the city fire department was evident. Through one-on-one media interviews and speaking engagements before local civic groups — such as the Lions and Kiwanis clubs — Rural/Metro's spokesman continued to emphasize the cost-effective, increased productivity benefits of a private fire department for the city. These groups were very receptive to the concept of privatization and the prospect of saving money, which Rural/Metro virtually guaranteed under its concept of operations.

The union, on the other hand, was taking the approach that only a public fire department that did not have to deal with profit considerations could really "care." "We Care" became the logo in their advertising and on T-shirts that union firefighters and their families and supporters wore at every opportunity.

The real emotional issue for the union membership was fear of losing their jobs if the city converted to a private fire department. And this fear was not entirely unfounded, since Rural/Metro's concept of operations requires less full-time fire fighters than municipal union fire departments, depending instead upon paid on-call reserves to augment the full-timers when needed.

About this time Dan Giblin, Senior Vice-President of Marketing for Rural/Metro, decided to launch an advertising campaign to run over a 30-day period beginning December 15. At the conclusion of this multimedia campaign, a second public opinion survey would be taken to measure the effectiveness of the advertising and its impact on changing public opinion. Giblin concluded that, since the first survey had indicated that nearly a third of the population were retirees, the advertising should direct an emotional message to their needs and concerns for emergency protection. The advertising also emphasized the cost-savings and increased productivity that Rural/Metro could deliver without compromising quality of service or response times. The initial survey had also indicated a relatively high level of education, which permitted the advertising to present a fairly complex message to an audience which could grasp its meaning and impact.

Three newspaper, two radio and one television advertisements were developed. On December 15, ads began running in three key area newspapers and on three radio stations. The 30-second television commercial ran over 300 times on cable television.

The objectives of the advertising campaign were to:

- Educate the public on the issue of privatization.
- Encourage community support for privatization and Rural/Metro.
- Create favorable public attitudes so the city council would feel justified in approving a contract with Rural/Metro.
- Counter information distributed by the union which the company considered erroneous.

Upon completion of the advertising campaign the second public opinion survey was conducted to assess any changes in the public's awareness and opinions on the issue of privatization versus municipal union fire protection. The results were encouraging and concluded that:

- The awareness level of the voting public increased dramatically between the time of the first and the second survey.
- People were aware of Rural/Metro's advertising campaign and the push for privatization.
- The increase in those favoring privatization was not significant; however, those opposed to the change dropped dramatically to less than fifty percent over the first survey.
- Most people believed a private firm would be more cost-effective. (This seemed to be the most significant change.)
- Other results showed a considerable drop in public support of unionization in the fire department and an overall increased receptiveness towards privatization.

Rural/Metro had successfully achieved one of its key objectives — to inform and educate the public on the differences and advantages of privatization over a public fire department. The city was heartened by the results, particularly since relations with the union firefighters had gone from bad to worse. Rural/Metro expected an RFP to be issued the following month.

Such was not the case. Charges and counter-charges were flying, and more lawsuits and legal claims were being threatened and filed. Contract negotiations broke down completely when the city's labor attorney would not meet union demands. He told a union representative that he could "...stick it right in his ear," and walked out of the contract hearings.

The city subsequently charged the union with engaging in an illegal strike for not responding to a general alarm that had occurred in early December. The charge asked that the union be decertified, fined $20,000 and charged for the city's legal costs.

The city continued to delay the release of an RFP and indicated it might wait until after the referendum, which now seemed a certainty to make the ballot for the November 1986 general election.

In mid–February 1986 Rural/Metro pulled its representation out of the city. Subsequently legislation was introduced that would have given all municipalities the option to consider privatization as an alternative to public services. Had such a bill been signed into law it would have effectively nullified the union firefighters referendum.

It did not become law. Instead, with the firefighters union lobbying against the legislation, it was assigned to a special committee for study, assuring the bill's virtual demise.

The city, continuing its fight, sued the union in an attempt to have the referendum on privatization declared unconstitutional. This effort also failed, and the referendum found its place on the November 1986 general election ballot. A "YES" vote would mean that the city would lose its option to privatize essential city services.

The firefighters' union campaigned vigorously to win the referendum, relying heavily upon advertising and door-to-door contacts. Balancing these efforts was a citizens' committee — chaired by the mayor — to keep the privatization issue in perspective, and to get the vote out to defeat the referendum.

The mayor was privatization's most visible and vocal supporter in his efforts to bring the issue before the public. While he never said he favored privatization, he was resolute in his determination to explore the "pros" and "cons" and present the issue to the public in an objective manner.

Prior to the referendum a hearing was held by the State Public Employees Relations Council on the city's strike charges against the union. The judge failed to uphold the charges.

Still, the private sector saw victory soon after. The referendum failed, and privatization and the city were winners. The voters overwhelmingly supported the city's right to retain the option to contract with the private sector. The city carried all of its five precincts. It was clearly a victory for the city, for privatization, and for Rural/Metro as a privatization pioneer.

This had a very sobering effect on the firefighters. With virtually no discussion, they signed a new contract with the city that was far less generous than what they could have had in the first place — a contract that reduced benefits and implemented a merit pay system for firefighters.

Rural/Metro will not see a Request for Proposal. The city and the union are now more interested in mending fences. But there can be little doubt that the city benefited from the efforts of Rural/Metro. The city was sincere in its efforts to look at privatization as a viable option to a traditional municipal emergency service, and greatly benefited from the efforts of Rural/Metro.

The privatization issue was the most expensive political battle in the city's history and in the 39-year history of Rural/Metro. Nevertheless, as Rural/Metro President Ron Butler concluded, "Even though we may have won a battle and lost the war, it was a battle worth fighting, not only for Rural/Metro but for privatization."

Case History—Scottsdale Fire Codes

The company's ability to demonstrate its fire prevention ethic through dramatic, innovative fire codes has set national standards and models in the process.

By working closely with the Scottsdale City Council, Rural/Metro was able to impact the city's development by engineering strict fire codes and the nation's most comprehensive commercial and residential sprinkler ordinances.

Far-sighted leadership, strict building and fire codes and a unique partnership between Scottsdale and its private fire department have seen the city evolve into a well planned, nationally recognized, progressive resort community of over 100,000 residents. Moreover, it has become one of the most structurally fire safe cities in the country. For instance, Scottsdale passed a fire code in 1974 requiring sprinklers in commercial buildings. That code remains strictly enforced.

And while pleased with this success, Bob Edwards, Scottsdale fire chief and a vice president for Rural/Metro, wanted to take the fire code a step further. In mid–1985, Chief Edwards persuaded the Scottsdale City Council to adopt what he calls "the most comprehensive fire code in the world." The city's ordinance requires an automatic sprinkler system in every room of every commercial, industrial and residential building in the city. The ordinance applies to all new multi-family residential and commercial buildings, as well as all single family homes and subdivisions. Chief Edwards calls it "the 24-hour fire fighter." It did not come easily.

Edwards had first considered a similar ordinance six years earlier, but due to considerable resistance, ". . . just had to put it on the back burner," he recalls. But in 1982 Edwards arranged a national test of two types of new quick-response sprinkler heads after convincing a Scottsdale builder to retro-fit two homes with them. Rural/Metro assumed full liability for the houses.

Over 250 interested parties from throughout the country and overseas attended what became a dramatic breakthrough test of life-saving, quick-response sprinklers for use in the home. Chief Edwards recalls it as "the first test of its kind with people sitting in a room without protective gear while a fire challenged a sprinkler system. It proved you could be in a room with a fire until it was extinguished by the sprinklers, and not suffer carbon monoxide poisoning, disorientation or be overcome by heat." City council members and building officials witnessed the drama, and the test became the nucleus of the new sprinkler ordinance campaign.

The Rural/Metro Marketing Approach

Growing from one fire truck and four men in 1948, Rural/Metro is currently approaching its 40th anniversary with a fleet of over 300 vehicles and over 1700 employees collectively known as "The Emergency People." Its contracts range from $160,000 to over $3 million annually for periods ranging in length from one to ten years. The company has over 95,000 fire subscription and 30,000 ambulance subscription customers comprised of individual homeowners and businesses.

In combination with the company's full-time/part-time paid reserve system is an ambitious fleet service program that provides not only major maintenance and refurbishing of its vehicles, but also fire truck and equipment construction when needed.

The company also contracts with ten fire districts throughout Arizona. The company has also found it strategically sound to expand its ambulance care to areas adjacent to existing operations throughout its various geographic regions. This not only meets expansion goals but also permits the sharing of administrative and management costs.

The company still relies on its time-tested door-to-door sales for fire and ambulance subscriptions supported by specialized advertising and direct mail. "Because we are targeting specialized markets we find direct mail very effective and comparatively inexpensive," Senior Vice President of Marketing Dan Giblin said.

The company does not seek out municipal fire protection contracts. They prefer instead to respond to serious queries from various government entities. Such, however, is not the case in ambulance operations. "We *do* look for potential ambulance contracts by making contact with key political entities in targeted states confined mostly to the sunbelt," Giblin added.

The company's marketing strategy has not changed much over the years, but has become more sophisticated and aggressive. While there is no magic marketing formula in the privatization arena, Rural/Metro has developed strategies over the years that have met the company's marketing objectives. Utilizing its well-established customer base in fire protection and pre-hospital care, the company markets its new services and products to that same group, according to Dan Giblin.

"Since pre-hospital ambulance care complements fire protection — often with both responding to emergencies — it's a natural link for us to introduce these customers to our newer health care products and services," Giblin said.

In conclusion, Rural/Metro will remain very active in the privatization arena and continue its growth and development in the emergency services field. Municipal governments and enlightened citizens and taxpayers understand the cost-effective benefits and increased productivity that privatization has demonstrated over the years in many areas that were traditionally government-operated. Privatization has not only arrived . . . it's here to stay.

15. Information Resources

David Krings and Charles Martin

America's government leaders are facing tremendous challenges today. How can the growing needs of constituents be met at a time when budgets are already constrained? How can productivity be increased and costs reduced to meet taxpayer demands for greater efficiency in government?

These challenges are having the greatest impact on government officials at the local level—because of initiatives such as Proposition 13 in California, the possible loss of Federal Revenue Sharing, federal/state budget reduction efforts, and a general trend among national leaders to view local government as the logical choice to provide any public services. At the same time, local taxpayers have expressed the clear determination to oppose tax increases, regardless of their desire to maintain or even increase service levels.

Faced with this predicament, officials at all levels are rethinking traditional government management and service delivery methods. While the opposing pressures of declining financial resources and increasing service demands are placing many government executives in a painful vise, this pressure is also creating opportunities to develop innovative solutions to these issues that would not have been possible in the past.

One potential solution attracting considerable attention recently is contracting for services with organizations external to the government. This article will concentrate on external contracting with a private firm—commonly referred to as privatization—but the analysis could also be applied to external services supplied by not-for-profit organizations or other governments.

*David Krings and Charles Martin, "Privatizing Information Resources in Government."
Reprinted with permission from* The Privatization Review, *Vol. 2, No. 2, Spring, 1986.
Published by The Privatization Council, Washington, D.C. (Printed by Maxco Publications,
Inc., Little Falls, New Jersey.)*

Government officials are now examining the basic question of service delivery to the public: whether to expend funds to improve internal delivery methods, or to use external sources to deliver certain services. There is a growing awarness in the public sector that government services do not always need to be supplied by the government. Many officials have found that it is sometimes more cost-effective for services to be arranged and funded by government but supplied through a third party with the specialized abilities to provide them more efficiently.

As a result, private companies are now providing myriad services for all levels of government, in such wide-ranging areas as trash collection, tax collection, food services, data processing, wastewater treatment, industrial development, park maintenance and health care. Most reports indicate that these efforts have produced substantial benefits for all the parties involved.

One of the growing areas for privatization is the management and operation of information resources—data processing, office automation systems and telecommunications. It is growing because the automation of information services can have a dramatic impact on a jurisdiction's ability to deliver services in a timely and cost-effective manner. In addition, improved access to data can provide government executives with the vital information they need to make critical management decisions in this era of changing demographic patterns, rising costs and reductions in funding.

Dozens of cities, counties, states and federal agencies are already working under such arrangements with private industry partners to increase the efficiency of their information systems.

When Is Privatization Appropriate?

Privatization is not the solution for every government service. And there is no simple formula to determining when outside contracting is appropriate. It is certainly true that not all public services can best be supplied by public employees. It is equally true that not all public services can be provided more cost-effectively or efficiently by outside contractors.

An analysis of internal versus external options is not easy. Cost and service comparisons must go beyond traditional "government department" budgets and the quoted prices in private contracts. True cost accounting is not common in government; as a result, in-depth research may be necessary to determine true program costs. Traditional "department" budgets, for example, do not include such direct costs as pension contributions and liability, or health insurance; they also exclude indirect costs such as payroll processing, recruiting and supervision.

At the same time, there are also costs involved for departments that have outside contracts that are not reflected in the actual contract. The contracts and vendors must be monitored, because the priorities of an outside organization may not always be consistent with those of the contracting government. Regular inspections, meetings and agreed-upon service objectives are a must for successful contracting, and all these efforts require expenditures beyond the stated contract price.

Service quality standards are also difficult to define and involve subjective judgments of alternative delivery methods. Every attempt should be made, however, to create "apples to apples" comparisons when evaluating the merits of internal versus external service solutions.

While these cost and service comparisons may present a challenge to government executives, the effort will be worthwhile, because it will permit a fair evaluation of the available options that should result in the greatest benefit for the government and its constituents.

Contracting for Information Resources

The need for effective information systems in government today, and the pace of change in information technology, pose their own set of challenges for government executives: how to meet the growing demands of departments for improved computing, office automation and telecommunication systems; how to get systems to work together; how to compete for scarce management and staff to carry out data processing projects; how to access strategic information to support management decisions; and how to develop an information systems strategy that will meet future needs.

These challenges are compounded by the limited-resource/service-demand squeeze in government. For example, government organizations must overcome the limited opportunities they are able to offer to information technology professionals. Salary caps, lack of clear career paths, and small staff sizes combine to limit career potential in government data processing operations.

In addition, the growing demand in the job market for professionals with computing skills is making it increasingly difficult to recruit and retain these individuals. Unlike the situation with police or fire departments, government is in direct competition with private companies for qualified managers and staff for their information systems. Even more difficult to recruit are skilled managers who understand both information systems and the unique requirements of government.

These salary and career limits often leave governments with the task of training entry-level personnel, who then move on to the private sector to benefit from the greater salary potential.

As a result of these limitations, local governments are frequently faced with a high turnover rate among their information technology professionals. Vacant positions may go unfilled for long periods of time. This resource shortage can lead to development projects that are behind schedule and over budget.

User departments begin looking for alternative solutions for their information system needs. This search often leads them to pursue separate, independent computing solutions, creating "shadow" data processing operations — and budgets — that develop with no overall coordination or compatibility, resulting in higher costs and lower efficiency.

Given these circumstances, it is not unusual for government executives to be dissatisfied with the overall effectiveness and responsiveness of their information systems. With the potential advantages of outside contracting, it should not be surprising that many governments are seriously considering — or already utilizing — privatization as a solution to their information resource problems.

The "External" Solution

A contract with an experienced external vendor operating in partnership with government can provide solutions to many of these issues. Private companies are often less encumbered by the constraints placed on local government regarding internal salary restrictions, limited career paths, and the sometimes cumbersome hiring processes mandated for government.

An outside company can also provide local governments with access to the most critical resource needed to accomplish their information service goals quickly and cost-effectively — experienced people. Private employers can offer the competitive salaries and career paths that attract qualified professionals, giving local governments the benefit of having the best people available in the market working on their information solutions. Privatization also relieves government of the difficulty and expense of recruiting and retaining these individuals.

Contractors can provide an additional benefit of a management structure and staff serving as backup to the personnel assigned to the local government's particular projects. With this support, the disruption caused by an occasional job vacancy can be significantly reduced.

While the cost per person may be greater using an outside company, the greater flexibility of a contractual arrangement offers potential savings because the right number of people with the specific required skills are hired only at the times they are needed.

In addition, an experienced vendor can offer proven methodologies, procedures and products that have been tested in similar organizations, and is probably serving other organizations with similar problems. The company can bring that experience to bear on the local situation, increasing the chances for success. That experience could also aid in the development of a strategic plan in conjunction with the government body for its information systems, and can increase the likelihood of that plan being successfully implemented.

Case Study: Peoria County, Illinois

A good example of contracting for information services – and its benefits – can be found in Peoria County, located in central Illinois, with a population of 200,000. In 1981, Peoria County was facing the same challenges confronting government bodies nationwide: rising costs, reductions in funding, and a growing demand from constituents for better and more cost-effective services.

County decision-makers saw improvements in information technology as vital to the overall improvement of county government. Like its counterparts in governments across the country, the data processing function at Peoria County was under pressure to meet increasing demands from county departments for improved computer services; many administrative operations were still being performed by hand.

The data processing department was handicapped in meeting these demands by limited resources and outdated equipment. Most of the staff's time was devoted to maintaining existing systems at a minimal level of performance, with no time left for new system development or enhancements.

A Long-Term Commitment to Improvement

Peoria County decided at that time to make a long-term commitment to improving its information systems. Part of that commitment was the hiring of a private firm experienced in information services – SCT Corporation – to manage and operate the county's data processing center and other information systems. SCT, of Malvern, PA, has been supplying information resource management services to governments across the nation since its founding in 1968.

The process began with the development of an evaluation team that studied the county's existing systems, helped establish its information system needs and goals, and started implementing short-term improvements. Another critical element that was introduced early in the process was a Users' Committee for the county's information services. This committee makes sure the improvement programs receive the support of county departments, support county policies, and provide a strong foundation for the future.

SCT then worked with the county to develop a strategic plan for its information systems, based on this evaluation and on discussions with the departments using the systems. A comprehensive "master plan" was drawn up that detailed the agreed-upon goals and spelled out the specific timetables and budget to accomplish them. The master plan has been updated annually since that initial drafting to reflect changes in county needs and priorities.

Once the plan was approved, the implementation phase began. SCT assigned an Executive Director to Peoria County, and experienced staff was brought in to undertake the improvement programs.

The Results of the Partnership

In the five years since that time, the Peoria County/SCT partnership has transformed the county's information resources into an efficient system that is meeting the demands of the county's departments and the constituents they serve. Dozens of applications have been added or enhanced, and the level of service delivered to the county has improved dramatically.

User satisfaction has increased as the problems common to local government data processing have been addressed. Improved communications, regular training programs, better documentation, and the knowledge that the data processing function has the ability to respond to departmental needs have effectively restored user confidence.

One indication of this improved performance is demonstrated by the statistics on the use of the computing staff's time. Prior to contracting for outside services, the data processing staff at Peoria was spending approximately 85 percent of its time on the maintenance of existing systems. Today, nearly 70 percent of the staff's time is devoted to new systems development and system enhancements.

The improvements in the county's information technologies have benefited nearly every county department. These improvements translate into more efficient use of staff time and increased control over county spending. Specific improvements include:

- Installation of a Financial Management System, helping the county make the best use of its financial resources;
- A new Alimony/Child Support System;
- An Automated Traffic Ticket System that increases staff productivity, improves cash control and automates records;
- Implementation of a new Payroll and Personnel System to provide more effective human resources management;
- Installation of a new mainframe and conversion of existing systems;
- Elections System enhancements to speed the election process;

- Policy for the use of microcomputers in county departments;
- On-line Physician's Order System for the county's nursing home to reduce clerical work and increase the accuracy of orders;
- Installation of a Jail Management System;
- Enhancement to Real Estate Tax Systems;
- Installation and operation of a new county telephone system.

These and many other improvements in Peoria County have demonstrated the effectiveness of a local government contracting for data processing services with a private firm. It has been so successful, in fact, that the county recently vowed to renew its relationship with SCT for five more years.

Privatization, or other forms of external contracting, is not the answer to every governmental service problem. However, it is an option that government decision-makers must consider if their constituents are to receive the level of services and fiscal responsibility they deserve.

The Peoria County experience is proof that substantial improvements can be achieved through privatization when the government body is committed to the solution, and when the parties involved work together as partners for the benefit of the public.

16. Public Parks

Joe Morris and Terry Stone

Golf courses and garbage collection seem to have few similarities, but they are two of the most common examples of local government's latest money-saving strategy—privatization. With increasing federal mandates and decreasing federal funds, local governments are turning increasingly to the private sector for cheaper management of public services. And public parks and recreational facilities are being targeted for privatization as they become too costly for local governments to maintain.

Grounds keeping, tree pruning, playground maintenance, and a host of other services come under the heading of parks and recreation. In addition, most parks and recreation departments provide summer activity programs for children, as well as craft and exercise classes for all citizens. Skyrocketing costs of personnel and maintenance, however, are forcing many local governments out of the rest-and-relaxation business; while investigating this trend, *American City & County* found that many parks and recreation departments are considering or have instituted public/private partnerships.

After all, says Leonard Ekimoff, administrator of recreation for Erie, Pennsylvania, saving money is the major benefit of privatization. "It's more economical than anything else," he says. "If we hire people, then we are subject to costly benefits, like insurance and pensions."

"There are definite economic advantages, which is the primary motivation that drives the public sector to deal with the private sector," says D. Michael Segrest, director of parks and recreation for Boulder, Colorado.

And money saved in one area can be applied to others, says Laurence Bicking, director of parks, recreation and properties for Cleveland, Ohio.

Joe Morris and Terry Stone, "Private Choices for Public Parks." Reprinted with permission from American City & County, *Vol. 101, No. 5, May, 1986. Published by Communication Channels, Inc., Atlanta, Georgia.*

"Where governments have constraints, economics are the first benefit of privatization. The more that is saved from the dollar, the more that is freed up for other services," he says.

"Parks and recreation services are looked at as a middle ground priority," says Billy Kendall, director of parks and recreation for Macon, Georgia. "Cities will be looking at this area very quickly for privatization of services."

In addition to contracting park services to private companies, some cities also allow civic groups to participate in park maintenance. The net effect is one of personal involvement, says Robert McCoy, commissioner of parks and recreation for Boston, Massachusetts.

"I think privatization has given services a more personal approach," McCoy says. "Traditionally, the cities did things for the neighborhood needs. By contracting out private services to neighborhood groups, it gets people more involved. They have more of a stake in what's going on."

In addition to saving the city money, community involvement has cut down vandalism in Boston's parks, McCoy says.

Equipment Savings

By contracting out maintenance, cities are also realizing substantial savings in equipment purchases and maintenance. "If a city does not have to buy equipment, it cuts down on inventory and maintenance costs. And with some heavy-duty mowers costing $15,000, that is a big savings," Kendall says.

"Private companies can offer substantial cost savings and efficiencies. If we have an area way off in one end of the city, we can allow a 'mom and pop' organization to mow and trim it, and save the expense of a city crew driving all the way out there and all the way back," says Chris Jarvi, director of parks, recreation and community services for Anaheim, California.

"The private contractors can build incentives into their operations where the cities cannot, because it is not considered appropriate to offer financial incentives to municipal employees," he says.

William James, director of leisure services for Altamonte Springs, Florida, says that using public employees to maintain the extensive landscaping surrounding the city's lift stations is too costly.

Similarly, in Marietta, Ohio, often several activities will be scheduled concurrently and hiring all the supervisors needed would break the budget. "Some nights we need five people in five different places to supervise recreational activities," says Marty Kitchen, recreational director. "I have 80 people on my seasonal payroll on contracts, so I pay a total of

$15,000 for all of them. There is no way we could ever cover full-time or part-time people on payroll for this amount."

Although privatization is a novel idea in some areas of the country, private-sector involvement has been in existence for decades. In California, where Proposition 13 forced municipalities to reexamine their financing structures, letting city contracts to private companies is an established practice. Because privatization is newer in some areas than in others, the effects on localities vary, Bicking says.

In California, Proposition 13 caused major budgetary reforms in the 1970s. But not every community turned to the private sector. For example, Anaheim was losing money with its parks program but subcontracting of services was not necessary, says Jarvi.

"We went with a work standards program instead," Jarvi says. "We developed standard practices, then looked at what we did and determined how much time it took. By doing all that, we were able to change our work methods."

In trimming time and methods of providing services, Jarvi says quality was still maintained. "We were able to cut back on the amount of work without changing the quality of the facilities offered. We just acted like the private sector—and found we could do the job just as effectively," he says.

Although many local leaders hail privatization as the answer to their fiscal woes, many others are critics. According to Bicking, the practice is an example of mismanagement. "I think privatization is being used as an excuse for poor management. A public agency should be able to compete or do better than a private firm," he says.

"Privatization is somewhat vogue in parks and recreation today," Cleveland's Bicking says, "and with the shift of revenue and action in Washington, we must be more astute business managers and be looking at the bottom line."

"Privatization is a hyped buzzword of recent times. We have bought paper, supplies, etc., for many years that way. It has been a long time since a pure separation existed between the public and private sectors," Segrest says.

Another drawback to contracting parks and recreation services is the paperwork. "The contract supervision," Bicking says, "is time consuming. If the government is less than efficient in providing services, then it may not be efficient in monitoring contracts."

In addition, "the work must be inspected," Altamonte's James says.

"You have to get your own shop in order, then compare your costs with those of private services," Jarvi says. "If the private sector is working smarter, sure they can undercut your costs, because they have advantages."

James says that privatization is not a panacea. "Once a level of service is established, one that the community is willing to pay for, the work should not be difficult to inspect." Drawbacks to privatization, however, are minimal, he says, even with inspections.

"The main loss is that of control over the conduct of employees and how they treat the public," Boulder's Segrest says. "There is also a limited control of servicing the public. And if you are not satisfied with the private company, you have to wait until the contract expires."

In addition, keeping public employees in parks and recreation is good public relations. If the employees are on site to answer questions about services, Jarvi says, the public has a better image of the department.

"The department needs to remain in contact with the people, so we leave our employees in the areas with heavy public use," he says. "When our people are there to answer questions and police the facility, it is just good public relations."

The private contractor, on the other hand, has a lack of rapport with the public. For that reason, providing the same quality of service as the municipality often is difficult, Jarvi says.

"Some private contractors are known as having a 'mow, blow and go' philosophy. They really do not have any incentive to get to know the public, and what that public needs and wants," Jarvi says.

Contract Considerations

Deciding what type of contract, as well as how to oversee the work, is important in privatizing services. "If you are contracting tree trimming, then it can be done on a per unit basis or on a time-and-material basis," Bicking says. "You have to monitor it carefully, and consider the cost of monitoring when evaluating the decision whether or not to contract out."

In Macon, Kendall says his department is still doing its work with an in-house work force, due to difficulties in getting contracts signed. "At one time," he says, "we looked into contracting out some services, but the way the specifications were written in the contract, the bids were too high. We discovered we could still do the work in-house for less money."

Marietta, Ohio, now is soliciting its first bid ever and is uncertain what will happen. When bids are too high to be feasible, the city calls in workers who have been laid off to perform maintenance tasks, says Bill McFarland, assistant service director.

"Our bottom line is to provide service to citizens at a lesser expense. For that reason, some of our activities are still in-house, and some we are seeking to contract," says McFarland.

With the city's increasing privatization, he says laid-off workers will have a much slimmer chance of being called back to work. "Day-to-day maintenance is hard to handle in non-privatized parks, and we are slow to respond to requests like changing light bulbs."

After laying off some employees in December, McFarland says his department's work force has stabilized. And with the main park's season just beginning, some of those workers are likely to work during the summer mowing lawns and maintaining pools. If the city continues to contract out services, however, these people will not have those opportunities, he says.

And due to an increasing number of contract specifications, smaller companies are being crowded out of the bidding, Kendall says. "Cities are trying to get comprehensive coverage, and so they have to go with the large companies that can provide all the services. And those companies are more expensive."

Most municipalities say they contract 10 to 20 percent of their parks and recreational services, mostly for ground maintenance. In Boston, the public-private partnership with the community has limited the contracts to heavy maintenance work, McCoy says. In addition to grounds maintenance, cities are also experimenting with contracts for recreational personnel.

In Altamonte Springs, James says specialized programs personnel are brought in from outside sources, rather than added to city staff, for areas such as gymnastics, baton and special educational therapy. "Privatization enables us to get better services in specialized areas, to bring in outside folks that have specialized training," he says.

"All our agencies contract for specialized services," Segrest says. "Skiing, scuba and other activities are contracted out. But that is nothing new, it has been done for years."

Marietta's Kitchen views short-term personnel contracting as most efficient. "Contracting works better with short-term programs. A few years ago we tried hiring an assistant director by contract, but he was only helpful in the office and could not be out at every gym during the evenings to supervise the activities. With contracting, I get more coverage for my money."

And in areas where contracts are limited solely to maintenance, further limits on the extent of privatization are encountered. "Our contracts are largely to maintain grounds that require heavy machinery," McCoy says. "They do the mowing and other maintenance, while the citizens' groups do lighter work. For example, a ball field might be mowed by a private contractor, but a local group may mend the fences, clean the dugouts and pull weeds around the area."

One charge leveled at the practice of privatizing parks is that of increased user fees due to the private maintenance cost. But that is not a problem in most areas. Cities such as Erie and Boston do not have any major user fees, so the practice has not caused much hardship to their citizens.

"The cost of user fees was never a problem here, because we really do not have any. Boston is a city where traditional things like parks are free, and it is hard to get that thinking turned around," McCoy says.

"When people pay, they have more of an initiative to take part in programs. User fees are used largely to offset costs, which are reduced by privatization," James says. "Specialized recreation—things above the minimum of recreational services where activities become specialized—are where user fees come into play."

In Boulder, user fees exist in all recreational areas, Segrest says, but there is a low-income program to ensure no residents are priced out of activities. But the city "does not set fees on the lowest common denominator, like many communities, meaning affordable for the poorest citizens. That is not feasible," he says.

"Many of our programs depend largely on groups of parents to coordinate," Kitchen says. "The parents coordinate, and the schools donate their facilities. We do not break even for such areas as the community swimming pool, though. We are getting closer, but we are not there yet."

Placating the Unions

In addition to fears of increased costs, municipalities are also having to allay union fears of lost jobs, McCoy adds. "When we began letting some services out, we had some concern from the union about loss of civil service jobs. We just had to get everyone in one room to tell them that it was not going to hurt them, that they would have less work and responsibility, and that it would take some of the pressure off the department."

Since parks and recreation have long been money-losing ventures for municipalities, any cost-saving measure is likely to take hold firmly. Public recreation should exist to a certain level, James says, but "there are some programs that traditionally are not going to pay their own way—and kids should not be left out. These programs will be traditional losers. If low income kids are left out, though, it defeats the purpose of public recreation."

The future of privatization in parks and recreation, as well as municipal services in general, will largely depend on the service suppliers, Segrest says. "There are different motivations for both sides of the issue: money for the public side, and services for the public. The two do not always work together. The future of privatization depends on the private sector—if it can maintain good services in a contractual relationship."

17. Prisons and Jails

Kent J. Chabotar

Prison and jail overcrowding is a major problem in counties and states across the country. The number of prisoners reached an all-time high in 1984. Inmates have been reported to be sleeping on floors in at least 18 states, and 31 states are operating under court orders to relieve prison overcrowding.[1] A national survey of more than 1,400 criminal justice leaders conducted by The National Institute of Justice (NIJ) in 1984 revealed that prison and jail overcrowding was their biggest concern. The view was held not only by corrections officials, but also by judges, court administrators, prosecutors, probation and parole officials and the police.[2]

Among the range of state responses to the problem, the most ambitious and costly efforts focus on increasing the supply of space.[3] State prison systems have reportedly added 77,476 beds over the past five years and plan to spend about $5 billion over the next 10 years to add another 104,688 beds. A number of states—Texas, Louisiana, New York and Minnesota prominent among them—have undertaken significant building programs.

Traditionally, state and local governments have financed capital improvements with current operating revenues or general obligation bonds. Yet, state and local governments are finding it more difficult to raise capital for prison and jail construction due to federal aid cutbacks, economic recession, and tax and debt limitations imposed by the voters. Increasingly, they are turning to the private sector for help and are exploring a variety of lease and lease/purchase arrangements for corrections facilities. All involve the acquisition of facilities rather than actually turning operations over to a private contractor.

Kent J. Chabotar, "Financing Alternatives for Prison and Jail Construction." Reprinted with permission from Government Finance Review, *Vol. 1, No. 3, August, 1985. Published by the* Government Finance Officers Association, Chicago, Illinois.

In 1984, Abt Associates Inc. as part of its program development contract with the NIJ, was asked to develop a monograph on emerging roles for the private sector in corrections. This monograph was intended to provide current information to corrections officials who were actively considering some form of private sector involvement, or might in the future. Corrections departments in all 50 states were surveyed by telephone to determine their use of private firms in prison industries, contracting for correctional services and facility operations, and financing new construction. A wide variety of vendors also were contacted for their views on the marketability of their products and services in the corrections field. Finally, Abt Associates staff surveyed journals, newspapers and other media to put this information in perspective.

The purposes of this article are to examine the private sector financing alternatives, discuss their comparative advantages and limitations in relation to traditional methods, and cite where and how they have been used.

Traditional Financing of Correctional Facilities

About 40 percent of the state prison systems until recently relied exclusively on the pay-as-you-go method for financing prison construction, about 50 percent financed all their construction with general obligation bonds and an additional 10 percent used bonds in combination with current revenues.

Although general obligation bonds have been considered a superior form of debt by investors because such bonds are secured by the full faith and general tax revenues of the government unit, there has been a trend away from general obligation bonds and toward revenue bonds in recent years.[4] Census Bureau reports show full-faith-and-credit debt as a percentage of total state and local debt declining from 87.6 percent in 1949 to 59.6 percent in 1973.[5]

Constitutional and statutory debt limitations have been significant factors explaining the shift away from general obligation bonds. Another is the requirement of a public referendum to authorize the issuance of bonds. Several problems have arisen with the use of legal controls on governmental debt activity, especially as they affect construction financing for correction facilities:

- The referendum requirement has proven to be an obstacle to financing projects that public officials and many voters—if not a majority— thought necessary. Detention facilities have not enjoyed popular support at the polls. In the November 1983 elections, 72 percent of all bond proposals passed; for jails only 40 percent passed.
- Referenda requirements delay construction programs. The California

Department of Corrections estimated that its state referendum requirement delays construction by eight to 10 months.
- Delay increases construction costs.
- Major consequences of debt limitations have been the development of
  nonguaranteed bonds and the birth of special districts and authorities
  that have been empowered to issue debt outside the legal constraints. As
  a result, there seems to have been little effect in restraining total government borrowing.[6]

Lease Financing Alternatives

Leasing is now considered an alternative to current revenues and
general obligation bonds in financing prison construction. For many years,
government units have used leases to finance everything from fire trucks
and computers to office buildings and schools. Because the leases are subject to annual appropriation (typically over a three- to five-year period) they
are often not considered a debt of the state or municipality and therefore
do not have to comply with debt ceilings and referenda requirements. New
forms of leasing arrangements have the potential of generating the millions
of dollars needed for correctional plant and equipment. However, before
resorting to leasing, governments have to compare leasing's full costs
(which are significantly affected by the length and type of lease) against the
costs of traditional financing as well as consider the legal and political
ramifications of leasing rather than buying.

Straight Leases for Correctional Facilities

In considering leasing, it is important to differentiate between straight
leases and lease/purchase agreements.

A straight or true lease is "an agreement in which the lessee acquires
use, but not ownership of leased property and the lease term is shorter than
the asset's useful life."[7] Lessors typically include banks, life insurance companies, real estate investment trusts and other private developers, although
nonprofit organizations have been known to lease facilities for juvenile and
minimum security offenders.

In exchange for an equity investment of as little as 20 percent of the
purchase amount, the lessor (the private owner) in a straight lease arrangement is able to claim tax benefits of ownership, such as depreciation, and,
in the case of significantly renovated historic or older structures, an investment tax credit.[8] Due to federal income tax restrictions, the lease term must
be less than the asset's useful life. A straight lease is frequently the most expensive financing alternative to the governmental lessee. This is because
ownership of the facility remains with the lessor during and after the lease

period. During the lease period, the lessor, if a private developer, must include costs in the rent that governments and other non-profit entities can avoid, such as taxes, insurance and higher interest charges on borrowed capital. Another factor increasing the costs of a straight lease is that, after the lease period, the asset's cash salvage value belongs to the lessor and not to the lessee as would be the case under other financing alternatives. This is a particular disincentive to straight leasing in the case of minimum security facilties which are more easily converted to other uses and thus have a higher market resale value. In straight leasing, the private developer reaps this profit and the government cannot use the salvage value to reduce the overall costs of the lease arrangement.

Straight leases are being used by 18 of the corrections departments contacted in the 50-state survey conducted by Abt Associates. About 4,000 total beds are being leased in modular units, community service centers and half-way houses in states such as Arizona, Colorado, Indiana, Kansas, North Carolina, South Carolina and Utah. Michigan (1,000 beds) and Pennsylvania (796 beds) alone account for more than 40 percent of the national total. No state is leasing a maximum or medium security facility. The flexibility which leasing offers for shifting between vendors and correctional approaches and for responding to fluctuating inmate populations was frequently cited to justify the use of straight leases. Some states have enhanced the cost competitiveness of straight leasing by permitting private vendors to finance up to 80 percent of the purchase price through tax-exempt debt, such as an industrial development revenue bond. (It should be noted that industrial development bonds are not available for facilities over $10 million, or up to $20 million if UDAG grant funding is included.) Straight leasing was also justified by survey respondents in terms of the lessee's ability to avoid building obsolescence, although most lessors consider this risk when deciding how much rent to charge. On the other hand, the California Department of Corrections has taken an opposite view:

> While the increased flexibility may, on occasion, justify the cost as it relates to obtaining office space, the Department of Corrections is interested in long-term placement of facilities at given sites. Ultimate ownership of the facility is in the best interest of the state given the more or less "permanent" nature of correctional facilities and the high cost of leasing.[9]

The straight lease concept is the basis for at least two other leasing arrangements: leasing with option to buy and sale-leaseback.

1) Leasing with option to buy—This arrangement gives the lessee the right to purchase the asset after each year of the lease period. In most cases, the rental payments are neither increased nor accelerated. Rather, the option's cost is realized when the lessee exercises it. The longer the lessee waits before exercising the option, the greater the total cash outlay for the asset

in that the optional purchase price deceases at a slower rate than the rentals accumulate.[10] For a state that may need time to negotiate with the legislature before purchasing a facility, the additional cost of leasing with option to buy may be tolerable. Missouri currently has this option on some of its straight leasing arrangements. And, the National Corrections Corporation has built jails in Wyoming and New Mexico which local governments have leased with an option to buy.

2) Sale-leaseback — This leasing arrangement involves government property that is sold to private investors and simultaneously leased back by the government for its use. It has been used mainly by governments to finance the renovation of older or historic structures. The provisions of the 1984 Tax Reform Act substantially reduced the attractiveness of this alternative to investors.

Lease/Purchase Financing

A lease/purchase agreement is the "financing and acquisition of a public improvement by a third party who then enters into a lease/purchase agreement with a political subdivision. It is a purchase agreement in the sense that the political sudivision receives title to the facility at the end of the lease period. The political subdivision generally retains control of the design, construction, operation and maintenance of the facility."[11] For correctional facilities, lessors are usually nonprofit entities — such as public authorities, joint powers authorities and nonprofit corporations — in order to take advantage of tax-exempt financing.

Lease/purchase financing is the newest and least tested option for expanded state and local corrections capacity. Because ownership technically rests with the governmental lessee, the lessor cannot depreciate the asset or receive tax benefits other than tax-exempt income from the lease payments. Unlike most straight leases, lease/purchase allows the property title to pass to the lessee upon payment of the final installment and can offer tax-exempt interest on the bonds used to finance the prison or jail, provided the third party or nominal owner issues the lease "on behalf of" the political subdivision.[12]

Lease/purchase financing has been promoted in recent years by leasing companies, brokerage houses and investment banking firms as prison and jail overcrowding has mounted and public officials have become increasingly unable to finance new construction through general obligation bonds. The volume of construction funded by this mechanism is still very small and largely concentrated at the local level. Many states, however, are actively considering lease/purchase financing of prison and jail facilities. Where lease/purchase financing is not permitted, legislation may be under consideration to change or clarify its status.

Lease/purchase financing in corrections has been stimulated by successful experiences in other fields. Examples include: office buildings in Los Angeles, San Francisco and Sacramento; port construction in Portland, Oregon; school buildings in Jefferson County, Colorado; telecommunications systems in Montana and Ohio; and a police station in Los Angeles.

The following steps are required to complete a lease/purchase transaction:

1. Government identifies a legal entity such as a public building authority or nonprofit corporation to issue revenue bonds (or certificates of participation) and act as a lessor of the correctional facility.
2. Government enters into a lease agreement with lessor.
3. Lessor raises capital in the tax-exempt bond market through issuance of bonds.
4. Government provides for construction and operation of facility and annually appropriates funds for lease payments.
5. Finally, government obtains title to facility when bonds are fully paid.

Exhibit 1 compares these steps to the typical general obligation bond process.[13]

Because a lease/purchase agreement is essentially an installment sale that restricts the government's ability to avoid completing the purchase, it is not an option that states are considering to maintain their flexibility to respond to changing correctional needs. Its only flexibility lies in permitting the government to acquire new facilities without following traditional public financing routes. It is often incorrectly assumed that lease/purchase necessarily involves the developer in the management and operations of the facility. However, it is simply a method for financing and constructing a facility that is turned over to the state or county to be managed as it may see fit. At this point, the lessor's role is frequently confined to administering the annual financial transactions. Since interest in lease/purchase financing is growing at the same time that the concept of contracting for facility management has achieved some prominence, combined construction and management packages may, however, emerge over the next few years.

One of the concerns of government units considering lease/purchase financing has been the ability to maintain control of both the construction of the prison or jail and the ultimate operation of the facility. California found that a "high degree of project control can be maintained by funding land acquisition and planning using traditional capital outlay funding and then going to bid on the financial underwriting and construction." Controlling the operation of the facility prior to ownership by the state could be incorporated in the lease agreement.[14] Don Hutto of the Corrections Corporation of America advises careful monitoring of building design and construction to ensure that it meets correctional standards and building

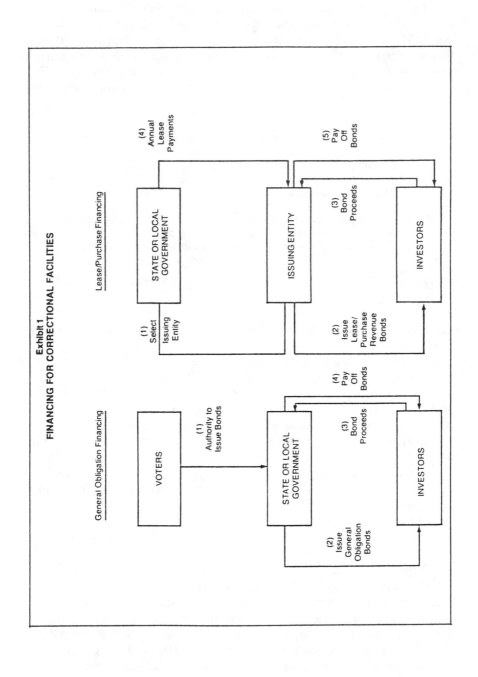

Exhibit 1
FINANCING FOR CORRECTIONAL FACILITIES

General Obligation Financing

VOTERS

(1)
Authority to
Issue Bonds

STATE OR LOCAL
GOVERNMENT

(2)
Issue
General
Obligation
Bonds

(3)
Bond
Proceeds

(4)
Pay
Off
Bonds

INVESTORS

Lease/Purchase Financing

STATE OR LOCAL
GOVERNMENT

(1)
Select
Issuing
Entity

(4)
Annual
Lease
Payments

ISSUING ENTITY

(2)
Issue
Lease/
Purchase
Revenue
Bonds

(3)
Bond
Proceeds

(5)
Pay
Off
Bonds

INVESTORS

codes since lessors may try to economize in unacceptable ways to keep costs down.[15] Another governmental concern has been the many legal considerations in lease/purchase financing, including: compliance with public bidding laws for property and equipment; compliance with usury laws with respect to the interest charged; liability for loss or damage; and what remedies are available to the holder of a lease/purchase contract upon nonappropriation.[16]

Two critical elements of lease/purchase arrangements are the legal entities used to finance and acquire the property and the market instruments sold to raise the necessary funds.

Legal Entities

Three common legal entities are a joint powers authority, public works board and nonprofit corporation. In addition, E.F. Hutton managed to secure tax-exempt status from the Colorado Attorney General's Office for lease/purchase bonds issued by Imperial Municipal Services Group Inc., a private corporation, for a jail and sheriff facility project in Jefferson County, Colorado. Finally, several states are experimenting with allowing financial institutions or municipalities to act as the legal entity, e.g., a city issues bonds on behalf of the state.

In many states, specific legislation is needed to authorize the establishment or use of such entities for prison and jail construction. The legal entity acts in the role of lessor or nominal owner from which the government unit leases the facility. After the bonds are sold, the lessor conveys all rights and interests to a trustee and its ongoing role is very limited. The lessor is not responsible for any ownership functions, such as operation, maintenance or inspections. No tax benefits, such as depreciation, are available to the lessor, although the property is not subject to real estate taxes since a state or municipality is the lessee and ultimate buyer. The trustee disperses construction advances, receives lease payments, forwards debt service payments to the bond or certificate holders and accounts for all revenues and expenditures connected with the transaction. The trustee (or trustee bank) is usually paid an initial fee out of bond or lease proceeds or an annual fee out of lease payments.[17]

Market Instruments

Each of the three financing structures—a joint powers authority, a public works board or a non-profit corporation—can, or could with legislative authorization, raise funds for prison and jail construction by the issuance and sale of two types of market instruments: revenue bonds and certificates of participation. Certificates of participation are used to split the financing of the lease into blocks of $5,000; they mature serially, pay interest semiannually and have prior redemption options much like the typical municipal bond. This is how the facility in Jefferson County, Colorado, was financed. Its entire issue worth $30.2 million was sold in three days at an 8.629 percent interest rate.

Shearson Lehman/American Express has modified the traditional fixed-rate bond or certificate with its "Daily Floating/Fixed Rate Certificate of Participation" which is issued by a nonprofit corporation acting on behalf of a government. In summary, this is a long-term instrument which is priced daily at 30-day tax-exempt commercial paper rates and which can be fixed at long-term rates at a time picked by the government to lock in the most favorable market conditions.[18] Because the government is willing to share some of the risks associated with interest-rate volatility, investors are willing to charge less interest for the use of their money.

Los Angeles County recently contracted with Shearson Lehman to use this mechanism in financing the expansion of its jail facilities. This $18.4 million issue will permit the creation of 700 additional beds at an initial interest cost of less than 6 percent. Another interesting feature of this arrangement is that the county set the rental payments assuming a higher interest rate of 12 percent and uses the excess rental payments over the actual 6 percent rate to prepay some of the certificates. The excess should allow the county to retire the debt in about 15 years, although the bonds do not mature until 2014. Richard Dixon, Los Angeles county treasurer, claimed that the county got two advantages from the structures: "...a very good rate and, associated with that, the economic savings from being able to retire our debt relatively early and lower our total debt service." The county's alternative, he added, would have been to sell 20-year fixed-rate lease/purchase bonds with a net interest cost of about 10 percent.[19]

Policy Considerations

Using revenue bonds and certificates to circumvent debt limitations has been challenged as stimulating imprudent fiscal practices, especially when they are sold for purposes that are not self-financing. A participant at the 1984 American Correctional Association (ACA) Winter Conference took issue with the proposition that rents paid under an annually renewable lease arrangement for the government's use of a privately financed corrections facility constituted the kind of secure revenue base typically required for the issuance of limited liability revenue bonds. Even if the government is not technically liable for the debts of the independent entity that issued the bonds or certificates and built the prison, a default by the entity on its obligations would discredit the government and might shake investor confidence in the creditworthiness of future bond issues. Large financial institutions are already becoming increasingly aware of the risk in leased assets. The Financial Accounting Standards Board ruled in 1976 that "capital leases," such as lease/purchase agreements where title to the asset transfers to the lessee at the end of the lease period must be shown on the balance sheet.[20] This ruling is officially applicable only to commercial enterprises but public officials are being urged to conform in the interests of fiscal prudence and full disclosure of governmental obligations.

In addition, the avoidance of public referenda and debate through the issuance of revenue bonds and certificates has been said to obstruct the participation of the citizenry in decisions related to the policy choices and long-term obligations of its government. In New York, a taxpayers' suit was filed against the state's Urban Development Corporation to prevent it from issuing revenue bonds after a general obligation bond issue for correctional facilities failed at the polls. Ominously for lease/purchase advocates, the taxpayers won on the trial court level, but the state's highest court, the Court of Appeals, dismissed the complaint for lack of jurisdiction and allowed the Urban Development Corporation to proceed with the $600 million bond issue. The Reagan Administration's tax proposals would also weaken the attractiveness of lease/purchase arrangements. It may be several years before we know whether lease/purchasing is rapidly increasing or has already neared its peak.

In examining the feasibility of using leasing as a means of securing additional detention facilities, it is important to consult independent legal counsel and financial analysts who are experienced in lease financing. The cost issues alone are very complex and require sophisticated investigation of construction costs, bond interest rates and expenses, cash flows and other technical matters. Moreover, professional judgment is needed to assess the potential impact on tax-exempt bonds and leasing schemes of proposed federal tax reforms, particularly the so-called "flat tax," which threaten to eliminate many of the tax incentives for real estate investment. Usually, only large jurisdictions have an in-house capability for this level of analysis, but others may contract for it from a professional association like the Government Finance Officers Association, a financial services firm precluded from bidding or a major accounting firm. All too often, however, the principal sources of such data are the investment bankers or real estate agents who are attempting to sell public officials on the merits of a proposed leasing arrangement.

18. Public Works

Karen B. Carter

How many plant managers have thrown up their hands in despair at some time or another and said "I'd pay somebody to take this place off my hands!"? During the last decade, a growing number of municipalities have done just that, and contracted a firm to take over responsibility for operation and maintenance (O&M) of their wastewater treatment plants. There are several firms that specialize in contract operations, and many consulting engineering firms have established a division within or a subsidiary without to take advantage of the market for these services.

In a climate of reduced federal spending, increasingly complex technology, and a new emphasis on compliance with discharge limitations, the task of operating and maintaining a wastewater treatment facility may be a significant burden for municipalities, especially those that are small or located in remote areas. Indeed, most plants operated under contract are ten mgd or less. The largest plant operated under a full O&M contract is the 60-mgd Oklahoma City treatment plant. Larger plants may not opt for a full O&M contract, but may instead contract out a part of the treatment process such as sludge handling. The city of Wilmington, Delaware, recently contracted for operation of one of the largest belt filter press installations in the nation. Other options have been contracts for maintenance only, or for supervision and administration of the treatment plant.

The typical duration of an O&M contract is five years, although many first-time contracts are for a single year. Most are paid on the basis of a monthly fee, and the contract includes a factor for annual increases. With few exceptions, the treatment plant staff becomes employed by the contractor instead of the municipality, so that few (if any) jobs are lost.

Karen B. Carter, "Private Contracts for Public Works." Reprinted with permission from Current Municipal Problems, *Vol. 13, 1986–1987. Published by Callaghan & Company, Wilmette, Illinois.*

Although the client (the city, town, or county, for example) still holds the National Pollutant Discharge Elimination System (NPDES) permit, the contractor is responsible to the client for the effluent quality. The "guarantee" of effluent quality in most contracts includes exclusions based on flow and waste strength, and may limit the dollar value of the contractor's liability. If the permit is violated as a result of negligence on the part of the contractor, any fines levied or other enforcement action taken are the contractor's responsibility.

The Objectives

Among the motivations for contracting out the operation of a treatment plant are compliance problems, financial considerations, and staffing problems. When a new facility is constructed, the municipality may feel that the expertise needed to operate it properly is unavailable locally, and may choose to turn the plant over to a contractor from the beginning. Robert Troxler of the Georgia Environmental Protection Division says that the greater flexibility in personnel management is one of the great assets of contract operations.

The city of Hood River, Oregon, turned their 3.5-mgd secondary treatment plant over to a contract operator two years ago for several of these reasons. Peter Harris, Hood River city manager, said that the major reason for the decision was to save money. When the city asked contractors to submit bids, they required at least a 10 percent savings compared to the projected cost of operating the plant themselves; the contractor they chose has saved them 30 percent. Harris said that Hood River is a small city with small resources, and a private contractor has larger resources (manpower and expertise) to draw on. The constraints of a union contract made it difficult for the city to make changes in the organization of the treatment plant staff, and a private firm would be free to make such adjustment as necessary. Harris says that operation of the plant by a contractor frees him to do his own job better, and notes that since contract operation began, no increases in sewerage rates have been necessary.

The Rocky River wastewater treatment plant in Ohio was once owned by the county, but is now owned jointly by four neighboring cities. While the county had a sanitary engineering staff to oversee plant operations, the cities do not. Contract operations provided the needed expertise, and shared it among all four cities.

Mike Wallner, the utilities director for Fort Dodge, Iowa, said that his city was principally interested in saving money when they considered contract operations for their 4.5-mgd (average flow) activated biofilm process. Before contract operations their annual operating costs were $900,000.

After $50,000 in capital improvements, operating costs have dropped to $500,000/yr. under the contract. The plant had been plagued by a variety of design, construction, operation, and management problems, and the Iowa Department of Water, Air, and Waste Management (the NPDES enforcement agency for the state) recommended that Fort Dodge consider contract operations to help solve their compliance problems.

Wallner believes that contract operations was the right choice for Fort Dodge, but does not believe it is appropriate for all plants. He stresses that cost savings should not be the sole justification, that contract operations is most needed when there is a problem. The treatment plant is now operating efficiently and in compliance with its permit. Wallner notes that although the plant was shifted from city employment to employment with the contractor, the plant is being operated by the same people as before. He says he can't help but wonder why the city couldn't have solved the problems itself.

At the 25-mgd tertiary White's Creek treatment plant in Nashville, Tennessee, contract operations was considered, but the city decided against it. The principal motivation was to save money, but concerns about the legal implications and liability were overriding. Jim Tarpy, assistant director of the department of water and sewer, said that the city's decision was not financial. He said that the contractors that submitted proposals to the city made a strong case for contract operations. However, a guarantee of effluent compliance came only with a requirement for a given influent quality, and the city was uncertain that such variation could be controlled adequately.

Tarpy says city management asked itself "How fine can the operation be tuned?", and why the contractor would be motivated to produce an effluent of higher quality than required under the NPDES permit. The city operates three large treatment plnts, and found that they could save the desired amount of money by diverting flow from the White's Creek treatment plant to one of their other plants. Like Wallner, Tarpy feels that contract operations are most viable when the problems are serious.

The Obstacles

A key concern voiced by municipal managers about contract operations is profit motive by private firms. What would prevent a contractor from shortchanging operation or maintenance for profit? Why would a private firm maintain plant equipment as well as the municipality would, when at the end of a five-year contract the contractor could simply walk away from a deteriorating plant?

Part of the answer, says Walt Colby, project manager at the 60-mgd

Oklahoma City treatment plant, is that a contract is really only as long as the notice required in the cancellation clause, typically 60, 90, or 120 days. Most importantly, contract operators live and die by their reputations. The business is in the early stages of its development, and the relatively few plants operated under contract are highly visible — a cancelled or un-renewed contract or a poor recommendation from a client can be instant death for a contracting firm. Unlike wastewater treatment projects funded under the Construction Grants Program during the last 13 years, contract operations is paid for 100 percent by the locality. The locality can usually choose to operate the facility themselves, where they wouldn't have had the choice to design or construct the plant.

Another major concern is control. Wastewater treatment plants often represent a sizeable fraction of the capital assets of a municipality, and the municipality is ultimately responsible for the condition of the plant and its effluent. It is difficult for a city manager to simply hand over the keys. Thom Day, district operations manager for contract operation of eight plants in the Pacific Northwest, makes the point that control depends on the quality of the reporting system. Day notes that the reporting procedure in many municipalities is not nearly as structured as that specified in an operations contract; the reports a city manager receives from the contract operator may be much better.

Like many things, control depends on who holds the purse strings. Jim Thompson, a city manager for 14 years and now operations services manager for a contract operations firm, says that as long as the city is signing the checks it has control.

Mike Wallner's question about how a contract operator can often succeed where a municipality has failed in operating a treatment plant with the very same staff is a good one. The unanimous answer from contract operators is that while they may have the same staff, they have the resources of a large professional organization — usually an engineering firm — at their disposal as well. Experienced help is just a phone call away.

Perhaps the most significant question that must be addressed in making the decision to turn a treatment plant over to a contractor is what effect that will have on all the people who work there. In most cases a contractor can operate a plant with fewer staff than is necessary under municipal management. Reduced staff requirements is one of the principal reasons contract operations can be less expensive.

Not only might they require fewer staff, but what is to prevent a contractor from moving in with a ready-made staff and putting all the local operators out of their jobs? Contract operators are extremely sensitive to this concern, and in every contract researched for this article there was a provision that gave the plant employees the option to work for the contract operator. If they chose to stay with the municipality, efforts were made to find them a suitable position in some other area of municipal government. In the vast majority of cases, plant personnel have chosen to become members of the contractor's staff.

Making the Change

Former municipal employees who have become contract operators say that the decision was a difficult one. Job security is a big concern, because the contract may not be renewed, or worse, may be cancelled. Of course, the contractor may offer the operator employment on another project, but suppose the operator is not in a position to relocate? Most contracts include a provision that gives the municipality the opportunity to rehire their own employees at the end of the contract if it is not renewed. The employee has no guarantee that his former employer would rehire him, but logic and practicality dictate that the municipality would want to obtain trained and experienced people.

Job security in a private firm depends on productivity and performance, and not usually on the protection of a union or civil service requirements. In Rockland, Massachusetts, the treatment plant employees voluntarily voted to leave their union, and negotiated with the contractor for the benefits they wanted. The employees of the contractor at the 32-mgd Fall River, Massachusetts, treatment plant have retained their union; relations between the contractor and the union have been successful to date. Indeed, unions may find that the flexibility of private sector administration makes negotiations easier.

Pension and retirement considerations are very important to employees who have been with the municipality for many years. Several contract firms have addressed this concern by making financial advisors available to municipal employees trying to make the decision. Often the benefits of pension plans offered by the contractor are better than the program of the local government. An innovative idea used by contractors to solve the dilemma for long-term municipal employees who want to keep the benefits of their government jobs is to lease the employee from the locality for the duration of the contract.

A private sector job may be more stressful than one for local government, because raises and promotions are not based on time-in-service, but on performance. However, the other side of this is the stress that municipal employees often experience as a result of the frustration of working for a bureaucracy slowed down by red tape. One of the principal benefits cited by converted contract operators is that of working for an organization run by people trained in engineering who appreciate the complexity of the treatment process. Valerie Bober, operations supervisor for the city of Lebanon,

Oregon, says that it is especially nice to work for people who understand that sometimes "you just have to fix it *now*."

Although salary and benefits can be better in the private sector, they are not necessarily so. In most cases they are commensurate because the contractor recognizes that it is important to be competitive with the local job market, and with the overhead expenses of the municipality. Bober says that her salary increased, but partially to compensate for reduced benefits, so overall she broke even. However, the private sector often offers far more opportunity for advancement, especially for employees willing to relocate to other plants for promotions. Two years ago Bober was a lab technician, and has been promoted rapidly into a supervisory position. Even in the same position, one day she was a "nobody" working for the city, and the next day she was an "expert" in a team under contract to solve the city's treatment problems.

This recognition factor is very important to Richard Harville, a former chemist for the Hood River, Oregon, treatment plant who is now project manager of the plant for the contractor. There seems to be a significant emphasis on employee motivation in contract firms—after all, to do a better job at lower cost, productivity is essential. Training programs are a large part of most operations contracts. Regularly scheduled classes are held at the plants during work hours on a variety of operations topics including safety. Operator certification is a major objective of training.

Variations

Some plants have found it beneficial to contract out only a portion of the total plant operation. Operation can be divided into liquid and solids processing, for example, or into operation and maintenance. In Albany, Georgia, a contract operator is exclusively responsible for maintenance of three treatment plants (20, 1, and 0.5 mgd), and 81 lift stations. The nine-person staff uses a computerized maintenance management system and sophisticated equipment tests to predict problems. The program includes preventive and corrective maintenance.

The contract at Rocky River, Ohio, is for supervision only. Asked why the city did not simply go out and hire a qualified plant manager, Mayor Earl Martin said that through the contract for plant supervisor services, the cities that own the treatment plant can draw from the resources of the entire engineering firm. In addition, the continuity of plant operation is not contingent on a single man—the cities have contracted for a plant supervisor, not just hired an individual. In this way the city obtained the benefits of the contractor's resources and kept their manpower within the city government. The contract, now in its third year, is renegotiated annually.

The city of Wilmington, Delaware, contracted out what is often the most troublesome aspect of wastewater treatment, sludge handling. The contract provides for operation of 14, 2.5-m belt filter presses that handle 220 wet tons of sludge daily from the 90-mgd treatment plant. Because the facility was brand new, the contractor provided the entire ten-person staff. The city felt that the complexity of the process exceeded the ability of their existing staff. Operation under the one-year contract began May 1. Instead of guaranteed effluent quality, the contract guarantees the quantity and quality of sludge produced and sent to the Delaware Solid Waste Reclamation Facility where it is mixed with solid waste and composted.

In Oklahoma City, operation and maintenance of the entire plant is under contract, but to three different firms engaged in a joint venture. The liquid process is operated by one firm, sludge treatment by another, and sludge disposal by a third. The city's management personnel believed themselves to be good "general practitioners," but felt that "specialists" were required to operate the sophisticated facilities.

The Miami Conservancy District in Ohio is seeking a very interesting contract. Not only do they wish to contract out the operation of their 11.2-mgd trickling filter plant, but also the farming operation they have established for sludge disposal. Sludge would be transported by pipeline seven miles to 800 acres of farmland where it would be land-injected as fertilizer. The district would like the contractor to be responsible for producing soy beans, alfalfa, wheat, and corn on the land on a rotating basis.

Some of the benefits of contract operations are the result of a unique variation on the theme, regionalization. The facility for heat treatment of sludge at the Gresham, Oregon, plant was shut down and the sludge was sent to the Hood River plant, which had excess sludge treatment capacity as a result of closure of a local industrial discharger. This cooperative effort was facilitated by operation of both plants by a single contractor. Several plants in Oregon, too small to afford sophisticated equipment or expert personnel individually can share the costs and benefits collectively.

Bulk purchasing of chemicals for five plants in New England is a benefit of regionalized contract operation. Joe Rego, administrator of public utilities for Fall River, Massachusetts, estimates that bulk purchasing by the contract operator has saved the city 25% in chemical costs.

Going Half Way

The treatment plant jointly owned by Boynton Beach and Delray Beach, Florida, is operated under contract by a *public* contractor. The contract for operation of the facility was originally held by Delray Beach, but after two or three years the city decided they did not wish to operate the plant itself. However, they were unable to convince Boynton Beach that a private contractor was the way to go. The compromise reached was to establish the South Central Regional Wastewater Treatment and Disposal Board as the contract operator.

The 25 employees who operate the $24-million facility (currently undergoing expansion to a capacity of 24 mgd) are not employed by the city but by the board. The board is a separate entity operated as a business, but without the profit motive inherent in private contracting. David Sloan, executive director of the board, says that because the board must continually compete for contract renewal against the services of private firms, they must operate efficiently and economically. Employees do not have the protection of a union or civil service system, and advance in their jobs through performance and productivity.

Theoretically the board ought to be able to operate the treatment plant as efficiently as a private firm, but without the overhead costs built into private contracts. This arrangement has the advantage of total direct city control; the staff may be hired and fired as individuals and do not come as a "package" as with a private contractor. However, such a public contractor does not bring to the city the multiple services and resources available from a private engineering or operations firm.

Future Prospects

The evidence is very favorable, but the jury is still out on the subject of contract operations as the universal solution to wastewater treatment in the U.S. One aspect that remains to be tested is the ease with which a municipality may take back responsibility for operation of its treatment plant. Although most contracts give them the option of rehiring the contractor's staff, there is no guarantee that the staff will accept the offer. If they did, would it be because they were tied by their property and families to that community and did not have the option to relocate with the contractor? Would the reverse transition from private to public employment be smooth?

Most contracts are undertaken because there are serious problems at the treatment plant or because the complexity of a new facility is beyond the expertise available locally. After the contractor has solved the operational problems and the plant is in compliance, and after the plant staff has gained several years of experience with the new facility, the municipality may very well be inclined to take over operation.

Contract operation is presently used mostly at smaller treatment plants with small staffs. At this level, staff reductions (lost jobs) associated with the increased efficiency of contract operation are minimal. Would staff reductions be proportional, and therefore more significant, in larger plants? Would the benefits of the associated cost reductions be overshadowed by the negative aspects of local unemployment?

Presently only about 100 of the thousands of U.S. wastewater treatment plants are operated under contract. Growth in the industry has been somewhat slow as cautious city managers watched and learned about this option. More information could soon be available as the business may grow rapidly in the climate of reduced federal support for pollution control projects and increased federal enforcement activities. Overall, the response to contract operations has been positive and the benefits are well documented, but it is only an alternative and not a panacea.

19. Refuse Collection

Eugene J. Wingerter

No municipal service is as visible or as regularly provided as is public cleansing. While most city residents might not see the refuse truck or street sweeper pass in front of their homes, they do notice the evidence—empty trash containers, better-looking streets, a more hospitable neighborhood environment.

City officials, elected and appointed, know these services are the most important they provide. They know this because when a mistake is made, and a given block is missed somehow by the collection truck or sweeper, the complaint phone calls pour in.

Keeping that importance in mind, it is interesting to note that these most important services are very often entrusted to private enterprise. This is especially true in refuse collection: two-thirds of all U.S. cities have their residential trash hauled away by trucks owned and operated by for-profit companies.

What are the reasons for entrusting these key services to the private sector? And why is this trend continuing and accelerating in the public cleansing field? There are many reasons, some of which vary with region and locale. The following three are probably the keys:

1. In the current era of restricted municipal budgets, the fact that private refuse collection is cheaper is overwhelmingly appealing. This is a fact that has been documented several times within the past 15 years.
2. Quality of service provided is important, and here, again, company-owned refuse collection efforts have been shown to be at least the equal of city-run operations. One reason for this: the private sector has, and uses, more flexibility in equipment purchasing and maintenance.

Eugene J. Wingerter, "Refuse Collection—The Privatization Alternative." Reprinted with permission from The Privatization Review, *Vol. 2, No. 1, Winter, 1986. Published by The Privatization Council, Washington, D.C. (Printed by Maxco Publications, Little Falls, New Jersey.)*

3. Workforce relations, which can be troublesome when a city does its own refuse work, are transferred to the company or companies which provide the actual service. Thus, a large headache is removed from the public works administrative effort.

Another contributing factor is the competitive nature of the business. There are as many as 10,000 refuse companies and perhaps 3,000 sweeping enterprises in the U.S. Cities with multiple service providers benefit from vigorous competition. Cities which contract for private sector collection or street sweeping do not have to worry about being "locked in" to the winning bidder forever.

The National Solid Wastes Management Association is not only heavily involved in preserving tax incentives that encourage privatization of waste-to-energy facilities, but sees refuse collection as the model among municipal services showing why and how public-private partnerships can help municipal governments and local taxpayers. In this belief, NSWMA is amassing documentation to become a resource to public managers on private waste service options.

To review the present status of privatized refuse collection in North America, let us now review data from recent studies comparing the cost of publicly run collection with that of private-sector refuse pickup. Later in the article, we will review three privatization "case studies," two from the U.S. and another from Canada.

The HUD Study

The "Comparative Study of Municipal Service Delivery," submitted to the U.S. Department of Housing and Urban Development in 1984 by Ecodata, Inc. (New York, N.Y.), studied eight different services for which cities can contract-out.

Note that Dr. Barbara J. Stevens, editor of Ecodata's study, was also a principal in the 1975 Columbia University study headed by E.S. Savas. The Columbia University study was done for the National Science Foundation. It reviews the most comprehensive, in-depth analysis of private and municipal refuse collection arrangements, covering 2,060 cities in 200 U.S. metropolitan areas. The findings and recommendations of this earlier work were a key in increasing privatization of refuse services, as it demonstrated the advantages of contracting-out for collection. Refuse collection by private contractors was found 29 percent less costly than service using municipal crews.

In the more recent study, Stevens and her Ecodata colleagues studied services such as traffic signal maintenance, street repair, turf and tree upkeep, and street sweeping as well as refuse collection.

After examining a number of California cities, they selected 20 Southern California cities for in-depth study. They matched 10 cities that provided their own services with 10 cities of similar size which contracted-out for the same services. The result: for seven of the eight services, contractors were from 37 percent to 96 percent more efficient than city employees (only in payroll preparation, the study found, did cities save money by doing the job themselves).

The main findings of the HUD Study as they apply to refuse removal include the following:

1. Significant cost savings were documented. On average, refuse collection by a municipal agency is from 28% to 42% more costly than contracting-out for the service. Note: the study included in the cost for contracting-out all costs of city administration (managing the bid process and supervising contractor performance) of such contracts and services (about 2% of the average contracts). The report concluded: "This finding is the result of statistical analysis where the effect of quantity of refuse collected, frequency and location of pickup, route density, and the quality of service provided are held constant."

2. Quality of refuse collection service was also ranked. It varied from a ranking of 11.05 (best) to 92.7. Average value: 34.3 for cities with municipal employees doing the collection, 38.2 for cities with contractors. The conclusion, as drawn by the researchers, was that the average quality of service provided by the two methods studied was almost identical.

3. Better management by private operators was confirmed. In comparison to municipal agencies, refuse contractors are:

   • able to achieve lower employee absentee rates (7.9% for contractors, vs. 13.4% for cities);
   • able to obtain lower equipment downtime ratios. Only 6.2% of the vehicles of contractors studied were in the garage for repair at any one time, versus 16.2% for the municipalities studied;
   • more likely to operate a one brand fleet of vehicles.

   Many cities find it almost impossible to achieve this kind of standardization, because of purchasing regulations. Standardization can lead to better equipment performance (and the lower downtime figure reported above) because mechanics working on the vehicles are able to learn quickly a great deal about the machinery on which they are working. In addition, the researchers found that contractor employees are more likely to achieve two full truckloads per shift than are municipal employees.

4. Of the 10 low-cost cities in the study, eight were contract cities. Comparing the low-cost with the high-cost cities, the Ecodata researchers identified several management factors that were shared by the low-cost cities but not common to the high-cost cities. These included absentee rates and vehicle downtime, as noted above.

Additionally, however, incentive systems were found to be important. Low-cost cities were more likely than high-cost cities to have their workers on a "go home when route is finished" incentive system. This helps account for the fact that low-cost city crews were more likely to complete two loads per truck than the others.

In short, the HUD study reconfirmed the earlier nationwide survey.

Canadian Study

About the same time as the HUD study, a similar study in Canada found the private sector even more efficient. "Residential Solid Waste Services in Canadian Municipalities," by Dr. James McDavid of the University of Victoria's School of Public Administration, was funded by the university. This study's conclusion: "Exclusive public sector (refuse) collection is 50.9% more expensive per household than purely private collection."

Focus of the study was 126 Canadian cities outside of Quebec with populations of 10,000 or more. (French-speaking Quebec, incidentally, is highly privatized.) McDavid found that 42 percent of these cities have private contractor-only collection; another 38 percent have some residential pickup performed by private contractors. Thus four of every five cities utilize private contractors for at least part of their residential refuse pick-up.

According to the study, private companies were four times as likely as municipalities to own and use 32-yard rear-loading collection trucks. These large vehicles can help lead to greater efficiencies. Privately owned trucks were of a more recent vintage as well: their average age, McDavid found, was 3.48 years, as compared with 4.47 years for city trucks.

In addition, private-only systems averaged a crew size of 2.2 persons per truck, versus 2.9 persons per truck for systems in which municipal employees did the collecting. And companies were three times as likely as municipalities to offer productivity incentives to their employees.

All of these differences added up to a significant variance in collection efficiency, the study found. Where crews in private-only systems collected an average of 1.25 tons per hour, the public employees studied were averaging 0.64 tons per hour. McDavid found that private collection operations were twice as productive as public efforts.

There were many other figures generated in this study, but perhaps the most interesting segment was McDavid's assessment of the advantages:

> Although less tangible, the element of competition may be the most critical factor in inducing increased efficiency. Private sector firms compete with each other for municipal contracts to collect solid waste.... This would be expected to keep costs down. Interestingly, in mixed settings (where some residential refuse pickup is done by private contractors and some by

municipal employees), municipal producers are consistently closer to private-only systems (in terms of cost per household) than are public-only systems... It may be that even where municipal producers dominate, but do not control all the residential collection, there will still be benefits from competition.

Three Case Studies

Based on the facts presented above, and on experiences of cities throughout the country in which private collection of residential refuse is efficient and provides quality service, one would think cities would be breaking down the doors of contractors in clamoring for service.

One problem the public cleansing industry faces in achieving increased privatization is that politics enters into the computations. To delve into these problems, we will now examine three cities which decided to move to private sector service: Knoxville, Tenn., Fullerton, Calif., and Richmond, B.C., Canada.

Knoxville, Tenn.

Working together with the private sector, elected and public officials in Knoxville have used contracting-out for refuse collection to cut $3 million from the city's budget over a four-year period.

Elected officials had heard for years that companies could do the job of picking up residential refuse at a lower cost, from national and local sources. They began to listen more closely in recent years, as budget tightening affected the city's ability to deliver key services.

In addition, city leaders were distressed by the rate of escalation in Knoxville's refuse collection costs. The budget for the last full year of operations, 1983–84, was $2.6 million; city officials say the increases were on the order of $175,000 to $255,000 per year.

One problem for the city was the maintenance of the existing satellite vehicle system. In a satellite collection system, small (one-ton) collection scooters feed larger trucks. If these smaller vehicles were spending a great deal of time in the shop, costs would rise due to overtime for both collection workers and mechanics, at the very least.

But Knoxville's mayor and city council didn't move blindly from municipal collection to contracting-out. They first authorized the Department of Public Services — which ran the municipal collection operation — to prepare bid documents. The bidders' responses would determine if the city collection operation was to be dismantled.

Herb Kidd, now head of the Department, was assistant director in 1983 and was involved in preparing bid documents. Because Knoxville had never contracted out for refuse services before, it needed input on contracts. "We contacted several cities that had recently contracted out for refuse services and asked to see their documents," he says. "We also spoke to several national companies, our likely bidders, asked them which cities had good contracts, and obtained copies of these as well. Then we sat down and took from each contract the things that we liked."

Every city is different; Knoxville's contract was unusual in that it asked for two prices: one for refuse pickup at curbside and in alleys (20,000 of the city-served stops) and another price for rear-door, carry-out pickup (26,000 stops). Note that the city has 180,000 residents.

What's more, the contract provided for six-night-a-week service to the downtown area, and it specified collection had to be performed between 9 p.m. and 6 a.m. The downtown area has no alleys for containers; food service concerns there just place bagged refuse on the curb, making overnight pickup a necessity for a sanitary environment.

Kidd notes that the city made only one mistake in its contract-writing process. "We allowed competing bidders 90 days to come in and look our city over. That was fine for two of the national competitors, which already had (commercial) operations in town. But for the others, I don't think that time period was long enough for them to become comfortable and familiar with our geography, streets, etc.

"Another problem was that the City of New Orleans had its contract out for bid at the same time. So the companies were stretched a bit. If we had it to do over again, I'd allow more than 90 days. That way companies not familiar with our town could learn more about Knoxville and perhaps submit a more competitive bid."

When the bids were received, Browning-Ferris Industries was the low bidder. After negotiations leading to a final contract were completed, Kidd sat down and computed the estimated savings through four years of the contract. His first-year estimate alone was enough to convince council members: $650,000 in projected savings in the 1984–85 fiscal year.

Holding up a final contract award, however, was a change in city administrations. In addition, city solid waste employees, who weren't enthusiastic about the switch, asked for a chance to voice their views.

In five public hearings before the city council, a few citizens and public employees presented arguments against awarding the contract. But in the end, Kidd says, "people couldn't argue with the dollar savings we could obtain."

According to Kidd and Browning-Ferris personnel, the city retained 37 and the company hired 37 of the 79 solid waste employees on the Knoxville payroll at the time of the switch. The other five reportedly retired.

Contract terms have the company's per-stop per-month price increasing minimally—from $3.00 in FY 84–85 to $3.05 in the third year of the contract. Either side can opt out of the contract after the third year is completed; but if Browning-Ferris agrees to perform the fourth year, it is committing itself to fulfilling the fifth and sixth years as well.

Per-stop per-month prices for the "out" years would be: $3.20 in year four, $3.35 in the fifth, and $3.51 in 1989–90. Then, in 1989, if both parties choose to continue, Knoxville residents will pay only 17 percent more for waste collection than they paid in 1984—which compares quite favorably with the city's experience of 8 percent to 10 percent annual cost increases when it ran its own operation (x to y over the contract life).

Kidd estimates the first-year savings at $400,000, with the city's decision to retain those 37 employees accounting for the lesser savings. Even with that factored in, however, Knoxville will save an estimated $650,000 in FY 85–86, $950,000 in the contract's third year, and "at least" $1 million in the fourth year. Figures for years five and six have not been estimated.

Knoxville's contract also gave it the option to sell to BFI all of its used refuse collection equipment—guaranteeing it a buyer, at a specified price. The city, Kidd says, did not need this additional service, because it sold its fleet at an auction.

Kidd says the switch to contract collection has been good for the city. "We've been able to do more with the public service personnel we have. It's allowed me, personally, to work better as a manager. I don't have to spend hours or days anymore working to resolve personnel problems and equipment problems in the refuse area. In addition, we're getting better productivity now from our remaining public service workers."

Fullerton, Calif.

Fullerton, California, has been enjoying private sector service much longer—its franchise collector, MG Disposal, has been servicing the city since 1959. The long-term relationship has enabled the company to invest in innovative technology such as use of front-end loaders for residential collection and a full range of collection and recycling services. MG Disposal and the city keep in close contact. That includes involvement in city planning. An MG Disposal representative sits in on planning meetings for construction projects. Any change in the city's neighborhoods that could impact on waste disposal service is thus known far in advance.

"We do not function merely as garbagemen," says owner Bob Gallio. "We are able to offer the city professional advice from a waste-management perspective. We try to solve problems before they develop."

A commonly heard complaint is that waste disposal is the last thing considered by planners. In the case of single-building construction, it sometimes is completely overlooked in design. "Our overall role is to make sure Fullerton residents and commercial customers are satisfied with their waste disposal service," says Bob Gallio. "Sometimes, that involves a lot more than quick and careful refuse collection."

MG Disposal is a good example of a long-term, essentially local response to harnessing the private sector to perform refuse collection. As Bob Gallio notes: "There's more to business than profit. You also have to put something back into the community. All of us are citizens and residents of Fullerton. We want to participate. Just as our employees wanted to be involved in building a better workplace, we want to have as much input as possible when it comes to things that will improve our town."

Richmond, B.C.

Richmond has nearly 100,000 residents; it serves as a bedroom community for nearby Vancouver. While other suburban communities had contracted out for refuse collection, Richmond had retained public employee service.

In the 1979–83 period, Richmond's population increased by about 12 percent. Population density increased as well: where 75 percent of all housing starts were for single-family homes in 1980, that figure dropped to 31 percent only four years later.

The move to privatization took a long time. In October of 1979, a report to the Richmond council's Public Works Committee noted that the collection service was exceeding its budget. Why? In the months previous, job actions were staged by the city employees, who were dissatisfied with working conditions. Changes were made in response to high costs and employee dissatisfaction, including the implementation of a modified task system.

Designed with the cooperation of union officials and introduced in April of 1980, this system grouped crews together. Once all of the tasks assigned to these crews were done, the workers were allowed to go home. They were still paid for an eight-hour day, provided hours worked did not exceed 160 hours in a four-week period.

According to Prof. McDavid, who researched the Richmond situation as part of the study referenced above, this modification initially led to increased productivity and reduced worker unhappiness. A four-month-long civic strike in 1981 hurt the good feelings, however. Municipal refuse collection was suspended over the period.

When the strike ended, there was a dispute over overtime hours required by the refuse cleanup. The task system was suspended for a time, and extra trucks were used to get the work done faster.

At the same time, Richmond public works officials began discussing modifying the task system. They believed that some municipal refuse collectors were ignoring speed limits, not taking lunch and coffee breaks, and skimping on daily vehicle maintenance to obtain to "go home early" benefit.

When the task system was reinstated, following the post-strike cleanup, directives designed to boost productivity accompanied it. In addition, an early September effort to cut the collection fleet down by one truck (from ten trucks to nine) resulted in a work stoppage.

Shortly thereafter, three refuse contractors interested in providing residential collection in Richmond made presentations to the city. The municipal engineer was instructed, by Council, to study the cost-saving potential of the proposals; but even before he completed his report, union officials appeared before the Public Works Committee to argue against contracting-out.

The union's argument was that residential collection productivity had increased in recent years, and contracting-out was not the solution to rising costs, because it posed new problems — including trying to make sure that service levels would be equal to those provided by municipal work crews.

The engineer's report, presented in late December, 1981, estimated a potential savings of $107,000 to Richmond through contracting-out — 7 percent of 1981 service costs. The report also noted specific changes that could be made to the municipal operation to make it more efficient. The Council Public Works Committee decided, based on the report, to hire a consultant to look at efficiency improvements that Richmond could make to the municipal refuse collection effort.

Three months later, the consultant made a series of recommendations, including reducing the number of trucks, possible elimination of back-lane service, and, in the long term, conversion to one-man collection.

These ideas — including reducing the fleet to an eventual six trucks — were soon being implemented by public works officials. Union officials, in late September, 1982, said they were opposed to the planned reduction (to seven trucks for the winter months).

In response to the city's decision to proceed with the reduction and other changes anyway, the union announced it was abandoning the task system. By early November, failure to complete daily collections was typical; crews and their union blamed it on unfamiliarity with new routes. Additionally, collection crews consistently refused overtime hours. Richmond was forced to put extra trucks on the road on a number of occasions.

The result: in January of 1983, the municipal engineer recommended to the Council that the city contract-out for refuse collection. In a 5-to-4 vote on the issue, March 14 was the date selected by the Municipal Council for private collection to begin.

Bids were received from four firms. Despite a great deal of activism by the union, including submittal of a petition with 17,000 signatures opposed to contracting-out, the Council upheld the award of the contracts — resi-

TABLE ONE

**Costs Per Household And Costs Per Ton
For Residential Solid Waste Collection In
Richmond, Before And After Privatization**

	Before Privatizing			After Privatizing
	1980	1981	1982	1983
Cost per household	37.47	45.85	46.24	31.72
Cost per ton	34.29	54.43	43.16	28.65

TABLE TWO

**Average Tons Of Residential Solid Waste
Collected Per Truck, Per Day, Before And After
Privatization**

Average Daily Tons by Season	Before Privatizing			After Privatizing
	1980	1981	1982	1983
Winter (Jan., Feb., March)	10.1	Civic Strike	10.8	Public and Private Mixed
Spring (April, May, June)	12.1	13.7	14.3	25.3
Summer (July, Aug., Sept.)	13.0	12.9	15.6	21.5
Fall (Oct., Nov., Dec.)	11.7	11.7	14.1	21.0
Overall Average	11.7	12.8	13.7	22.6

dential services to Haul Away Disposal Ltd., and container service to Smithrite Disposal Ltd., both divisions of Laidlaw Industries, Inc.

The five-year contract with Haul Away covers 26,141 households initially. See Table One for the costs to Richmond before and after privatization; and Table Two for the average tons collected per truck by municipal crews (before) and company-employed workers (after).

Summary

Privatization of refuse collection works. It can help a given municipality save money and eliminate workforce relations problems; it can help stretch municipal public works budgets to get more done with the same dollar.

Many other public cleansing services can be successfully shifted to the private sector, with significant savings. These include operation of refuse processing and disposal systems (such as resource recovery plants, waste transfer stations and sanitary landfills), street sweeping, sewage sludge dewatering plant operation and hauling, and more.

With the contracting-out of refuse collection as a backdrop, other services can successfully be privatized. Cities are looking to private industry for solutions to the modern problems of urban life.

In the public cleansing area, industry is ready, willing, and able to solve these problems while keeping service levels constant, saving municipalities money, and making a profit.

20. Street Sweeping

James Mills

More than half of America's cities, towns and state highway departments could deliver more for less by contracting out street and highway cleaning services, according to national survey data and numerous interviews for *American City and County* magazine during a three-month period.

Cities that enjoy high employee morale and dedication experience low absenteeism and run efficient maintenance operations with low equipment downtime and high equipment use. They often can compete on both the cost and performance levels, survey and interview respondents indicated. The research indicates that when all these conditions are present, in-house service will be as economical and effective as contract services.

"The fact is, there are few cities that can objectively make these claims and prove them," says Bernard Crotty, San Francisco's superintendent of streets. "We have a relatively efficient, cost-effective street cleaning program. I'm not sure, however, that our performance would be superior to that of a professional private company."

The national survey on street cleaning practices was mailed to more than 5,500 cities and counties nationwide. Since response was voluntary, the results were subject to a margin of error. Consequently, a telephone survey was also conducted based on a representative sample of 50 cities. The project was co-sponsored by Moore and Sons, Inc., of Southhaven, Mississippi, and Organization Management Consulting, of Scotts Valley, California.

"We have invested considerable funds in research related to sweeping equipment performance and needs," says Ralph Luebke, president of

James Mills, "Contract Street Sweeping Is a Viable Alternative." Reprinted with permission from American City & County, *Vol. 99, No. 7, July, 1984. Published by Communication Channels, Inc., Atlanta, Georgia.*

Moore and Sons, Inc. "The results of the OMC survey confirmed our own findings. First, sweeping equipment performance and reliability must be improved. Second, contractors are an increasingly important market for this equipment."

The survey showed that the primary reasons for improved performance under contracting are greater equipment utilization and repair and maintenance efficiencies. When improvements in one or both of these areas are not achievable through contracting, in-house service may serve the taxpayer better.

The movement toward contract sweeping is catching on at a slow but increasing pace, according to a survey. "There has always been a market for contract sweeping by private industry," says Peter Block, director of corporate communications for Browning Ferris Industries. "We believe that the slow tilt toward privatization of services, which were once exclusively municipal, is on the verge of becoming a full-scale movement. Street sweeping is the next most popular — if that's the right word — stage in that movement since private waste collection."

Recent evidence of B.F.I.'s determination to provide quality contract sweeping services are acquisitions of two respected contract sweeping companies, Atkinson Enterprises of Indiana and Empire Sweeping Company of Ohio.

The survey data and information obtained in interviews indicate that contractors could capture between 25 percent to 35 percent of the municipal market in the next five years. If this potential demand were to materialize rapidly, there is not expected to be an adequate supply of reliable, professional contract service personnel to meet the demand. Therefore, contractors are placing top priority on operations personnel recruitment and training.

Where It Has Caught On

Contract street and highway cleaning is not new — particularly in Massachusetts and Southern California. In addition, spring cleanup contracts have been in force for years in many snow belt communities. Now, however, what was once a limited regional practice is being used nationally.

The city of Newark converted to contract sweeping after lengthy analysis and a careful specification development process. Councilman Henry Martinez praises Alvin Zach, Newark's director of the department of engineering, and DeJana Industries, Inc., the contractor, for providing the cleanest streets in recent memory.

"We have the cleanest streets I've seen in 10 years and I believe it will get even better," Martinez says. He explains that elected officials and management were dissatisfied with the performance of their operation. Equipment breakdowns, inability to discipline employees, budget constraints, positive experience with private waste collection and reduction of work week hours were among the factors cited for Newark's interest in contracting.

Newark's equipment use was low due to operator abuse and lack of control over the general services department's fleet maintenance division. "We are very pleased with the contractor," explains Zach. "He has gone out of his way to help get the program off to a good start."

According to Zach, the only problems encountered in the conversion were related to street parking signs, a few routing questions and some vagueness about the contractor's role in leaf removal.

An element of Newark's approach emphasized by Martinez and Zach is competition. "We retained over 60 percent of the street cleaning program in-house," says Martinez. "Now our employees know that they must compete with the fine performance of DeJana. This has helped improve the quality of their work."

Still, the obstacles of equipment maintenance efficiency, equipment replacement costs and employee accountability remain to some extent, according to Martinez. As a result, Newark may increase DeJana Industries' share of the city's street sweeping.

DeJana Industries' sweeping service program is managed by the company's president, Peter DeJana. "It is a high pressure, demanding contract and it is going well," states DeJana. The Long Island firm, with experience in highway sweeping, snow removal and municipal street cleaning, anticipates growth in its municipal sweeping operations in the years ahead.

Texas Highways Covered

In Texas, the state Department of Transportation allows each district maintenance superintendent to decide how to best get the job done in each area. In Houston, freeway cleaning was contracted out over a year ago and was recently re-bid by Universal Services, a local company. The Dallas County District opted to contract its highway cleaning services this year. Atkinson Enterprises of Indiana, now a B.F.I. subsidiary, won the annual $2.4 million contract.

"For the first time, we know the roads will be swept when they are supposed to be swept," explains Mike Heise, assistant superintendent of maintenance for the state's Dallas County District.

The reasons cited by Heise for the Texas Department of Transportation decision were equipment downtime of 40 percent despite a rigorous preventive maintenance program, a state quota on employee levels, increased litter in urban areas and dollar savings.

"We budgeted $3.9 million and were pleasantly surprised," Heise says.

Heise explains that the district will continue to clean low volume freeways and the city of Dallas will be responsible for its sections of road. "We are confident that when the Republican convention comes to Dallas (in August), Atkinson will have its portion of the freeways clean and free of hazardous material," Heise says. He explains that the timing of the decision to contract was influenced by the convention and the need to present a clean image to retain and attract investment.

Evesham Township, New Jersey

This south New Jersey community of 25,000 has not been able to clean its streets properly in the spring until this year. "Now we have a mess off our hands and cleaner streets," says George DeChurch, Evesham's superintendent of public works.

Reilly Sweeping, Inc., of Morrisville, Pennsylvania, was awarded the township's street cleaning contract after a cost analysis and contractor pre-qualification and bid process. "Jerry Reilly is saving us about 40 percent of what it would cost us for a well run in-house operation," says DeChurch. "My power and prestige are increased by performance, not by empire building. Our contractor performs and responds with promptness."

Jerry Reilly is encouraged by the expressions of interest in his company's municipal services. "I think those of us who are professionals in this business are finally beginning to get our story across. Common sense tells you that a $70,000 piece of equipment that only works 10 hours to 20 hours a week, seven months or eight months out of the year, is uneconomical to own, operate and maintain."

Reilly agrees with DeChurch that elected officials want performance at a reasonable cost. "If I don't deliver, I don't get paid and that threatens my bondability," he says. "If an in-house operation doesn't deliver, there is little, if any, recourse."

The OMC research survey responses support Reilly's contention that smaller cities and towns are usually better off when serviced by a sweeping contractor. Thirty-five percent of the cities with populations under 50,000 indicated an interest in contracting out the service. More than half of those smaller municipalities who indicated no interest had purchased new equipment within the last two years. Smaller city and town equipment downtime averaged more than 30 percent, twice the contractor rate.

Hampton, Virginia

Browning-Ferris Industries responded in April, 1982, to the city of Hampton's need to upgrade its attractiveness. The city's elected officials became image conscious in connection with their economic development plans and invited contractors to bid on cleaning and maintaining Hampton's 825 curb miles.

The city had sweeping equipment, but could not maintain any regular schedule. Budget cutbacks, equipment downtime, the cost of unit replacement and the advantage of commanding performance in exchange for payment are cited as reasons for contracting out the service.

"In the beginning, it took longer than anticipated to clean the city," says B.F.I.'s Hampton street sweeping chief Fred Snyder. "The program has been running smoothly ever since initial cleanup was completed."

Hampton's assistant director of public works, Edmund Pancyrz, agrees. "They have gone beyond the call of duty to respond to our needs. And that's what you want when you make these kinds of changes. You need cooperation and teamwork on everyone's part."

Pancyrz cites an innovative contract provision that has helped to reinforce the cooperative spirit. If the contractor does not complete all of the curb miles required in a given month, a payment reduction is set aside in a reserve fund/special sweeping service account. The funds in the account are used to pay pre-determined hourly rates for special cleanup and parking lot sweeping requests.

"This way, the contractor at least knows he will get so much a month in cash to meet his cash flow needs, even though he may incur more labor and operations expenses than planned," Pancyrz says. "Smaller, independent street sweeping companies need this kind of support. It helps to assure their financial stability and service reliability in a fair way."

Mesa, Arizona

In June of last year, Mesa contracted out all of its routine street sweeping to Waste Management, Inc. The contract, valued at approximately $400,000 a year, called for once-per-week sweeping of main streets and thoroughfares and once-every-three-weeks sweeping of residential streets. The new contract will not include residential sweeping.

"This year, we decided to change our method of sweeping to a combination of city and contract services," explains Mesa Transportation Director Arnold Harring. Harring says the city's elected officials and senior management are in favor of contract services.

Harring was encouraged to investigate the possibility of reducing costs by contracting out street cleaning. "Our in-house program was excellent," he says, "but if we could cut costs by contracting and still retain excellence, the city felt we should."

The first year was a learning experience with mixed results, according to Harring. The job was done, but not without problems. Furthermore, the cost savings were not as dramatic as expected. The kinds of problems encountered can be traced to the city's specifications and expectations and the contractor's understanding of them, Harring explains. Questions relating to performance standards and special cleaning needs arose.

The new bid specifications being developed will incorporate the lessons learned from the first year's experience. The new program will provide for a competitive environment and improved methods of quality control, according to Harring.

Mesa's experience illustrates the importance of specifications to a successful contract street cleaning program. Provisions related to personnel experience, equipment, routing and special needs, as well as performance, should be carefully thought out, survey respondents concurred.

San Jose, California

Silicon Valley's most populated city, San Jose, chose to eliminate residential street sweeping after Proposition 13. Citizens are encouraged to clean their own street frontage while the commercial and main arterial streets are mechanically swept.

Last year, San Jose completed a six-month trial program with San Jose Commercial Sweeping. The company's owners, Leonard Vella and Frank Dorsa, also own majority interest in Mr. Air Sweepers, a parking lot air sweeper manufacturer. Now, they are expanding their contract sweeping services in other cities as Universal Sweeping Service.

"The pilot program allowed us the opportunity to identify problem areas and assess alternative approaches to the contract's job specifications and other terms and conditions," says Floyd Gier, head of the San Jose Neighborhood Maintenance Division.

Gier says the city is now negotiating a contract with Universal Sweeping Services for ongoing services. Gier explains that the city's policymakers did not believe a competitive bid was necessary or in their interest.

There are many other public entities that contract out street cleaning that are too numerous to list. They include counties, military installations and universities, as well as cities and state highway departments. There are also many that have chosen not to contract for services.

Campbell, California, is an example of a smaller city that uses a contractor for back-up and construction work purposes when necessary.

Otherwise, the city does its sweeping with public employees and equipment.

Hank West, Campbell's field maintenance supervisor, has analyzed his situation this way. First, it is important to have a good operator for the city's one sweeper. The sweeper does a 30-mile route, five days a week, and is seldom out of operation because of the operator's skill and dedication.

"Production is high, downtime is low, and maintenance is prompt and effective," says West. "Consequently, our cost is exceptionally low and our performance is reliable."

Larger cities such as San Francisco continue in-house sweeping services for other than economical reasons. Jerry Costanza, the city's deputy director of finance and administration, explains his thinking this way: "We have a strong civil service tradition and a union that supports the city's leadership. Private contractors are profit oriented, whereas the civil servant is dedicated to the common good. One must consider the intangible benefits of having an in-house, civil service operation. The idea of evaluating contract street cleaning has never been seriously suggested."

Costanza's comments reflect what is probably the biggest obstacle to service privatization, namely, union opposition and conventional interpretations of public and private sector motivation. Newark represents what can happen when these obstacles are confronted. The Newark contractor's operators belong to the same union. Contractor responsiveness and dedication is assured through the contract's terms and specifications. Councilman Martinez of Newark observes, "Performance is paid for. Non-performance doesn't cost the city taxpayer. That's black and white. Before it was gray."

21. Transit

Ralph L. Stanley

Privatization, the transferring of government services to private, profit-motivated enterprises, is currently receiving an in-depth examination in the federal government. At the Urban Mass Transit Administration (UMTA), we have reached conclusions which were so positive that we now advocate increased public/private partnerships in the field of mass transportation. UMTA today is a catalyst for this policy idea, and the laboratories are the cities, towns and counties across the nation.

There is much discussion about privatization of government services in context with the Administration's budget proposal, particularly such aspects as the sale of government holdings. Mentioned frequently are the Naval Petroleum Reserve, the Tennessee Valley Authority, and portions of the Postal Service. These trial-balloons are really bottom-line motivated actions to increase productivity, profitability and efficiency, much like a troubled company would spin off units ill-suited to their overall business agenda.

I prefer to think of privatization as a vehicle by which to inject competition into public transportation, emphasizing the creation of public sector/private sector partnerships rather than divestiture, and on competition rather than public or private monopolies. For example, in Phoenix, Arizona, it might appear to the observer that public transportation was not available on Sundays, because no buses are on the streets. This public service is indeed provided—it is simply camouflaged. Rather than run fixed-run bus schedules on low-demand days like Sunday, the city leaders contracted with a local cab company to provide demand response service at a subsidized rate.

Ralph L. Stanley, "Time to Get Back on Track—The Need for Competitive Services in Transit." Reprinted with permission from The Privatization Review, Vol. 2, No. 2, Spring, 1986. Published by The Privatization Council, Washington, D.C. (Printed by Maxco Publications, Inc., Little Falls, New Jersey.)

For low-density Phoenix, privatization by contracting-out to local companies was one method of holding down spiraling transit costs while maintaining and even improving the quality of service. City management estimates it saved $700,000 annually, or nearly five percent of its total transit budget, by implementing this paratransit (taxis and vans) idea. Then Phoenix went a step further and awarded the operation of the entire bus system to St. Louis–based American Transit Corporation after having received bids from both private and public providers.

Private sector involvement in mass transportation is no longer an abstract idea nor a scheme dreamed up to reign in spending. As the Phoenix illustration demonstrates, it is fast becoming a working reality which produces results.

Other municipalities across the country are pursuing similar experiments. In Chicago, private "club" buses carry over 5,000 commuters a day from the suburbs to the Loop. In New York, 700 private buses bring 100,000 workers into Manhattan daily. Today, after twenty years, UMTA is working to rekindle this kind of enthusiasm for free enterprise in public transit. We see it as the key to mass transportation's survival and as the best hope for continued mobility in the years to come.

Those First Steps

Included in the Urban Mass Transportation Act, passed by Congress in 1964, is legislative language which encourages private sector participation in the federal transit program "to the maximum extent feasible." These provisions have been greatly ignored by most transit authorities. On October 22, 1984, UMTA issued a policy statement renewing our commitment to achieving this goal.

The objectives of our policy statement are several: First, we want to promote competition for services by requiring that public transit authorities provide interested providers with fair and timely consideration. Second, we want to encourage businesses to become more involved corporate citizens by assisting local governments to control those factors that affect the demand for transit, such as the promotion of ridesharing. Finally, we want to explore areas where private capital formation can come into play in the development, building, and maintenance of transit systems.

Shortly after issuing its private enterprise policy, UMTA created the Office of Private Sector Initiatives (OPSI) to assist in its implementation. By this action, we seek to develop a greater reliance on the eagerness, energy, strengths, resources and insights of the private sector in sharing transportation responsibilities. Our efforts to get OPSI up and running came under siege in the House of Representatives last year. Had the attack been successful, our program to promote transit privatization could have been quashed.

During hearings in the House Appropriations Committee, Bob Carr (D-MI) offered an amendment prohibiting UMTA funds from being used for private sector feasibility studies. Responding to this, concerned Washington policyshapers, spearheaded by the Heritage Foundation, banded together in support of our initiative. Armed with the argument that in a time of federal fiscal uncertainty, there was no foundation for cutting off the exploration of cost-effective transit alternatives, privatization supporters prevailed and the amendment was watered down and made harmless.

The Private Sector Initiative, now just over a year old, is charged with fostering acceptance of the concept while coordinating implementation. Strict enforcement of the policy will be monitored both by field ombudsmen and through the complaint process at UMTA headquarters. Of great importance is the office's activities to encourage local planning organizations to explore private sector alternatives that have not been attempted, using the UMTA grant dollars they receive. This is a priority.

Why the Need to Privatize — What Happened Along the Way

We are doing this now in response to the economic realities looming on the horizon and the certain impact on mass transportation. After 20 years and $46 billion, transit's share of work trips was still in decline. As we searched for answers, we found that a potent tool was already available in the form of the private enterprise mandate.

In his first State of the Union address, President Reagan unveiled his simple but long-held belief that it was high time that the federal government curtailed its intrusive presence upon the people. Otherwise, America would never move out of its dreadful economic predicament. This "New Federalism" was based on the belief that the federal government had undertaken too many responsibilities to which it was unsuited and unable to carry out effectively. This idea held that local governments, closer to the people they serve, were much better positioned to meet the needs of the people than was Washington. A dialogue between the federal officials and state and local leaders was needed to redefine their roles. This was a call for greater reliance upon the private sector, in the forms of public/private partnerships and volunteerism, to offset inadequacies. The response of the people was overwhelmingly positive.

When UMTA looked at itself, as the President directed, several aspects of the federal mass transportation program fell into the category of misallocation of responsibilities. One in particular was the federal provision of transit operating assistance to local governments. Another was the absence of private service providers. Public-private cooperation is the product of the strengths of both sectors.

In the public transportation world, transit's primary lenders — governments at all levels — are suffering from declining resources and revenues. Since 1964, the federal government has invested $43 billion in public urban transportation. Local and state governments have chipped in billions more. Today fares cover only 38 percent of transit costs; 62 percent are from public subsidy. Yet, during that expansion period, public transportation ridership decreased from 3.7 percent of all urban travel to 3.2 percent.

Another factor which will give real insights into the efficiency and effectiveness of transit service resolves around the issue of labor compensation. Research conducted by the Urban Institute in Washington, D.C., examining total compensation of a number of transit occupations in comparison with similar occupations in the private sector, both transit and otherwise, reveals that the compensation of public sector transit employees can exceed that of their counterparts in the private sector by 50 to 100 percent.

Additionally, while ridership, the best measure of return on investment, did not increase — transit costs went through the roof. Between 1970 and 1983, total transit industry operating expenses increased from $2 billion to $9.7 billion — a five-fold increase. In this same period, as the record shows, the cost per mile of operating transit systems rose almost twice as fast as the inflation rate. This is quite a painful, but realistic, thought when one recalls the double-digit inflation and 21 percent interest rates of the late seventies. It would appear that public transit management failed, when tested by a never-before-experienced twist in the economy, which shattered their business-as-usual cocoon. Clearly, an alternative to increased subsidies was called for.

On the broad national front, in 1980, the country's economic outlook could have been described by no other word than bleak. Yesterday's policies of depending on big government for a helping hand had not worked.

That year's election ushered in a new approach. Central to the program was the need to reduce government spending, coupled with a reduction in personal taxes, that would restore the taxpayer's purchasing power, thereby re-stimulating the economy — all principles of a free-market system. Skepticism prevailed from the outset, but finally the program began to take hold and pay off. The engines of American business had been restarted.

Four years later, the breadth and strength of our economic recovery was better than predicted. The inflation monster had been put back into its cage, and more Americans found jobs than at any other time in our history. The recovery had truly developed into an expansion.

But with this enormous growth and recaptured prosperity came deficits of unrecorded proportions. The central problem was the government's burden on the economy. Whether government borrowed or taxed to address the deficit issue, it would still be taking the same amount of money from the private sector. The weight and expense of government was still a hindrance to the economy's ability to grow. The Administration's resolve to further reduce spending held firm. But the very real need to sharply reduce government spending had always been countered quite effectively by political pressure and complete enactment of cuts were never achieved. The real question was never whether we should bring the deficit down, but how.

Enter Gramm-Rudman and Fiscal Discipline

The how was recently signed into law. It's entitled "Gramm-Rudman-Hollings," the landmark legislation structured to bring the federal budget in balance by 1991. It means compulsory fiscal discipline for the federal government, similar to what has existed all along at the city, county, and state levels of government.

While questions exist as to the law's constitutional validity, the adverse judgment issued by the special three-judge panel will have little immediate impact, since the justices delayed their ruling pending an appeal to the Supreme Court. That review is expected in early summer.

Regardless of the outcome, in my opinion, the balanced-budget measure holds the key for any potential continued economic growth that the U.S. might ever hope to have.

To what extent this legislation will effect the federal government's mass transportation activities is yet to be seen. But if history is any guide, it will have an effect. All the more reason to look to the future and to explore privatization.

Mass transit has grown into a public expense of staggering proportions. Gramm-Rudman will no doubt rectify this situation either by intimidation or by the triggering of across-the-board cuts, if budget targets are not met. Legislators will have to demonstrate a willingness to set new, more stringent priorities and carefully prune the transit program for UMTA to remain in business. Gramm-Rudman-Hollings, in essence, provides the federal government with something that it has never had—a bottom line.

Experiments & Results

Our advocacy at UMTA of privatization in the field of public transportation should not be misinterpreted. I do not see competition or contracting-out of services as a panacea. I can say, however, that in most instances in which the private sector took over a service, it has been more efficient and less costly. Increasing the use of private operators in transit offers the opportunity to save money and improve service by injecting a time-tested motivator into its workings — incentives. Competition is the means to the end — the end being effective services to the public at a reduced cost, producing greater mobility.

Academics agree with this premise. A recently completed study by Dr. Roger Teal of the University of California's Institute of Transportation Studies found cost savings ranging from 20 to 60 percent in sampled communities where transit services are contracted with private providers. The services included fixed route, demand-responsive, elderly and handicapped, and commuter in various communities across the country. The following three examples show the inherent results when communities have had the foresight to experiment with solutions to their own problems:

> *El Cajon, California.* This city of roughly 74,000 inhabitants in the greater San Diego area used competitive bidding to select the operator of the community's entire public transportation service. After conducting a competitive bidding process for service, El Cajon determined that a local business could fulfill the community's transit needs at two and a half times less than the cost figured by the regional transit agency.
>
> *Dallas, Texas.* The city and the Dallas Area Rapid Transit Authority (DART) are shifting some services and maintenance to the private sector. For example, DART contracts some commuter service to the Trailways Company. That action took place in 1984, and since then 200 more suburban circulation service buses have been brought on line by private operators. Additionally, it contracts maintenance functions to the Ryder Corporation.
>
> *Norfolk, Virginia.* One of the fastest growing communities in the Commonwealth, Norfolk has reduced its subsidy per passenger by as much as sixty-four percent on certain fixed transit routes, by switching to privately contracted demand-response service, much like the efforts of Phoenix described above.

While not "made in the USA," privatization is frequently associated with British Prime Minister Margaret Thatcher's own successful transfer of government functions back to business. It's worth noting that the British have had a great impact on the way America views public/private partnerships. Our English friends have been working with great success towards the development of these partnerships on many different fronts, such as the job creation initiative the Reagan Administration has embraced, Urban Enterprise Zones.

In specific transportation terms, the *London Regional Transport* is in the midst of systematically returning a great deal of its mainline transit service over to private operators. Recently LRT let contracts for service on 13 routes, to which both public and private operators bid.

It is not that the private sector is superior to the public sector; it is that competition is superior to monopoly.

Time to Get Back on Track:
Transit Privatization: Where it Began—or Should Have

There are those who view our thrust toward competition as revolutionary, when in fact it's been around far longer than my agency itself. From a historical perspective, private industry involvement has been intended since UMTA's creation. Passage of the Urban Mass Transportation Act of 1964 signified the federal government's first official involvement in the transportation aspect of urban policy. The Act served as a prelude to the many other "Great Society" government programs, which we know now have become totally unyielding. The "Great Society" era was a jubilant period, a time when our nation's compassion for the needs of her people was matched by her cash reserves. However, the mood changed as the Treasury's surplus soon evaported due to the country's expanded involvement in Vietnam.

The bill was written as a solution to the long decline in the viability of local transit systems. These systems were for the most part being operated as highly regulated private monopolies, which came to suffer heavily from the effects of over-regulation and the automobile age and suburbanization of America.

Privatization and its potential, even in 1964, were recognized by the bill's architects when they included the "maximum extent feasible" clause. The UMTA legislation focused primarily on providing assistance to state and local governments in their efforts to finance the purchase of failed or failing transit systems.

Unfortunately, this road paved with good intentions by the Johnson Administration and the 88th Congress led to a tragedy of sorts, and just the opposite happened. Local governments began turning to Washington with greater and greater frequency. Every transit problem became something for the federal government, easing the demand for creative, locally inspired solutions from community leaders. Before long, the federal government was not only providing capital assistance to local transit agencies, but actual operating assistance as well. The old private monopolies were replaced by new public monopolies. The actors were changed but the problems remained. As for the bill's instructions to privatize when advantageous, by and large the intent of the private sector involvement clause has gone unheeded for these past two decades. Federal funds were poured into the creation of regional public transportation authorities, with little regard for industry inclusion.

The Case for Competition: Real Measures Needed

Just as the needs of the public in the sixties hastened a response on the part of the government, the same is true today. The reasons for competition are many, but principal among them are the demands for services while the government is unable to fund at ever-increasing levels.

Put simply in political terms, privatization means unleashing free-market forces and using private competition and local initiative to meet local needs. My commitment as a member of the Reagan Administration is to put competition in the driver's seat of mass transportation instead of letting government take the taxpayers for a ride, as the current federal-subsidy system has done.

We cannot lose sight of the issue before us, that of our future mobility. As a people, our transportation network has grown as our commuting habits have matured. The need for new services to keep pace with our desire for better mobility is ever-present. Transit can no longer be held synonymous with suburb to inner-city trips. Suburban circulation is becoming vastly more dominant than movement from the "burbs" to the center-city.

Just a moment of thought will substantiate this point. Did the high tech businesses of Massachusetts locate in downtown Boston? Is North Carolina's Research Triangle on Main Street in Raleigh? No, it's the outlying metropolitan areas which are experiencing this new job growth, and that's where a new transit need has developed. Another example can be witnessed in Tyson's Corner, Virginia. This once undeveloped cross-road on Washington, D.C.'s perimeter is now a booming business area that has half the office space of downtown Baltimore. In accordance with this business migration, answers are needed to meet the travel demands of those who dwell in these mushrooming growth areas.

Another category in need of expanded service is for those who are handicapped and for our elderly. Adequate service designed to meet their needs is long overdue. Also, late night and weekend service is essential for those Americans who have the will and the desire to seek employment and work — if only they could reach their job locations. These demands, and their expense, must be dealt with.

As these and other pressures continue to rise, the federal government's fiscal resources to support such systems have been severely restricted. Funds in Uncle Sam's coffers have been diminished to the extent that the responsive solutions to the mobility question must be developed now. Most definitely, a new direction is necessary.

As I see it, public transit agencies' options toward a solution are these:

- They can raise fares and lose additional riders, while risking political fallout.

- They can cut service, which again could lead to a similar end result.
- The agencies could cut corners by deferring maintenance or capital improvements, but this is likely to come back to haunt them. A case in point is the situation now facing New York City, which is in the midst of a multibillion dollar program to overcome past deferrals.
- Perhaps transit authorities can acquire new public funding, but that only postpones the problem.
- Or finally, they can develop new forward-looking strategies that will improve productivity and save money.

If we are to continue up the ladder of progress while at the same time coping with the reality that government can no longer afford to maintain its previous financial posture in total transit involvement, privatization, via competition, can be that new strategy.

My strong belief in the abilities of the private sector and competition is obvious. The business community has a major part to play in the process, for the fruits of their endeavors can be enormous.

Business Community as Better Corporate Citizens

Businesses should recognize the demand for dependable transportation, not only from customers but from employees as well. The business community can have a positive impact because of their ability to control and manage factors that affect the demand for transit. The role of business in affecting demand components such as working hours, parking policies, and public transit passes for employees can be an important element of this desired cooperation. Many business concerns are moving toward the development of these strategies by supporting ridesharing programs, thereby enhancing their corporate image within the community. Hartford, Connecticut's success along these lines is noted time and time again as evidence of the business and community leaders' ability to organize, plan, and carry out these necessary travel improvements.

Increased Private Investment

Another major area of impact which the business community can have on public transportation should be mentioned. Private investment in public transportation by the financing of transportation infrastructure is another opportunity we have to move progressively forward. This includes capital funding.

Private capital is increasingly being considered as a solution, as public officials and private investors meet to plan for tomorrow. Developers in numerous instances have come to realize that a shared financial contribution to transit projects and their costs is not only good public policy—but good business as well. Those who benefit from public transit investment should share its cost. This underlying thesis is also a dollars-and-cents motivation. Quality examples can be seen in Orlando, Florida, and in Washington, D.C. In both cases, the transit systems are designed to enhance land development, from which the private investors expect to profit.

> *Orange County, Florida (Orlando).* Only two years ago, Orlando was set to pursue federal funding for a $500 million light-rail line. They have now entered into a preliminary franchise agreement with Matra, a diversified military contractor, which is developing design, construction and private financing plans for a twelve-mile rail line. It is expected that Matra will receive an exclusive franchise to build and operate the system, at greatly reduced federal capital costs and no federal operating subsidies.
>
> *Washington, D.C.* This project entails rail service to Dulles International Airport. The airport area, currently underutilized, is considered an ideal future growth center. Two separate, and unsolicited, proposals have already been received to build and operate a rail line connector to the airfield.

The picture I've painted is not all rosy. There have been setbacks. One of these, which called for the building of a high-speed rail link between Los Angeles and San Diego, did not move forward as planned. Perhaps the development potential and or financial support were not sufficient. However, the L.A. project's fate should not deter further private sector involvement, and it seems that it has not. You see, this type of creative undertaking does not have the luxury of past precedent. They are experiments of sorts, and when experimenting we learn from both our successes and from our failures—but nonetheless, we learn.

Planned Implementing Legislation

Just before 1985 came to an end, UMTA was awarded Senator William Proxmire's (D-WS) much publicized "Golden Fleece," his citation for wasteful government expenditures and use of taxpayers' funds. In accepting the award, I agreed with the Senator that there was a degree of waste at UMTA and told him that we earned the "fleece" the hard way—"we paid for it." I reminded him as well that we earned his trophy with his help and that of his colleagues on Capitol Hill. Despite the cost-efficient budgets that UTMA has submitted to Congress for the last four years, Congress still has had difficulty showing the same kind discipline in the approval process.

Funds for expensive new systems were appropriated, especially in selected politically powerful districts, for "pork-barrel" purposes. A frightening example of this "bring home the bacon" method of governing is now located in Miami, Florida, in the form of a one billion dollar rail line. The system has attracted only 10 percent of its envisioned 200,000 daily riders.

The Mass Transit Administration will spend 25 percent less on formula capital projects in this fiscal year than in the fiscal year before. Yet, as a result of the irresponsible earmarking of new start monies by Congress, UMTA is faced with outrageous demands on its resources.

Secretary Elizabeth Dole has transmitted to Congress legislation to continue the federal mass transit program, including the law that provides for the mass transit portion of the Highway Trust Fund. DOT's proposal, which would fund UMTA by continuing to dedicate a penny per gallon of the nickel gasoline tax that was passed in 1982, will be frugal. It will also be far more flexible through a proposed urban mobility block grant. This block grant approach will allow state and local authorities to decide whether to spend their allotted funds on transit or highway needs. And as has always been the case, the trust fund will back those selections with a stable source of revenue.

An essential part of this reauthorization bill from my perspective, also aimed at enhanced efficiency, is UMTA's new language geared toward private sector participation. Five key areas to be addressed are:

- Private enterprise requirements which would upgrade UMTA's existing private sector policy to the level of statute. It would require opportunity for private providers to participate in service decision-making before the public hearing stage; that public operators consider using private operators to provide federally subsidized service; and that fair cost comparisons be made in evaluating the costs of public and private operations.
- A competitive services element for each urbanized area receiving federal funds, that a portion of service from both operations and maintenance must be reserved for competition each year. A gradual percentage increase would evolve, beginning with 5 percent of the local transit operating budget the first year and increasing to 20 percent by the fourth year, remaining at that level thereafter. Local mechanisms would be required to select and compete for services with equitable participation by public and private operators.
- Private operator representation on transit boards would be called for to the extent allowed by state and/or local law.
- Charter buses would be affected by a strengthening of the existing charter bus prohibition to explicitly prohibit use of federally assisted facilities and equipment for their use.
- The present section 13(c) of the UMTA legislation should be repealed, which would significantly improve the efficiency of labor in the transit industry while retaining all existing federal, state, and local labor protections.

On the competitive services proposal in particular, assuming the low end of savings as referenced before in the Teal study, coupled with the 5/10/20 percent formula to be targeted for competitive bidding, we would estimate that a potential savings of one billion dollars could be realized over a period of four years.

These proposals will be the subject of vigorous debate by Congress. I welcome this exchange. In fact, I'm anxious for it to begin. Hopefully it will cause a re-examination of the failed course of the past and produce a policy and program more in step with the future. These strong but flexible provisions will return the federal transit program to its original intent — that of a limited involvement by government when and only when local government and the private sector cannot do the job.

Conclusion

Good public transportation is not simply the provision of certain types of service, but involves coordination of the efforts of many, public and private. The most effective approach to improve transit must start with close coordination between the public and private sectors at all levels of the process, from planning to funding to operations. Our proposals to stimulate competition will nurture the diversity of local responses to local problems, while unleashing the creative energy of small entrepreneurs and the support of major businesses. We in the Administration are dedicated to making the program both a reality and a success.

I believe that, in addressing transportation problems, the blending of the profit motive of private business with the public interest responsibilities of government will lead to more efficient solutions than through either pubic or private provision alone.

The American Public Transit Association, the lobbying arm of the industry, has a slogan which is "Transit Means Business." I believe in that slogan; that's why I want to see transit conducted like a business — carried out with a healthy dose of competition.

22. Wastewater Treatment

Douglas Herbst and *Lanny Katz*

Introduction

Since 1983, the concept of privatizing wastewater management facilities has progressed from an idea that seemed worthwhile to reality — more than 10 transactions have now taken place. Given this experience, a detailed comparison can be made of this alternative to the "classic" financing approach — EPA Construction Grants Program funding.

At first, privatization was not meant to compete with grant funding, but rather to be an alternative for those communities whose only option was 100 percent local funding. In light of developments in the Construction Grants Program since 1981, it is arguable whether this remains totally valid. Using three recently concluded privatization transactions as examples, this article will show a comparison between the privatization approach, grant funding, and 100 percent local financing, and discuss the implications of these comparisons.

A Historical Perspective of the Construction Grants Program

In its first nine years, the Construction Grants Program was the supreme example of how the federal government, through the disposition of huge amounts of money, could stimulate a much needed and desirable effect — the planning and construction of hundreds of wastewater management facilities, and the concomitant improvement of water quality.

Douglas Herbst and Lanny Katz, "The Privatization of Wastewater Treatment — Three Case Studies." Reprinted with permission from The Privatization Review, *Vol. 2, No. 2, Spring, 1986. Published by The Privatization Council, Washington, D.C. (Printed by Maxco Publications, Inc., Little Falls, New Jersey.)*

During that time, the Construction Grants Program budget averaged over $5 billion a year, with a grant percentage set by law at 75 percent of eligible costs. In many states, matching grants sometimes increased this percentage, in some cases to 90 percent of eligible costs. These costs included the planning, design, and construction of the treatment facilities and major conveyance and collection systems for both existing need (actual flow) and planned growth (future flow). Even with grant budgets of $5 billion per year, priority systems were necessary to select those projects most deserving of grants, and some communities waited several years before receiving grants.

Since 1981, the grant picture has changed markedly. Efforts to curb federal spending have had their effect on both the size and nature of the Construction Grants Program. Eligibility criteria have been tightened to exclude collection systems, portions of conveyance systems, and costs for future growth.

The most significant change has been the recent reduction from 75 percent of eligible costs to 55 percent of eligible costs. In addition, total annual federal expenditures for the program have been reduced to half of previous levels ($2.4 billion).

The impact of these changes is the shortening of the list of "fundable projects" each year.

Construction Grants, Privatization, and Local Financing

As it is currently structured, the grant program's use of the term "55 percent grants" is somewhat misleading. Because of eligibility criteria, the percentage grant of total project cost in all cases is less than 55 percent, and in some cases far less than 55 percent. Therefore, in any comparison of alternatives, the grant must be looked at in terms of its effective percentage, i.e. the grant amount (55 percent of eligible costs) divided by the *total* project costs.

We have chosen three communities that have recently selected privatization of their wastewater management projects. All three concluded negotiations in late 1985 and are proceding with development. Using available information, and after consulting with the respective state regulatory agencies about eligibility criteria, we have developed a comparison of costs to the community that would have occurred under 100 percent local financing and EPA grants.

One major assumption which was applied was that these communities would have been in the fundable range on the state priority list during 1985. Another assumption was that there was no difference in time from the development of the project to the granting of funds or consummation of the privatization contract. As to the first assumption, none of the communities were, in fact, in the fundable range. The validity of the second assumption is arguable, but may be implicit in the project descriptions.

East Aurora, New York

The Village of East Aurora, approximately 15 miles southwest of Buffalo, New York, had an inadequate wastewater treatment facility. The Village was not on the New York State Priority List for grant assistance. Therefore, no federal or state funding was available. The existing facility needed upgrading to attain the required discharge permit limits as well as an expansion to 3.5 mgd (million gallons per day) to meet the Village's continued growth. The Village was also under a consent order from the New York State Department of Environmental Conservation.

Faced with the prospect of 100 percent local financing, and with plans and specifications virtually complete, the Village decided to examine the feasibility of privatization in March 1984.

The Village proceeded with procurement and in December 1985 signed a contract with a privatizer. Tax-exempt bonds totaling $7.4 million were issued to finance the project.

Western Carolina Regional Sewer Authority (WCRSA), Greenville, S.C.

The WCRSA had an inadequate wastewater treatment facility serving a rapidly growing area. The existing facility was at its design capacity (1.5 mgd) with marginal performance.

The original plant was built in the 1960s, and, as the area developed, the plant was expanded and upgraded several times. Some EPA grant assistance was involved in a previous expansion/upgrade and helped provide interim capacity until a long-term solution could be selected. The Authority's Facilities Plan, completed in the mid–1970s, called for improvements to be made at the existing site.

As the need for another expansion/upgrade became apparent, further EPA assistance was sought. The project was ranked low on the priority list, and further grant assistance was years away. This low ranking, combined with a consent order and the increasing need for service to permit the continued growth, presented a major problem to the Authority. The Authority amended its Facilities Plan and concluded that the needs of the service area would best be served by the construction of a new 4 mgd facility. With a new facility and a new site, approximately 8 miles of trunk sewer would be needed to convey flow to the new location.

The South Carolina Department of Health and Environmental Control (DHEC) preferred that the existing facility be improved and stated that only 1 mgd of additional capacity would be eligible for construction grants (to meet existing needs of 2.5 mgd). DHEC held that if the Authority built new facilities, only 1 mgd of the proposed 4 mgd facility would be eligible, and the trunk sewers would not be eligible.

Given the above reality and to assist in this analysis, a hypothetical scenario was also evaluated to present a more readily identifiable case to compare with other similar projects. This scenario viewed the new facilities without regard to history and site-specific circumstances. It examined the project in accordance with Federal regulations, with funding limited to existing needs (in this case 2.5 mgd).

In March 1985, with design approximately 50 percent complete, WCRSA examined the feasibility of privatization and found the option attractive, as compared to local financing. WCRSA proceeded to procure a privatizer while simultaneously completing design plans and specifications. By August 1985, the Authority had completed designs to give to a shortlisted group of privatizers for final proposals that would include firm price quotes for construction. In December 1985, the Authority concluded negotiations and signed a privatization contract. Construction is expected to begin in mid–1986.

Pelham, Alabama

This small suburban city just outside Birmingham has experienced explosive growth in the last 15 years. Between 1970 and 1980, the city grew from 900 residents to over 7000 residents. Less than 20 percent of the population is served by any type of centralized-systems, mainly small package plants installed in several developments. The remainder (over 2000 homes and businesses) use septic systems or cesspools. Faced with continued growth because of its location and attractiveness, but limited because of the lack of facilities, the city government decided to begin planning a wastewater management system.

In April of 1985, the city's consulting engineer completed a preliminary master plan calling for a wastewater system of collection, conveyance and treatment of up to 6 mgd by the year 2000. With no chance of being in the fundable range in upcoming years, and with eligibility limited to the treatment facility and possibly a portion of a major interceptor, the city decided to examine privatization. A rapid procurement process was initiated. The privatizers were told, "be flexible, be innovative, have the majority of the existing population served by January 1987, and keep the costs affordable during the initial years when the user-base is small." Seven months later, a contract was signed, at a firm fixed price, based on preliminary engineering. Sixteen million dollars of tax-exempt bonds were sold, and construction began in February 1986.

The Economic Comparisons

To calculate the effective grant percentage that these projects might have received, total capital costs must be evaluated. For East Aurora and WCRSA, the costs used are those estimated by the consulting engineers from plans and specifications. In the case of Pelham, no estimates had been made because of the preliminary nature of engineering investigations prior to the city's decision to privatize. Therefore, capital costs guaranteed by the privatizer were used as a base amount, and inflated by 15 percent to account for a two-year period during which the city would have prepared a facilities plan, had it approved, and prepared detailed plans and specifications and had them approved. No assumption was made that the base amount (the guaranteed cost by the privatizer) is less than would have estimated for a publicly financed project.

From the total capital costs, ineligible costs are then subtracted, to derive those costs upon which the EPA grant (of 55 percent) would be calculated. The grant amount, in dollars, is then divided by total capital costs to derive an effective grant percentage. Table 1 shows the results of these calculations. In the best case, East Aurora, the effective grant percentage is 42 percent, reflecting the fact that most of the facilities would be grant-eligible. In the actual funding scenario for WCRSA, the effective grant percentage is extremely low (7 percent) because the majority of the costs are ineligible (trunk and relief sewers and excess capacity). In the hypothetical scenario, the inclusion of a greater portion of flow (2.5 mgd) as eligible and limited eligibility for the conveyance system based on existing needs increases the effective grant percentage to 33 percent. In the case of Pelham, the low effective grant percentage (20 percent) reflects the ineligibility of the collection system and a portion of the interceptor costs.

Table 2 presents the annual debt service costs for the projects. Under the 100 percent local financing alternative, they are based on financing the total project costs at tax-exempt rates available at the time. Annual costs under the grant approach are based on the issuance of bonds for the portion of total project costs not covered by the construction grant (see Table 1 for these dollar amounts). Finally, annual costs under the privatization approach are those which had been guaranteed by the privatizers.

In Table 3, these annual costs for both privatization and grant funded

Table 1

Project Costs and Effective Grant Percentages

	Total Project Costs	Eligible Project Costs	Grant Amount (55%)	Remaining Amount — Local Share	Effective Grant Percentage[3]
East Aurora	$ 5.310.000	$4.098.588	$2.254.000	$ 3.056.000	42%
WCRSA No 1[1]	$15.082.000	$2.040.600	$1.854.000	$13.228.000	12%
WCRSA No 2[2]	$15.082.000	$9.003.800	$5.142.000	$ 9.940.000	34%
Pelham	$13.594.000	$4.993.000	$2.746.000	$10.848.000	20%

(1) Actual Funding Scenario

(2) Additional Funding Scenario

(3) $\dfrac{\text{Grant Amount}}{\text{Total Project Costs}}$ = Effective Grant Percentage

Table 2

Average Annual Debt Retirement Costs

	100% Local Financing	Grant Approach[1]	Privatization Approach[2]
East Aurora	$ 576.000	$ 320.000	$ 354.000
WCRSA No 1	$2.000.000	$1.800.000	$1.350.000
WCRSA No 2	$2.000.000	$1.353.000	$1.350.000
Pelham	$1.778.000	$1.419.000	$1.236.000

(1) Debt Retirement Costs of Funding Local Share

(2) Capital Charge Portion of Privatization Service Charge

Table 3

Annual Savings of Debt Retirement Costs

	Grant	Privatization
East Aurora	44%	39%
WCRSA No 1	10%	33%
WCRSA No 2	32%	33%
Pelham	20%	30%

projects are expressed as a percent annual savings compared to 100 percent local financing. What can be seen is that under privatization, savings are relatively constant (although the three projects involved three different privatizers) while the savings under a grant-funded approach are, of course, heavily dependent on the size of the eligible portion of the project and virtually equivalent to the effective grant percentage. Several points must be emphasized:

- The economic comparison has dealt only with capital costs. The growth of contracting-out of municipal services through operation and maintenance contracts for wastewater facilities indicates that there is economic benefit associated with private-sector involvement. Since operation of the facilities is an integral part of privatization, there is likelihood that further savings can be realized with privatization.
- The additional economic benefit of risk avoidance by assignment of risks to the privatizer has not been addressed. The allocation of project risks must be carefully considered by local governments when evaluating their options. Under 100 percent local financing and a grant-funded approach there is little or no allocation of risk.
- Most importantly, the comparison of grants to privatization was done assuming that grants were available to the three communities. In fact, a grant was effectively unavailable to Western Carolina because of their low position on the priority list. East Aurora and Pelham were not on the priority list.

National Implications

Having seen how privatization competed with hypothetical grant-funded projects in three specific examples, it is interesting to speculate on the implications of these results nationwide. Clearly, for communities like those described, outside the fundable range of the Construction Grants Program, privatization can be a timely and cost-effective solution to needs. Even when in the fundable range, many communities may, because of low effective grant percentage, find privatization to be the more cost-effective alternative. It is impossible to gauge how many fundable communities would opt for privatization, if given the choice. Public policy and political considerations are integral components of any community's decision to proceed with wastewater facilities construction, but it could be argued that at least a portion of these communities would take advantage of the opportunity.

The consequence of such action is obvious. Grant funds reserved for such projects would be available for other, lower-ranked projects, currently below the fundable range. This would spread federal resources further than the lower grant percentage and tightened eligibility criteria already imposed would allow. The concept of using private-sector involvement to stretch or replace government assistance for wastewater facilities construction leads to further speculation regarding the possibility of blending privatization with government assistance under prospective revolving loan programs. While only in a formative stage, and admittedly without regard to any specific legislation that would allow it, preliminary analyses indicate that blending privatization with loans to the communities could extend loan funds between 10 percent and 83 percent (depending on various loan scenarios), while maintaining user charges at the same levels as those projected under direct loans for capital investments.

The 1984 Needs Survey (a biennial report submitted to Congress by the U.S. EPA assessing the capital investments required for wastewater treatment facilities) estimates that over 30 billion dollars is needed through the year 2000 for wastewater treatment facilities nationwide. The staggering need takes its place among the other competing infrastructure needs, placing a heavy burden on already stretched state and local government budgets. Add to this the reduction and ultimate elimination of federal assistance, and the need for new and creative concepts for financing and constructing wastewater treatment facilities becomes clear.

Privatization is one such concept which needs to be brought out of the background and into the forefront as an alternative for state and local governments. When it is properly evaluated and fully understood, privatization will present a viable alternative for solving the nation's water pollution problems.

These results — affordable wastewater treatment services, more efficient use of federal and state funds, and in effect, an enhancement of government funding — can be achieved if privatization continues to be economically attractive to both the public and private sector. One way to assure this is for Congress to recognize the clear public purpose nature of privatization and retain current or comparable tax postures for privatization projects.

Part Four: The Precautions

23. Uses and Misuses

Robert W. Bailey

\

When a consensus was reached in the late 1970s that redistribution through taxation and budgeting was becoming a less attractive policy for state and local governments in the United States, a series of new, off-budget policy instruments were advanced to provide localities and the Federal government with other ways to act in the presence of fiscal restraint. In both public policy and the academic literature, *limits* became the watchword — limits not only in fiscal resources but also in the ability of government effectively to influence social or economic direction: the limits of *état* power. Strategic planning, land-use planning, exactive zoning, community-sponsored public benefit corporations, public development corporations, public-private partnerships, and many other initiatives can be gathered under this umbrella. Indeed, not since the first half of the nineteenth century has such intense activity been seen in these areas.

One of the concepts in vogue is privatization. Although the concept itself is unclear, it might be tentatively defined as a general effort to relieve the disincentives toward efficiency in public organizations by subjecting them to the incentives of the private market. There are in fact several different concepts of "privatization," but this theme unites them all. Depending on the emphasis of the advocates, the theoretical grounding of privatization comes from either public-choice theorists, students of monopolistic behavior in economics, or political scientists with a prescriptive view of interest-group analysis.

This essay presents some of the limits to privatization; not so much to reject the concept — the introduction of a policy instrument can only be beneficial for the professional public manager — but to reduce its ideologi-

Robert W. Bailey, "Uses and Misuses of Privatization." Reprinted with permission from Prospects for Privatization, *The Proceedings of The Academy of Political Science, Vol. 36, No. 3, 1987. Published by The Academy of Political Science, New York, New York.*

cal character to practical guidelines. For privatization is not new. It has been tried and, at least in four cases in New York City, has not always succeeded.

Clarifying the Concept of Privatization

When words become political weapons, they often lose their clarity. *Privatization* is no exception. At least four identifiable policy initiatives are associated with privatization in current public-management discussions. No one of them excludes the others.

The first might be called "load-shedding through privatization." This is the oldest notion of privatization and the one most often used. Simply stated, it is the transfer of a service or operation from a public agency to a private organization. The classic example has always been sanitation services. E.S. Savas has argued that the private pickup of solid waste would result in greater efficiency. The traditional argument is that a network of private organizations, in competition with one another, would create an incentive for cost containment or even reduction. At least in New York City, according to the argument, the growing influence of public-employee unions, through their ability to withhold services or through campaign activities, had undue influence over managerial prerogatives. In collective bargaining, the "scope of bargaining" had expanded, and labor had become involved in decisions that in the past would have been left to management. By privatizing the service, this influence would be put into a more proper perspective. Similarly, the argument over education is that privatization through a "voucher" system would lead to more effective schools, since parents, who would have control over the disposition of educational resources, could choose from a number of different educational offerings. Obviously, schools would then attempt to upgrade their educational effectiveness; if they did not, they would fail to establish credibility among parents and could not attract enough students to succeed. In education and sanitation, advocates of privatization see the monopolistic nature of local-service delivery as the greatest impediment to government effectiveness. Competition is the recommended remedy via privatization.

The second definition is associated with the current debate in Western Europe and is less germane to the American discourse. In Europe and in most of the rest of the First and Third Worlds, governments hold state owned enterprises (SOEs). These institutions can be either fully or partially owned. What separates them from their American counterparts is that many of these SOEs are equity corporations, that is, they issue stock or some other instrument that can be shared with nonstate organizations. Many of the airlines in the world are owned by state entities in partnership with private investors. In Israel, the government is often in partnership with the Histradut, the organization of labor unions. Their jointly owned corporations often form partnerships with other organizations—public or private or even international, such as the Jewish Agency. Privatization here relates to the relative position of the government in SOEs. In Britain, Prime Minister Margaret Thatcher's government has privatized many SOEs by selling up to 100 percent of the Crown's ownership. In France, Prime Minister Jacques Chirac has "privatized" some of the financial-services industry that President François Mitterand's government had "nationalized." In many cases, such as Italy, the government has an overall holding corporation that manages the state's role in SOEs. A direct application of this concept of privatization is not useful in the United States. Public benefit corporations (PBCs) are found in the United States, but not since the last century has there been a significant number of public-private equity corporations. Although there are similar issues of political and managerial accountability of PBCs and SOEs, they remain fundamentally different. American public benefit corporations usually issue debt, serviced by revenue streams derived from their activities. In the American environment, debt—not equity—is the key to understanding SOEs.

The third definition—one recently added to the nuances of privatization—is the sale of assets. The Reagan administration has proposed liquidating some of the Federal government's holdings to either raise revenues or end subsidies. The sale of Conrail in the Northeast and oil lands in the West are the best examples. Suggestions for the sale of home mortgages held by Federal financing corporations and the privatization of Bonneville Power and Tennessee Valley Authority facilities have also been made. What is really being proposed in these "privatizations" is the liquidation of assets for their cash value. The problem, though, is determining the market value of the asset being liquidated. In California the Federal government wants to sell lands with oil reserves at only eight times their cash flow, normally considered quite a low price by market analysts. In the Northeast, the sale of Conrail has become a political problem because one of the groups offering to buy it is a consortium of unions involved in rail transport. The government has not been enthusiastic about the offer and has been leaning toward one made by Norfolk Southern. But even if the political problems can be solved, there are others. Conrail, for example, has extensive real property holdings throughout the northeast corridor. In some cases—such as northern Philadelphia and Hudson County, New Jersey—how that land is used will have a tremendous impact on development patterns. Liquidating Federal assets for their cash value may provide some temporary relief to budget problems, but it may also have important negative effects on the public interests of localities. Here, too, privatization is a complicated policy whose long-term effects may outweigh short-term gains.

The fourth definition is "privatization" by contract. Here the concept becomes even less clear. It is an operational notion of privatization — in which a traditional responsibility of government is maintained but conducted by a private firm — and yet the *état* power of government is responsible for both the policy and the financial success of the "private" actor. The traditional source of such privatization has been in the provision of social services. Because most social services were begun by religious and voluntary organizations, there was a base of service and experience when government began to take on these responsibilities. In many cases, services for children, families, drug and alcohol dependency, and other social needs can best be delivered by these groups. The government contracts with them for their services, and referrals are made through family courts, criminal courts, government social-service agencies, and other organizations. A more recent example is the contracting out of research and analytical services. The U.S. Department of Energy privatizes, or contracts out, over three-fourths of its total budget. The bureaucratic advantage is that people are off-budget. They do not show up in the headcount or the budget and are outside the civil service system. The flexibility offered is enormous, of course, but so is the opportunity for abuse. On the state and local levels, there has been considerable pressure to privatize the management of special facilities, particularly convention centers, park lands, and sports facilities. In Tennessee an effort has been made to privatize the management of the state's correctional facilities. Privatization has been hailed as a way to reduce the operating costs of large facilities, relieving managers from the need to deal with public-employee unions and offering the "economy" of private market values — as it has in all four definitions.

Each of these definitions could be further refined and additional nuances introduced. The focus here has been more operational than ideological. Public managers do not really need an explication of the theoretical underpinnings of privatization, since their experience will likely diverge from it. Indeed, that point needs to be pressed: the ideological advocates of privatization so overstate its applicability, or so cloud it as a concept, that practical public managers who might choose to use it as a feasible policy instrument find themselves on the defensive among others who have been aroused to oppose privatization on ideological grounds.

The Twin Themes of Efficiency in Public-Choice Theory

Despite the confusion of what exactly is meant by the term *privatization,* there is a clear unifying thread in all its uses: maximization of efficiency. The assumption among advocates is that, inherently, private managers can deliver at lower costs services similar or superior to those of public managers. One can understand this. The constraints on public managers are tremendous—certainly greater than on private managers. There are the constraints of labor, the press, and the citizenry, all of whom hold public managers to a higher standard of accountability than private managers. And yet it should be pointed out that public management is simply different from private management. No homogeneity exists in the criteria of policy choice as there is in the private sector. There is no objective way to establish the price of public services and thus no basis for comparative analysis among competing activities for the investment of slack public resources. The government is required to be more open than a private organization. In short, the two are not directly comparable. A different set of skills is needed, as private managers learn when they take on previously held public responsibilities.

This standard point of debate in the difference between private and public management noted, the intellectual grounding of advocates for privatization should be taken seriously. Particularly in the large American cities, monopolies are formed by local governments to deliver services. The tendency for these monopolies to perform like all others—whether public or private—is great. The organization tends to absorb resources on internal preference scales. Since there is no need to create new products, innovation is low and research and development is neglected. Clients have few ways to express their preferences and no alternative when minimum service desires are not met. Because there is no unifying criterion of policy making in the public sector as there is in the private sector—i.e., profitability—assessing or pricing the comparative worth of services is difficult. In fact, the public sector offers one of the few arenas where service providers regularly generate their own demand. Thus the Pentagon generates Soviet threats as the Soviet military establishment generates American threats; and special education evaluation committees recommend services for 95 percent of the students referred to them.

The monopolistic nature of much of local service delivery is matched by a monopsonist character. Often, the local government is the only purchaser of a service or commodity. This is less to the advantage of the local government than it should be—that is, in establishing a monopsonist price—but it also opens local government to additional noncompetitive restraints. The actual service providers are unified through unions or professional associations. As the sole or major purchaser of services, local and state government may become hostage to the inefficiencies of single sellers or services. The monopsony reinforces the tendency toward internal preference scales and creates an extraordinary imbalance of power between the bureaucracy and the individual.

The combination of monopolistic government and monopsonist providers led in some cases to an imbalance within the public sector itself. In what political scientists call policy arenas — service areas where third parties come together to effect their interests — the combination resisted community responsiveness or, in the case of schools, responsiveness to parents and even resisted the fiscal authority of central political authorities. This dynamic contributed to New York City's financial crisis.

While all these patterns could be affirmed by more research elsewhere, there is also an irony. The same intellectual traditions that provide the underlying arguments for privatization — public-choice theory, theories of the firm, and monopolistic behavior — also provide an argument against it, at least on the state and local levels. While the pressures working against the effectiveness of local administration revealed by these traditions are clear, the same traditions reveal latent and indirect pressures toward efficiency. Charles Tiebout, in his classic 1956 essay on local expenditures, celebrated the relative fragmentation of jurisdictions in American federalism.[1] He noted that there would be individual or household-preference tables for public goods and individual or household resources available for tax effort. Both of these would vary but would be the underlying influences in deciding between what Albert O. Hirschmann, fifteen years later, would call "exit and loyalty."[2] Young families, for example, might be willing to suffer high taxation if the quality of education in public schools was superior to that in surrounding school districts. Senior citizens, most of them on fixed incomes, would likely prefer lower taxes and might tend to rely on the church and family for social services. Single people would likely prefer few services and low taxes.

According to the public-choice tradition, an incentive toward efficiency comes from different jurisdictions providing an equivalent array of services at different tax efforts. If one jurisdiction can meet the preference schedule of an individual, household, or organization at "Y" tax effort and another at "$1.12 \times Y$," other things being equal, that individual, household, or organization will tend to move into the first jurisdiction or, located in the second, tend to "exit." As the difference between jurisdictional efficiency variables increases, it will inevitably meet "inertia advantages" and make it irrational for the individual, household, or organization to remain settled. Obviously, these factors will become more potent as inertia advantages are mooted by depreciating capital, a larger family, a change in jobs, or other factors that put location on the decision agenda.

The point here is not so much that monopolistic behavior is unobserved in the public sector — surely it is — but that public entities are limited monopolies: limited by jurisdictional borders. Geographic fragmentation presents an incentive ultimately and, over time, toward efficiency. There is, then, a tension between two competing implications of public-choice theory: one indicating that the monopolistic nature of local-service delivery will naturally tend toward inefficiency, another indicating that the geographic limits of states and localities create an incentive toward efficiency. Which of the two themes is more potent at any one time is to be determined empirically by social scientists. What is interesting for us here, however, is that the tradition on which advocates of privatization rest their most persuasive arguments is in itself ambiguous on the long-term outcomes that limited local public-service monopolies might effect. One conclusion might be that intervening variables — such as the quality of public management — might have greater influence over public-sector efficiency than either of the discussed theoretical implications of public-choice theorists.

Lowering Expectations for Privatization: Four Cases from New York City

Although privatization is now discussed in a theoretical framework, much of what is being advanced has been in effect on the subnational level for many years. Four cases from the experience of New York City indicate that the promises held out for privatization may not be fully met. The intent here again is not to dismiss the concept of privatization but by reviewing it in real rather than ideological terms to see its actual utility. The four cases are commercial refuse, proprietary vocational schools, school transportation services, and management of sports facilities.

Commercial Refuse

There are two major structures of solid-waste removal in New York City. The city's Department of Sanitation removes the solid waste of the residents and not-for-profit organizations of New York. Private carters service the sanitation needs of commercial enterprises, including office buildings, restaurants, and retail outlets. This current dual structure of sanitation service is the result of privatization. In 1957 the city turned over delivery of sanitation services for commercial enterprises to private firms. Individual firms bid for contracts among commercial establishments needing sanitation services, and dozens of carter firms sprang up in New York.

From a theoretical standpoint, the citywide monopoly held by the New York City Department of Sanitation was broken up and an opportunity to provide the services previously delivered by the department was opened. The result, however, has not been fully beneficial. By the mid-1980s the efficiency expected by the privatization of commercial refuse had not been achieved. The proliferation of private carter companies is really misleading, since many are owned jointly by holding companies. In addition, either through formal or informal arrangements, the city has been divided into service districts or routes. Carter firms have agreed not to compete for business on the routes of other carters — an anticompetitive action. "Stops" — commercial establishments needing private carter services — are regularly sold between private carters if they decide to change the routing of their trucks or leave the commercial-refuse business entirely. There have been continuing rumors and several indictments indicating that organized crime has influenced the anticompetitive action of some private carters.

Even if the suspicion that organized crime is involved in private carting services is untrue, the efficiencies claimed for the privatization of the trade-waste industry have certainly not been obtained. Clients have no alternatives. When a mailing went out by the city to owners of commercial establishments, it was found that many were being overcharged by their carters, including a major office tower in midtown Manhattan. The lack of competitiveness puts upward pressure on carting fees. The monopoly has simply been switched from a public one to a private one. In addition, what might be expected as a benefit of privatization — that private carters would not have to deal with public-employee unions — is also hampered. Although there may be many private carters in New York City, there is only one union — the Teamsters. Its contract is citywide and binds nearly all private carters.

In 1987 it is clear that the privatization of commercial refuse has not achieved what might have been hoped for in New York City. The current policy discussions on commercial refuse concern greater regulation, particularly in regard to hazardous waste. Many private carters do not handle dangerous materials, such as asbestos and hospital wastes, in a proper manner. Despite a predisposition against taking on additional government responsibilities, the Koch administration is seriously considering eliminating the private carters.

Proprietary Vocational Education

Although one can point to a specific policy choice in the privatization of commercial refuse collection in New York City, no such decision was made about private vocational schools. There has been a conscious decision to regulate these schools, however, and to provide financing for them. An accumulation of regulatory and legislative initiatives in New York State leaves the clear impression that government wishes to meet the short-term, adult vocational-education needs being generated by the economy through private services.

Since the early 1980s the number of private vocational and business schools in New York State has skyrocketed: from 28 in 1980 to over 100 in

1986. Proprietary business and vocational schools offer training programs lasting from a few weeks to two years. Their curricula range from driver training, air-conditioning repair, and computer assistance to business skills. Many of these schools have long traditions and have made important contributions to their students and communities. But many have not.

Fueled by third-party payments—mostly student loans, New York State tuition assistance, and Federal Pell grants—the educational offerings of these schools have often been investigated. In some cases, there have been charges of outright fraud. Their primary market is students over the age of eighteen who have either dropped out of the public-school system or are among the new wave of immigration from South Asia or Spanish-speaking areas of the Caribbean and South America. The enrollment is overwhelmingly black, Hispanic, and female.

The State Education Department is responsible for regulating proprietary vocational schools in New York, but its resources are strained, and many of these institutions are afflicted with national chains and operate outside the jurisdiction of the department's officials. Compounding the problem is the fact that most of the state's inspectors are in Albany, while most of the schools are in New York City.

In a series of investigations conducted by state and city consumer-affairs advocates, legal-aid attorneys, and legislative staff, patterns of poor services and fraud were revealed. Many schools assessed students in terms of their potential for aid—and thus tuition—and were only secondarily interested in establishing needs assessment for their education. Some schools coached students skills tests during admission. Often students would be directed toward programs longer than they initially requested, thus ensuring eligibility for state and Federal assistance. Students were never informed that equivalent or better services were offered at their local community colleges at substantially lower cost. They were encouraged to incur debt. Some students signed loan applications without ever knowing that they were applying for a loan, and recruiters were paid a per head fee for students applying to schools. One school continued to recruit students and accept their tuition even though its lawyers were planning to file for bankruptcy.

The experience with private vocational schools in New York State over the past ten years raises some serious questions about privatizing educational services. Given the third-party payments available to students using these schools—essentially a form of the voucher system advanced by advocates of privatization—there was little incentive on the part of either the schools or the students to ensure the quality of education. Most students drop out. Since the schools can fill empty seats with new students and obtain new fees, the proprietors do not attempt to bring dropouts back to class. There is no evidence that competition has enhanced the career options or the quality of education for these students. The competition seems to be among the schools for students with the most potential for state and Federal aid. Of all sectors of the education community in New York State, proprietary vocational schools appear to be the least honest and the least effective.

School Transportation

School transportation services in New York City are private. Although the city's school district provides for free transport of most of its pupils, the Board of Education contracts out the service. Five major bus companies compete for such services and the one overwhelming actor is Varsity Bus Company. Despite efforts by the Board of Education to expand the number of potential vendors and thus increase competition, there has been no dramatic increase in the number of bidders for school contracts. The capital and start-up costs for a new firm are high. Necessary safety equipment increases the costs, leaving both the school system and the vendors with difficult trade-offs between children and profits. Despite efforts to get minority and small firms into the school transportation business, the situation remains the same: one firm dominates the market and four others provide whatever check there is on monopolistic abuse.

Even if the city's Board of Education could expand the number of potential bidders, there is a hidden monopoly in the school transportation market. Although five bus companies are operating in the market, the real driving force behind the bidding process is the contract provisions between the drivers' union and the five companies. The two principal costs in delivering transportation services are the cost of the buses — again a near monopoly situation — and the cost of labor. While the drivers' union may strike the bus companies, they are also striking against the school system, pressuring the Board of Education to accept higher vendor fees, different work rules, or other contract demands legally binding only on the bus company. In reality, however, at least in labor terms, there is a clear monopolist-monopsonist relationship: the union is the sole provider of services, and the school system is the sole purchaser. Competition among the bus companies, even if effective, would have influence only at the margins of this transportation market. Privatization here has had only minor effects.

Management of Sports Facilities

If one of the definitions of *privatization* is contracting out managerial and analytical services, then current activities in sports-facilities management are germane. For many communities, sports and convention facilities have become signs of pride and have involved heavy capital investment. They are seen as part of the infrastructure cluster needed if a city is to obtain or keep a reputation as a regional center. How sports and convention facilities are built and managed is now generally seen as an aspect of economic development. Indeed, the Lilly Endowment in Indianapolis, Indiana, advised and partly financed the city's efforts to become "the amateur sports capital of the United States." One need not be a sports enthusiast to recognize its economic and business aspects.

One trend in all of this is for government — either a general-service government or a public benefit corporation — to build these facilities and contract out their management. There are several advantages to this. At its best, contracting out management puts personnel practices outside the civil service system and public-employee collective bargaining. Greater flexibility in personnel assignment and compensation packages should become available for the private manager of a public facility. In addition, there will be an incentive to maximize utilization of the facility, since private managers will make more money. The public manager would not.

Although the proper application of this concept of privatization holds out some hope for a more efficient use of important public infrastructure investments, again the New York City experience with private management of public facilities has been negative. The general-service government of New York City built two major sports facilities in the 1960s and 1970s: Shea Stadium at 24 million 1961 dollars and the new Yankee Stadium at 127 million 1974 dollars. They are managed in the on season by the principal tenants of the stadiums — the New York Mets and the New York Yankees — and in the off season by the New York City Department of Parks. In both cases, the on season is now only half the year, since two National Football League franchises, which had used the facilities at other times of the year, have left the city and play in the Meadowlands complex in New Jersey.

The terms of private management of both stadiums are laid out in great detail in tenant contracts with the city and give both the Yankees and the Mets broad authority over the management of these facilities. Among these are decisions on prices, concessions, scheduling, hiring of non–Parks Department personnel, use of office space, sale of advertisement and television rights, and many other issues. Thus, for at least half a year, the management of these stadiums is privatized. The privileges were so extensive in the case of the Mets that the subtenant for over twenty years, the New York Jets, claimed that its principal reason for leaving the city was management quarrels and poor contract provisions exercised by the Mets franchise. The New York Yankees, whose contract precluded use of the city-owned Yankee Stadium by any other organizations unless approved by the Yankee management, recently threatened to leave New York City if the city does not build more parking space for spectators. In addition, since the city did not negotiate either a share in television rights for the use of its own facility or an agreement that television rights would not be sold to pay-television operations, the Yankee organization has sold the rights to more than 200 games to a local sports cable enterprise with no revenue derived for the city. Even worse from a political vantage point, most of New York City is not yet wired for cable television. Fifteen years after it was rebuilt, the new Yankee Stadium can be seen as a direct public subsidy to a private business organization.

This experience is not frivolous. Better management by the city of its own sports facilities would have increased utilization, enhanced revenues, provided greater managerial flexibility, and provided some political accountability to fans who can no longer watch a baseball game at home. Although the relationship between the Department of Parks and the Mets and Yankees has always been described in terms of tenant and landlord, it might be better termed as the privatization of facilities management. In this way it could be seen how New York City can get more out of its investments, and other jurisdictions can avoid its mistake. Proper privatization of management to an independent firm might have given the city a better bargaining position and a greater revenue stream. The lesson to be learned from New York City, however, is that if the privatization of sports and convention-facilities management is to succeed, it should not be privatized to the principal tenants.

What to Watch Out For

The point in these four cases is not to reject all aspects of privatization but simply to show its limits. It is true that in New York City other factors — such as union strength, the scale of the city, and its politics and government — may have mitigated the potential privatization offers to other jurisdictions. Expanding the tools available to state and local — and even Federal — public managers can only yield good results. The wise application of privatization, however, is a difficult enterprise and should be weighed against local needs, the matrix of obligations and resources the manager confronts and the effects that privatizing may have on different groups in the jurisdiction or on other jurisdictions. One can be certain that New York City's experience requires public managers to ask questions and not to treat privatization in an ideological fashion. At least ten issues should be considered before policymakers and public managers make a commitment to privatize.

1. Hidden monopolies. Hidden monopolies mitigate the efficiencies expected from the breakup of a public monopoly. These monopolies could be in labor or in available vendors who might contract to deliver a service, or they could be in material necessary for the provision of a service. Surely, when there is a sole bid from one contractor, the potential for savings from contracting out will not be achieved. The potential for voucher systems to give parents an increased voice in education policy will likely be undermined in those states with a strong teacher's union. Hidden monopolies will work against the goals of privatizers. They will either have to accept this reality or be willing to bear the additional fiscal and political costs of breaking up a set of private monopolies in addition to the public monopoly.

2. The continuing need to regulate. Government will still need to regulate a delivered service even though it has been privatized, since privatizing a service does not leave the government without responsibilities. Issues of public safety, public health, and quality of service will arise. Private hospitals and nursing homes are regulated by every state, and it could be argued that they should be regulated even more. In the Northeast, where there is a strong tradition of private higher education, the private nature of colleges and universities does not preclude state regulation and licensing of higher educational facilities. In fact, it requires it. Meeting the public need through private action will inevitably lead to greater regulation of private activities, regardless of who delivers the service. There will always be a need to regulate such activities to ensure that the public need outweighs private interests. And costs will thus be incurred.

3. The availability of a vendor. Many advocates of privatization assume that a vendor will always be available to purchase a government asset or to contract the services needed to be delivered. But no organization wants to take on the responsibility to deliver services that, for the most part, lose money. No organization could deliver solid-waste management services for the city of New York — or any other large city in the United States for that matter. Despite the proposal by John Silber of Boston University to contract with the Boston School Board for the management of the school system by the university, no private organization has sufficient capital or human resources to deliver educational services to the children of any large city, county, or small state. No organization is large enough or has sufficient private capital to operate a privatized national airport or a system of air-traffic control. And these are comparatively easy cases when compared with the Social Security system, the U.S. Postal Service, or the publicly owned utilities throughout the country.

4. Transition costs. The theoretical literature on which privatization is based assumes perfect knowledge and mobility and that individuals will seek Pareto-optimality. Transition costs are rarely mentioned. But the public manager must face a different set of issues and assumptions, including the costs of disruption associated with transition, potential labor problems, vendors' failure to deliver, vulnerability to litigation caused by tort actions in transition, or poor management. Consider the potential loss of life – and the costs of litigation – during a transitional period if air-traffic control was privatized. Anyone who has ever overseen the transition from manual systems to integrated data base-management systems understands the loss of productivity, unintended costs, labor problems, and innumerable other issues that sometimes lead to questioning whether computerization was a good idea in the first place. Transition is a real, sometimes inestimable cost that could far outweigh the potential benefits of privatization. The public manager understands this. The theoretician may not.

5. *Loss of economies of scale.* Economies of scale may be lost if the operations of a government monopoly were transferred to many smaller private operating companies. The argument for *small* is efficiency through competition; the argument for *large* is economies of scale. Again, New York City refuse collection is an example. As the largest purchaser of sanitation trucks in the country, New York City can negotiate bulk sales with lower per unit costs. Moreover, the purchase is so attractive to manufacturers that they will cooperate with city officials in designing equipment particularly beneficial to New York. This allowed productivity managers to move from three-person trucks to two-person trucks in the Department of Sanitation, thus saving millions of dollars in labor costs and enhancing services. The fragmentation of educational services would also likely increase per pupil fixed costs for facilities, support services, transportation, nonpedagogic personnel costs, and other expenses. Although large public bureaucracies impede efficiency certain economies can be gained from the scale of public organizations. One option is to break up the organization to control bureaucratic inefficiencies. The other is better management to attain the full potential of scale.

6. *The problem of estimating market value.* If a public organization is to privatize (liquidate) some of its assets, how does it establish the price? The Federal government, for example, wishes to sell off certain oil properties in California, but their claim to market value is low when compared with standard measures of corporate analysis. In many areas of the country, localities are selling underutilized schools to developers. What is their value? Obviously, it could be argued that the price should be set in a competitive process. But if the asset is so large that only one or two consortia can bid – as in the case of Conrail – is the price set fair? And if the price is not at maximum yield, what has been gained by privatizing it? Is the government obtaining public-sector efficiency or subsidizing a private consortium by selling public assets at lower than market value? A traditional problem in public management has been the inability to set a price for the value of public services. In some cases, at least, the same may be true of public assets.

7. *Contract compliance.* How does the public manager ensure that a

privatized service is meeting the terms of the contract? Although contracting out a service or management of a capital facility may offer certain benefits, it does not eliminate public responsibility. Contracting out daycare services does not end public responsibility for fiscal efficacy or — in the worst case — child abuse. In the latter case, is the government open to criminal or civil action because of the acts or omissions of its vendors? Like the regulation of services privatized, contracting out requires public monitoring of quality and the achievement of the public interest. If a locality contracts any services, an obligation remains that the providers abide by state and local health and education regulations, offer services as described in the contract, and review financial records. There will be auditing requirements, program evaluation, and investigatory needs if corruption or criminal activity is possible. All of this will add to costs and detract from services. As a practical matter, contract compliance will require a managerial unit to oversee vendor actions — another hidden cost of privatization.

   8. Lost opportunities. In privatizing a service or an asset, the government may lose opportunities to effect better service or to act more efficiently. One reason the private sector may be perceived to be more efficient in the use of its resources is that there is an internal incentive for managers to lower per unit fixed costs and raise utilization rates of capital, i.e., profitability. There is no such incentive in the public sector. In fact, there is a disincentive. Even the effective public manager tends to see capital as it contributes to the provision of service he or she oversees, not its overall potential. Thus school buildings, sports and convention facilities, park land, and other government-held assets are underutilized, because the public manager is not focusing on maximum utilization but on minimization of cost in service delivery. In addition, effectiveness is rarely tied to utilization rates of capital, partly because — in most jurisdictions — the capital budgeting process is separate from the operating budget process. Maximum utilization of a sports facility, a convention center, a school, or a university could just as easily be obtained by public managers if they were more entrepreneurial. By privatizing either the asset or its management, options may be closed off that were never explored in the past.

   9. The costs of failure. It is possible that many private actors who wish to take over public services will fail either from lack of quality — in which case government regulators will have to decide whether to cancel a contract — or because of bankruptcy, leaving clients without services. In either event, the public sector will have to provide the service as before privatization or bear the transition costs as the service is transferred to another private actor. It is clear that the service was of sufficient import for government to provide in the first place — before it was privatized — and so one can be fairly certain that there will be political pressure to guarantee service delivery. Again, a series of new start-up costs, transitional costs, legal costs, and the loss of service — a nonfiscal cost borne by clients — will follow as the inability of the private actor to meet public needs reminds public managers of their responsibility.

   10. The limits of governance. Privatization redefines the relationship between what is public and what is private, what is of the commons and what is not. It also changes the relative sets of social incentives and their relationship to the governing process. In the end, an unexpressed but present sense of legitimacy is also being privatized. From Adam Smith to current public-choice theorists, an ongoing effort has been made to provide an intellectual framework for the mobilization of private interests to the public purpose. In Smith's time, the application of the seeming reason of the market over the whims of the monarchy held out the promise of higher productivity and even "peace," the arbitrariness of the crowns being tempered by the reason of the market. The source of inefficiency and arbitrariness in public management today may well be the alliance of service providers, public-employee unions, and entrenched bureaucrats that has become the windmill against which privatizers are fighting. And yet economics does not exhaust governance. Privatization certainly offers the possibility that it will enhance efficiency and buttress the command, control, and accountability processes of the public sector. But it comes at the risk of a transition of allegiance from the state — in the French sense of *état* — to private actors. If the private actors are community-based, intermediate organizations, the outcome may be socially beneficial. If not, a sense of public legitimacy will have been squandered for marginal productivity enhancement — a trade-off that not only is unquantifiable but is even more dangerous to effective governance.

Conclusion

   Privatization adds another policy instrument to the tools of the public manager and policymaker. If fully aware of the hidden costs, the potential for failure, and the inadequate guarantees for obtaining the efficiencies that theory indicates will accrue, policymakers can decide to privatize. For the public manager, it should not be a matter of ideology, however, but of informed judgment based on experience in public management and on policy analyses more exacting than is currently presented by advocates of privatization.

   Americans' ideology often outpaces their behavior. George Kennan and Walter Lippmann saw it in foreign policy; Mark Roeloffs, on a domestic level. Americans may celebrate the market place, its ability to satisfy a wide variety of needs and desires, its tendency toward efficient

distribution and utilization of resources, and its openness to those of sufficient means to obtain access. But Americans do not subject the things they
hold most valuable to the market. The nurturing of children, the care of
the elderly, the obtaining of basic educational skills, the provision of a
minimum standard of living, minimum health care, and nutrition standards, for example, are not left to the market. For these, they rely on family, church, or state. It would, of course, be an exaggeration to claim that
Americans delegate exclusively to family, church, and state the things they
hold most dear and to the market those things they can do without; nevertheless, the point is made. Americans let the market establish the price of
pork bellies, not the future of children.

It is true that Americans have always mobilized private interests for the
public purpose. But they set limits on the process. Entrepreneurial generals,
with self-financing and standing armies, would never be tolerated by the
American people. And yet that fits the privatization model. Although
privatization may provide a good tool for the public manager and add an
interesting dimension to the political discourse, the concept—even after
eventual clarification—will not offer as much as its advocates claim. Privatization will be applied only to things that the American people are not
willing to risk; that includes every policy and program that several generations have put into place to protect themselves from the whims, uncertainties, instabilities, and unintended consequences of the marketplace.

24. Two Different Concepts

Ted Kolderie

Privatization is currently a hot topic, much in discussion and highly controversial.

Professional journals and business magazines have been filled with articles about it. Whole books have been written about the idea—some boosting it, such as E.S. Savas' *Privatizing the Public Sector* or Stuart Butler's *Privatizing Federal Spending;* some condemning it, such as *Passing the Bucks* by the American Federation of State, County and Municipal Employees. Centers are being formed to study or to promote the cause. Privatization now threatens to displace "partnerships" as the number one topic where people gather to talk about the contributions which business can make to the solution of problems which beset government.

Privatization is a live issue on the agendas of state, county, and city governments. It is becoming an issue in political campaigns. During the past year some particularly unusual and controversial proposals—especially, involving prisons—have brought privatization more to the attention of the media and of the general public. It is closely covered now, for example, by the *New York Times* and has become a favorite target for newspaper and magazine columnists, who tend to treat proposals for privatization as assertions that the market can replace government.

The discussion, the reporting, and the comment would be more helpful if there were some clarity about what the term privatization means. Much of the discussion is quite unclear—largely because two quite different ideas are being expressed by the use of the same word, and very different interests with very different implications for public policy are represented by those different ideas.

Ted Kolderie, "The Two Different Concepts of Privatization." Reprinted with permission from Public Administration Review, *Vol. 46, No. 4, July-August, 1986. Published by the American Society for Public Administration, Washington, D.C.*

This article is an effort to sort out those two conflicting definitions of privatization.

What Are We Talking About Privatizing?

Typically in a discussion about privatization it will be said that the Postal Service, or transit, or the fire service, or some other service should be "turned over to" the private sector. No useful discussion is possible in these terms. What does "turned over" mean? What precisely would be "turned over"?

Government performs two quite separate activities. It is essential to be clear which activity would be dropped under privatization. Is it the policy decision to *provide* a service? Or is it the administrative action to *produce* a service? Is government to withdraw from its role as a buyer? Or from its role as a seller?

We cannot talk simply about a public sector and a private sector. Only a *four*-part concept of the sectors — combining providing and producing, government and non-government — will let us have a useful discussion about the roles of public and private and about the strategy of privatization.

An example will help. Let's take the service called security. There are two pure cases and two mixed cases.

Case 1: Government does both — The legislature writes the law and provides the money; the Department of Corrections runs the prison. Neither function is private.

Case 2: Production is private — The City of Bloomington decides to provide security when the high school hockey teams play at the city arena, and it contracts with Pinkertons for the guards.

Case 3: Provision is private — Government sells to a market of private buyers. The North Stars hockey team wants security at Metropolitan Sports Center, and it contracts with the Bloomington city police.

Case 4: Both activities are private — A department store decides that it wants uninformed security and employs (or contracts privately for) its own guards. Government performs neither activity.

Case 1 is the pure-case public sector. The policy decision is governmental. A public bureau, at the same or at a different level, produces the service.

Case 2 is immediately recognizable as the — still controversial — system of contracting.

Case 3 is less familiar, although examples of government agencies selling to private buyers are in fact fairly common.

Case 4 is, again, well understood as the pure case of private agencies selling to private buyers.

The vocabulary *can* be confusing. Nothing is as troublesome as the ambiguous use of the word "providing." Some people talk in one breadth about society providing medical care for the elderly and in the next describe doctors as the providers. Avoid such confusion: That way madness lies.

One distinct activity of government is to *provide* for its people. In other words: policy making, deciding, buying, requiring, regulating, franchising, financing, subsidizing.

A second and distinctly separate activity of government may be to *produce* the services it decides should be provided. In other words: operating, delivering, running, doing, selling, administering.

Each activity can be broken down into several parts; each of which might be privatized separately.

The *production* of a service is the less complicated of the two. It can be divided, for example, into the line service and into the support service; into the labor and into the equipment and facilities; into the work itself and into the management of the work. Any of these can, in turn, be divided into parts; the way a city might divide its refuse collection among several haulers or the management of its pension funds among several banks.

The *provision* of a service is more complicated. A service is publicly or socially provided (a) where the decision whether to have it (and the decisions about who shall have it and how much of it) is a political decision, (b) when government arranges for the recipients not to have to pay directly for the service themselves, and (c) when the government selects the producer that will serve them.

The service is privately provided (a) where individuals and nongovernmental organizations make their own decisions whether or not to have it, (b) where, if they choose to have it, they pay for it in full out of their own resources, whatever these may be, and (c) where they select the producer themselves.

Clearly there can be mixed cases. Government may make a service available but let citizens decide whether to use it; or the financing may be shared between public and private, with users paying a part and government paying a part of the cost; or some individuals may be asked to pay the cost in full themselves while government pays the full cost for others; or government may pay the cost but allow the user to select the vendor, and so forth.

Services provided publicly may be financed through taxes, as schools are. But government also uses nontax devices. One of these is regulation: Government provides us with clean restaurants by requiring their owners to clean them at their own expense. Franchising is another: Government provides to all parts of a city a uniform level of service by creating a monopoly that permits a utility to average its prices, overcharging some residents so as to subsidize others.

With this distinction clear, we can now look separately at what it means to privatize both provision and production.

Privatizing Production

Let's begin with the simpler activity of service production. Here privatization means simply that a governmental agency that had been producing a service is converted into, or is replaced by, a nongovernmental organization. This can occur either where the agency is selling to private buyers or where it is selling to government.

The British Example

In Britain privatization means transferring to private parties the ownership of a state industry that had been producing very largely for private buyers.

Over the years a number of private industries had been socialized by successive Labor governments, becoming British Steel, the Coal Board, British Gas, British Air, British Telecom, etc. These state industries served each other and the government, of course, but did business very largely with private firms and private households.

These are now being sold; sometimes to other firms, sometimes (through a stock issue) directly to individuals, sometimes to the workers. This "selling off the family silver" has been both popular (especially the sale of public housing units to their occupants, which has transformed tenants into owners) and profitable for the government.

As state industries, these enterprises had been under pressure to hold down their prices. Thus, year by year, deficits arose which the government had to cover. Year by year, the effort to limit the subsidy, as a way to force these industries to reduce their costs, had failed. So the Thatcher government decided to privatize these service producers. As private organizations, these industries will have to earn their revenues and will be forced to control costs and improve services in ways that, as public organizations, they were not.

The American Application

A few proposals for the sale of government enterprises have appeared here. Conrail is to be sold. President Reagan has proposed the sale of others, including power distribution facilities and selected petroleum reserves. But in this country (though called public utilities) the major energy, transportation, and communications systems (except for the Postal

Service, TVA, and such distribution systems as Bonneville Power) have been in private ownership. The scope for the kind of privatization under way in the United Kingdom—transforming government-owned sellers of private services back into privately-owned sellers of private services—is limited in this country.

Here privatization has come to mean mainly the government turning more to private producers for services for which government remains responsible and which government continues to finance. It has become simply a new name for contracting.

Contracting itself is not new in American government. It is traditional in public works at all levels, and it has been common in the rapid growth of human services since the 1960s. What is new is the proposal now to expand the practice and to apply it to service areas in which it had not previously been considered. There are proposals, for example, that a county board might privatize its hospital by turning over the management (or ownership) to, say, Hospital Corporation of America; or that a city might retain a private firm to finance and to operate, as well as to design and to build, a new waste-water-treatment plant; or that Tennessee might bring in the Corrections Corporation of America to run its state prisons.

These facilities and services would be turned over to private organizations in the sense that private organizations would run them (that is, become responsible for service production). But the responsibility for provision, the policy side, would remain governmental.

Issues in Privatizing Production

The debate about this idea of privatizing production is now fully under way. While it has its ideological side, most of it is intensely practical. It is very much a clash between competing producers, both of which want the government's business.

The organizations of government employees, which would like to hold on to the business, say privatization will mean poorer service at higher cost. The American Federation of State, County and Municipal Employees has been running ads in the magazines read by city public-works directors, warning about the dangers of contracting, and has mailed copies of *Passing the Bucks* to 5,000 government officials.

Private firms that would like to get into the business say that privatization (contracting) offers better service at lower costs. In 1985 a number of firms created the Privatization Council, with offices at 30 Rockefeller Plaza, New York. The council sponsors conferences and publishes a journal, the *Privatization Review,* to promote this concept of privatization.

The problem is complex, falling roughly into six parts.

The Question of Competition

What actually happens as a result of a shift to contracting depends largely on whether the change is only the substitution of a monopoly private supplier for a monopoly public bureau or involves also the introduction of competition among producers.

If the change is simply from one monopoly supplier to another, then neither cost nor performance is likely to change very much. The government as buyer is still caught with a sole source arrangement. Some of the privatization in Britain has been of this sort. British Telecom has been sold to private owners, for example, but other communications companies have not been allowed to enter the market freely to compete with it. It is privatization without competition.

An argument can always be heard for this. Private and public organizations alike are quick to tell you how much better they could serve you if only they did not have to compete for your custom. But an effort at privatization should try to make the producers competitive. (Efforts are needed periodically to make even *private* industries competitive. The deregulation of railroads, aviation, over-the-road trucking, banking, health care, and telecommunications in the 1970s and 1980s was such an effort.)

The Question of "Creaming"

A common charge against privatization is that it will result in service going only to the easy and profitable customers, while the difficult and unprofitable customers are neglected.

This reflects a failure to distinguish between providing and producing. Creaming is a problem when producers sell to private buyers. It should not be a problem where government is the buyer. Government can get the service it wants to pay for. It will have to pay for what it wants. But if government wants rockets to the moon, it can get rockets to the moon. If it wants daily mail delivery to Lost Butte, Montana, it can get daily mail delivery to Lost Butte, Montana.

Government *will* have to be a smart buyer. Creaming, like corruption, *can* occur if the government is careless. Private contractors and public bureaus alike may tend to avoid the difficult work required in the poorer neighborhoods of a city. The government must be careful to specify the work it wants done, and it must inspect the work to make sure it gets what it wants.

The Question of Corruption

When a government buys from private producers, efforts must be made continually to detect and suppress anti-competitive behavior and the

use of public office for private profit. The same is true when the producers
are public.

We tend not to talk about corruption in the relationship between
elected officials and their bureau. But this is also a noncompetitive arrangement, with the potential for problems (if, for example, wage increases are
exchanged for contributions at campaign time). One good way to protect
the public interest is to separate the governmental provider from its
producers — public bureau or private contractor — through free-choice-of-
vendor or voucher arrangements.

The Question of Cost

Where competition is introduced, costs are normally expected to fall.
Thus, privatization of the producer side should be appealing not only to
business firms eager for a chance to sell to the government but also to
managers frustrated by a costly and unresponsive public bureau and to
citizens eager to see service made more effective without an increase in their
taxes. And probably competition does reduce costs per unit.

As the discussion goes along, however, concern is arising about a cost-
increasing effect of contracting. This comes through strongly in the book,
Privatizing Federal Spending by Stuart Butler, head of domestic policy
studies at the Heritage Foundation in Washington. He argues that contracting expands "the spending coalition" that drives up the federal budget.

Moving the supply (producer) function out of government may replace
a muted bureaucratic pressure for bigger programs with a well-financed,
private-sector campaign. This significant drawback means that contracting
should be viewed with caution as a means of privatization. Contracting can
lead to more efficient government, but it does not guarantee smaller
government.

How you view contracting depends on what you are trying to do. If
you think programs ought *not* to be expanded, you will probably want to
resist its use. If you favor larger public programs, you may find it highly
strategic to expand the use of this form of privatization.

A good example of this just now is in the field of corrections. One
group wants to put more people behind bars and is advocating contracts
with private firms to build and operate state prisons. Another thinks the industry of locking up people (especially, kids) has already grown too large
and wants to block contracting. The two groups disagree — except in their
belief that contracting would mean more jails.

The Question of Control

Opponents of contracting argue that a government has better control
when it *owns* its operations; that is, when the workers are permanent

employees. Proponents argue that control is better when operations are handled by contract, because on contract — since an affirmative decision is required periodically to continue the relationship — the producer is always at risk.

The Question of Community

The term privatization — even if only of service production — suggests to some people that the public purpose of a program is somehow lost. Proposals are quickly drawn into an ideological debate — attacked as further eroding the sense of community in contemporary society and for intensifying the individualistic ethic of our time.

Here again the error lies in confusing production with provision. So far we have been talking only about a privatization of the *producer* role. The sense of community is not lost in this kind of privatization — unless the public character of a service depends on its being delivered by a specifically governmental producer. In some service areas and for some people, it may. This is clearly a reason for the resistance to contracting of prison services. Also, to most people, public education means a school run by government.

On the other hand, no strong feeling exists today that the public character of the program is lost if people needing medical care do not go to the county hospital or if people needing housing are not required to live in the project owned by the local housing authority.

When we're talking simply about nongovernmental *producers,* the social commitment to a program is generally maintained and, as we have seen, may even be enlarged. Hence, this kind of privatization does not put community seriously at risk.

The danger to community comes from the other major concept of privatization, to which we now turn.

Privatizing the Provision of Service

It is quite possible, of course, to privatize the public role in the provision of benefits and services. Government would simply withdraw from (or reduce) its role as buyer, regulator, standard setter, or decision maker. People (or certain people for certain services thus privatized) would then be on their own to decide whether or not to have a service and to pay for it should they decide they want it.

Since the essence of government lies in this first function, of deciding what it will provide — what it will require and buy and make available; where and when and to whom and to what standard — *this* is the real (as Butler says, complete) privatization.

For those who care about government maintaining a strong policy role, health care is not privatized when the county board contracts the management of the public hospital to a private firm, when it sells the hospital to a private firm, or even when it closes the hospital and buys care from the other hospitals in the community. The responsibility to provide is truly privatized when the county board says it will no longer pay for the care of the medically indigent.

The Methods for Privatizing Provision

Government can withdraw from the provision of service in a variety of ways.

First, it can withdraw from the production of a service and not at the same time redesign that program into a purchase-of-service arrangement. This is load shedding, in the vocabulary of alternative service delivery. A city that simply stopped plowing snow out of alleys or stopped inspecting restaurants would be privatizing production and provision simultaneously.

Sometimes this occurs. Sometimes it does not. When government reduced its role in the production of housing (i.e., stopped building more housing projects), it redesigned public housing into a program in which it pays the rent for low-income families in privately-owned houses and apartments.

Second, government can reduce or withdraw from its role as provider by introducing fees and charges for a service it continues to produce. In many cases the financing responsibility will still be shared between tax-payers and users. But the proportion paid by users will rise. It is a kind of creeping privatization.

Charges can be introduced at a flat rate for all, regardless of ability to pay. Or they can be introduced for some people and not for others, or set at a higher rate for some than for others. Discount transit fares for the elderly, sliding fee scales for day care, and checks to some people for winter heating bills (while other people pay full rate) come quickly to mind.

A similar privatization occurs as tax liability is extended to cover the cash payments received and the cash value of services received under benefit and entitlement programs. Above a certain income level, for example, social security payments are now taxable, and Colorado's Governor Richard Lamm has suggested this as a general policy where the pressure to offer services and benefits universally in the first instance cannot be resisted.

The Reasons for Privatizing Provision

Who would want to do anything so cold-hearted?

Actually, two very different interests, both deeply concerned about equity and about community, are coming together to reduce or limit the role of government as provider in America and in other western countries.

The first of the two efforts to limit the scope of government rises mainly from social and political concerns. In recent years some representatives of the poor and disadvantaged have increasingly resisted government housing, health care, and other social-welfare programs. For them effects are what count; not intentions. For the people they represent, programs have too often operated mainly to enlarge the income, status, and power of the industry of bureaucratic and professional service producers, whether governmental or private.

These advocates resist the idea that we find our community through politics and resist the extension of law and regulation that steadily deprives nongovernmental and nonprofessional institutions of the right to care for themselves and for each other in ways that private communities always have. Their efforts to maintain these rights for individuals, families, and voluntary organizations form an important part of the support for privatization.

The second and more conspicuous of the forces arises from the effort to restrain public expenditure—to relate needs and wants to what the city, state, or nation can realistically afford to pay.

The combination of client advocates, the media, and the political process has worked powerfully to turn needs into rights, rights into entitlements, entitlements into programs, and programs into budgets. At the same time, the combination of international and interstate economic competition, taxpayer resistance, and the need to stimulate entrepreneurship and investment has worked powerfully to constrain the resources that come into the economy and the amount available for public service provision.

In almost every country, public services have come under pressure. Something has had to give. One response has been to reduce services across the board, making no distinctions among users. Another is to shift from a universalist to a selective approach in social policy—that is, from a policy that makes services available to everyone at no charge regardless of ability to pay to a policy that asks those who can afford to pay to do so and reserves the limited public resources for those who genuinely cannot.

The latter approach, privatization, enhances equity better than an across-the-board reduction in service levels. It also eases the concern about what could happen to democratic institutions in a society in which more than half of the people have their incomes politically determined.

The people who want to limit what government provides are not necessarily cold-hearted. They are skeptical about public officials' tendency to justify programs in terms of intentions. They worry about government's ability to drive out its competitors with the offer of free services. They seek to reduce the proportion of decisions made in a political process which they see as incapable, realistically, of resisting the pressure for irresponsible decisions to pay for services with other people's resources and to increase the proportion of decisions made in a process where private parties make responsible decisions about the use of their own resources.

The clear requirements for the success of a social policy of this sort, however, are almost certainly the provision of an adequate income to the poor — through transfers or through work — and the maintenance of community standards to those whose service is being paid for socially. It is hard to see that the effort at privatization is yet adequately sensitive to the practical and ethical importance of this idea of social equity.

A Reasonable Program for Privatization

Privatization can serve a useful purpose. It also carries some dangers. The effort should be to secure the former while avoiding the latter.

A reasonable program would involve some privatization of service production combined with some privatization of service provision.

Implementation of such a strategy would focus mainly on (a) maintaining the right and enlarging the responsibility of people to provide for their needs privately, where they can and where they wish; and, where government *is* responsible, (b) enlarging the opportunity for elected officials and for citizens to secure those services from private producers as well as from public agencies if they wish.

First, in the area of service *provision,* such a program would involve:

- Being selective. *Targeting eligibility* to those in need.
- Continuing to use *fees and charges with income offsets* for people of low income.
- *Taxing benefits,* where benefits are granted universally in the first instance. (All of the above will privatize financial responsibility and thus help restrain expenditure.)
- Fixing — *appropriating — the revenues* for programs and managing the eligibility as demand for the service changes. Commonly, today, programs fix the eligibility so that with a rise in demand it is the appropriation that becomes the variable.
- *Introducing voucher systems* or other user-side subsidies that privatize and thereby depoliticize the vendor-selection decision where the service is governmentally paid and even where it is governmentally produced. This will guard against the problems that can arise in contracting, where elected or appointed officials select the vendor. It will also indicate more clearly the sort of service people really want.

Second, in the area of service *production,* such a program would involve:

- A policy to *avoid sole sourcing,* whether the supplier is governmental or private. This will ensure competition. A public-bureau arrangement is essentially a long-term, noncompetitive, sole-source contract. (Note that it is possible to have competition without privatization. A government can contract with other governments, and free-choice-of-vendor arrangements can be introduced where the choice is simply among public agencies. Governor Rudy Perpich's proposal in 1985 for open enrollment among public school districts in Minnesota is an example of the latter.)
- An effort to *disaggregate the elements of a service.* Breaking up a service into pieces will enlarge the opportunity to use different kinds of suppliers. This will allow changes to occur more gradually and thus lower both the political pain and the risk involved in service redesign.
- *Divestiture.* A public policy body that serves also as the board of directors for the public agency producing its service is caught in a dual role which can at times become a conflict of interest. Separating the roles of provider and producer can make it easier to privatize production. This will be useful even in a general-purpose government organization, freeing the elected board to concentrate on policy and on ways to reduce the cost and to increase the quality of service. It is especially needed in single-purpose agencies such as transit commissions and public school districts.
- *Capitation.* Paying the producer a lump sum, up front, and allowing that organization to keep whatever it does not need to spend introduces an incentive for producers to innovate. Teachers, for example, say that if given this incentive they would move quickly toward peer-teaching, independent study, parent involvement, the use of community resources, differentiated staffing, and new learning technology.
- *Co-production.* In voucher arrangements clients can do much of the work themselves. They need not be required to spend the money on professional service. This will encourage strategies of prevention and self-help that can be, at the same time, less costly for payers and more supportive for users.

In Conclusion

Such a program ought to be possible.

For the moment, however, both the private leadership and the political leadership are mired in the old ways of thinking. Both are bogged down by traditional concepts of government that are insufficiently sensitive to needs for economy and responsiveness and by concepts of a private role that are insufficiently sensitive to the need for equity.

A new concept, combining equity in the provision of services with competition in their production, has yet to be articulated politically.

25. Problems

Harry P. Hatry

Admittedly, public officials should periodically consider options for greater use of the private sector for delivering their services. This is good public policy and good public management.

But public officials should also examine existing instances of private sector delivery and consider the option of switching *back to public employee delivery*. This is also good public policy. For a number of reasons, private delivery can become inefficient or have quality problems.

The Best of Times, the Worst of Times — to Contract

Our work at The Urban Institute indicates that the appropriateness and success of using a particular privatization option is *highly situational.* Success depends on many factors that are individual to the particular public agency, in the particular location and at the particular time. Success of a privatization approach depends on:

- The current level of performance of the current delivery system. A government agency may indeed be delivering the service quite efficiently and with good quality — leaving little room for improvement. (As hard as some people find it to believe, often public employee delivery *does* work very well.) In other situations, the service may be inefficient or of poor quality. This is the situation that provides the major opportunity for successful change.
- The way the option is implemented. Without good implementation even the best ideas will go awry. For example, in a switch to contracting, the quality of the request-for-proposal process is key to assuring that a

Harry P. Hatry, "Privatization Presents Problems." Reprinted with permission from National Civic Review, *Vol. 77, No. 2, March-April, 1988. Published by the National Civic League Press, Denver, Colorado.*

capable contractor is selected. And a sound, sustained contract administration and monitoring process is essential to assuring that contractor performance remains up to par.

Threat of Privatization Is Often Enough

I believe that the major advantage of the privatization movement is not that the private sector can reduce costs or improve service to a great extent, but that consideration of privatization encourages public officials and public employees to innovate and to break down obstacles to improving public employee efficiency.

Increasingly, examples occur where employees and their unions agree to changes, such as reductions in the size of garbage collection crews, when faced with a city council threat to contract the service.

Other governments have introduced procedures that involve direct competition between public and private agencies. In the "Phoenix Model," public agencies such as the City of Phoenix Public Works department submit proposals that compete directly with bids received from private firms for services such as garbage collection and street sweeping. (The City Administrative Services codified this in January 1985 as "Management Procedure: Procedure for Preparing Cost Estimate City Services Under Consideration to Be Performed by Private Industry on a Contractural Basis.")

In a third approach, Kansas City, Phoenix and other cities have split their work, such as garbage collection, into districts, some of which are served by private contractors (if they win) and some by public employees. The city reports on comparative costs, encouraging competition between public and private service providers.

Private Isn't Necessarily Cheaper

Lower cost with improved efficiency is the most frequently given reason for contracting. I am not convinced, as some others are, based on the evidence thus far available, that privatization lowers costs in most instances. Hospital care is one of the few areas that has been extensively studied in recent years. A University of California study of contracting the management of public hospitals in a number of counties in California did not find evidence that the contractors had achieved cost savings. The study did find evidence that the private firms were better at securing revenue.[1] Last year's National Academy of Sciences study of private versus public hospital care found that "studies of hospital costs that control for size (and in some cases for case mix and other factors) show for-profit hospitals to have slightly *higher* expenses than not-for-profit public and private institutions."[2]

The Urban Institute recently worked with two states (Delaware and Maryland). In three of the four programs that the states considered for a change to contracting, we found that state employees were likely to achieve costs similar to or lower than the private sector. In one, food service for inmates of Delaware's prisons, we surveyed ten other states that had contracted for inmate food service. Six reported higher costs with contracting, three lower, and one reported about the same costs. Delaware's own current costs appeared to be similar to those expected if the service were contracted. The department is still considering contracting, its motivation being the difficulty in hiring prison kitchen supervisors and, secondarily, the desire of some prison administrators to reduce the administrative headaches in arranging for meals.

Columbia University's classic 1970s analysis of solid waste collection costs found higher *average* unit costs for public employee delivery than for contractor-delivered service.[3] But it also found that the most expensive delivery method was delivery by franchised firms — firms that dealt directly with households and not through a government. The more recent Ecodata study of Los Angeles County private vendors were also, on average, cheaper. In all these comparisons, however, averages hide the fact that in some cities the unit costs were lower for public employee delivery than in some contracted cities.

Vouchers, while often an excellent way to give consumers more choice, do not necessarily involve lower costs. It depends on how the government sets the value of the vouchers. Hennepin County (Minnesota) in its trial of day care vouchers found that total costs increased when it switched to vouchers.

It is dangerous to generalize as to the success of privatization options. There will be situations where a switch will be worthwhile and cases where it won't be.

Three Important Potential Problems with Privatization

Three major potential problems in privatization are almost always raised by public employee unions. While these problems are acknowledged by advocates of privatization, they are often treated too casually, as if they were easy to overcome, only minor inconveniences. These three problems are: 1. potential for corruption; 2. possibility of reduced quality of service; and, 3. possibility of reduced access of disadvantaged citizens to services.

Corruption

High financial stakes introduce great temptations to individuals to engage in illegal action. We have frequent examples—New York City's Parking Violations Bureau; recently, in the District of Columbia, in all sorts of contract awards; and, over the years, the City of Chicago has had its share of problems. The American Federation of State, County and Municipal Employees (AFSCME) has taken great pains to document numerous instances of hanky-panky in public sector contracting.[4] The possibility of corruption can be reduced by establishing sound procurement procedures, and in the case of divestiture, by installing appropriate regulations. Nevertheless, the threat remains.

Possible Reductions in Service Quality

Again, when substantial payments are involved, a natural temptation is to do whatever is necessary to maximize profitability and skimp on quality to save dollars, particularly in for-profit organizations. This temptation becomes even greater when a firm gets into financial difficulties. This sometimes happens even with private nonprofit organizations. The principal protections against poor quality are performance contracting and adequate performance monitoring. The need for these protections has been noted by both proponents and opponents of privatization. A classic example of this problem is recently shoddy aircraft maintenance in deregulated airlines facing major financial problems. Some airlines have been assessed large fines for inadequate maintenance.

However, it is much easier to say that monitoring is needed than to provide it. Most government contracts I have seen in recent years have very weak or non-existent performance requirements. To make matters worse, performance monitoring of contracts is very sparse.

Possible Reduced Access to Services for Disadvantaged

The incentives to private firms—particularly for-profit firms—are to avoid clients for whom securing payment for services is likely to be difficult, and to avoid clients who may be particularly difficult and expensive to help, such as disadvantaged clients.

This problem has become particularly acute in the delivery of medical services. Persons without medical insurance or other funds have reportedly been turned away from private hospitals and even from emergency room care. The National Academy of Sciences study cited earlier concluded that access is a major national concern. The study found that for-profit hospitals served fewer uninsured patients and had a smaller proportion of uncompensated care than non-profit hospitals. The researchers felt that although the percentage differences were small among the types of providers, they could nonetheless "translate into large numbers of patients: Data from four of five states demonstrate that not-for-profit hospitals provide two or three times as much uncompensated care, on average, than for-profit hospitals. (Both types provided less uncompensated care than public hospitals.)"[5] Debate continues about what laws and regulations should be introduced to encourage or require private hospitals to admit patients regardless of their ability to pay, particularly emergency-care patients.

This problem can be alleviated through contractual and statutory requirements and the provision of subsidies. Alleviating the problem, however, will often reduce the benefits of privatization.

Conclusion

Privatization should be viewed as neither panacea nor poison. It is simply one tool available to public officials. Before they attempt to apply it universally, there are points they should remember:

- The success of privatization is highly situational, dependent on local circumstances and how well the new approach is implemented.
- Periodically consider options that involve greater use of the private sector.
- Periodically consider switching *back* from *private* delivery to *public* delivery.
- Give serious attention to the three potential problems of privatization-corruption, reduced service quality, and reduced access of the disadvantaged to services.

Perhaps the main virtue of the privatization movement is that it encourages public employees to improve their own productivity in order to help ensure their own competitiveness in the face of privatization. Increasingly, the message to the public sector is that if a service has problems in efficiency or quality, the agency needs to "shape up or be shipped out." The net result should be less costly and higher quality services for all the public.

26. The Unions

Joe Morris

Negotiations with unions often are long and bitter, with neither side emerging with any clear gains. In recent years, new twists on old themes have served to make negotiations even trickier. But despite the emergence of such issues as privatization, most communities have managed to strike a balance with their organized workers.

One key issue in current negotiations is contract length and pension plans. In Hartford, Connecticut, City Manager Alfred A. Gatta says the pension plan was the toughest item in the latest round of union talks. Although most cities have a standard age of 65 established for receiving pension benefits, many unions are attempting to have that age lowered.

The issue of contract length is also a heavily debated issue. Although most cities prefer a two- or three-year contract, most unions maintain a one-year agreement. Some cities are reaching longer agreements, but they are sacrificing in other areas.

Occasionally, the sides are so far apart on an issue that all negotiations fail and a strike results. A strike does not have to be crippling. Many municipalities have developed strike contingency plans to ensure continued service. These plans include establishing an area to act as a control center in the event of a strike, and cutting services to the essential ones. In addition, municipalities can amend their water and sewer contracts to allow outside maintenance work if a strike should occur.

For example, a contingency plan for solid waste disposal during a union strike might include establishing temporary dump sites for solid wastes. When Etobicoke, Ontario, experienced a strike in July 1984, the alternative dump sites were sprayed with insecticide and deodorizer, and

Joe Morris, "Privatization and the Unions." Reprinted with permission from American City & County, *Vol. 102, No. 7, July, 1987. Published by Communication Channels, Inc., Atlanta, Georgia.*

notices were distributed to residents about emergency garbage collection and the locations of the temporary sites. The city also tied heavy-duty plastic to the fences surrounding the dump sites to minimize the visual impact of the trash.

After several weeks, the strike was settled. Because the city had been prepared adequately for the strike, there was little public inconvenience, so the union did not have much popular support. The city did suffer losses, however. More than $300,000 in construction work had to be carried into 1985 due to the strike, and maintenance and survey work fell behind as well.

Subcontracting public services to the private sector is still in the exploratory stages in most areas of the country, but the issue has sparked much interest, especially among unions. The issue of privatization also has become prominent in recent years, as more cities contract out traditionally city-provided services. Garbage collection, major construction work and landscaping are three areas often contracted to the private sector. Other city services such as road patching have remained largely in the public sector.

Privatization also is becoming a more frequent issue during contract negotiations, when many other issues that union workers consider important are discussed.

"Salary increases, health costs and job security are always prominent issues," says Robert H. Goodin, director of public works for Rockville, Maryland. "The unions are concerned about privatization as well, and they should be. If their work's not up to par, then they have no business providing the service. It's doing a disservice to the people if they hang onto a service as a matter of it being their turf."

In Rockville, city leaders are investigating the privatization option more and more. This trend is occurring in other areas of the country as well. In the West, contracting city services to private-sector businesses has become commonplace.

Carson, California, for example, is known as a "contract city." Although some of its workers are represented by unions, the city contracts out a majority of its services. According to City Administrator John R. Dangleis, many cities in the Los Angeles area operate in this fashion.

"It's called the Lakewood plan," Dangleis says. "Lakewood was incorporated in the early 1950s, and the city entered into contractual agreements with the county of Los Angeles for sheriff's services, police and fire protection, and other services. They also decided to provide some of their own services, such as parks and recreation."

Carson's arrangement is similar to Lakewood's. The city is covered by the Los Angeles County Fire District and therefore has no fire department. The sheriff's department, and engineering services also are contracted out. Carson does maintain its own parks and recreation department. In addition to contracting out major functions, the city sublets many smaller jobs.

"We also contract out for consultants and other services like sidewalk paving and major tree-trimming jobs. We have a staff that takes care of roadside trees and the parks, but if it's a job the size of a third of the city, then it's much easier to contract it out," Dangleis says.

In Lancaster, Pennsylvania, privatization is not an issue at all, says Howard F. Goldberg, city manager. "We're involved in it some, but there's really no problem with the unions. Our main issues are wages, benefits and work hours."

There are no unions in Auburn, Alabama, so if the city contracts work outside its own work force, there is usually no dispute, says Douglas Watson, city manager.

"None of the employees here want to organize," Watson says. "We work so that they don't feel like the union is necessary. The unions have never been strong historically in the South; they don't go back several generations." While unions are not as strong in the South as in the North, they do exist in the larger cities such as Atlanta and Memphis, he adds.

In the North, unions are strong and any major issue they question is likely to hinder negotiations. In Hartford, Connecticut, privatization was not a major topic of discussion in last year's negotiations, but likely will be during the next round of talks, says City Manager Gatta.

"We're looking at that (privatization). I expect it to become a bargaining issue, a union issue that has to be addressed," Gatta says. Hartford is considering contracting services for sanitation, data processing, golf course management and cemetery management.

The novelty of the idea also means the city will spend more time examining the issue before making any decisions. "It's a new field and there are conflicting reports. It deserves a lot more study," Gatta says.

"You have to deal with union interests — it's a matter of negotiating," he adds. One reason the unions may not protest privatization strongly is the service areas that are contracted out. Because most union employees are not in the highly subsidized jobs, there is not much argument from the unions, Dangleis says.

"If we picked up a function the union has a lot of employees in, they would probably not be thrilled about that. We just haven't made great inroads into their work force," he adds.

Although most municipal officials say privatization has not caused too much of a struggle with the unions, that is not to say unions support the idea. In fact, most unions are adamantly opposed to privatization, says Edward Handman, director of public relations for the AFSCME Local #37 in New York City.

"There's been an attempt to privatize, but they're doing it piecemeal," Handman says. "No city has done it completely. It's more than getting away from unions. It's stripping the city of its ability to do things. We'll always fight it. The public is paying billions of dollars for things that could be done much better in-house."

In the face of such arguments, some cities now are providing their own services after experimenting with subcontracting in the private sector. Lancaster subcontracted its trash collection service for many years, but when the contract was due to be renegotiated, the city re-examined its own capabilities, Goldberg says.

"We had gotten an excellent bid before, but when the new bids came in 1985, we realized that we could collect it cheaper ourselves," Goldberg says. Although the city now collects trash at designated points, it still contracts out its curbside garbage pick-up service.

There are many arguments for contract cities, as well as for full-service municipalities. But those who have lived or worked in both types of areas say each system has its strong and weak points.

"I've lived in both and seen them work," Dangleis says. "Full service cities can function as well as contract cities. Contract cities say they save money on staff and overhead. But when they contract out services, the contractor pays benefits, so they pay for things sooner or later."

"The bottom line is productivity," he adds. "If we in the public sector can compete with the contractual suppliers, then we have a way to maintain the traditional control over services provided."

Time for Negotiations

Aside from dealing with specific issues in union negotiation, there are other factors to be considered. One key issue in union dealings is time. With contract negotiations occurring frequently—most cities renegotiate every two to three years—municipalities are finding themselves spending more time working with unionized employees on contract items and grievances. In Jackson, Michigan, the personnel office spends a "substantial" amount of time in negotiations with unions, says Walter Vaclavick, city engineer.

"We have a number of unions representing the city workers," he says. "Our public works contracts are for three years, with negotiations from March to August. That usually ties up two days a week for the office during that time." But that time is better than in Hartford, where contract negotiations require an "extraordinary" amount of time, Gatta says.

When the police and fire unions negotiate, even more time is spent, Vaclavick adds. Although Michigan state laws prohibit striking by those unions, they are allowed to seek an arbitrator during contract negotiations. This requirement makes both sides somewhat recalcitrant, Vaclavick says. In addition, contracts also mandate that privatization cannot take place if union jobs are threatened.

"We do quite a bit of subcontracting, but we don't get a beef from the union unless there's a threat of layoff," Vaclavick says. Jackson has also added some previously contracted services to its city workload, including snow removal.

In essence, municipalities that suffer strikes can prepare themselves in order to minimize inconvenience, but little can be done to prevent losses in services. With negotiations occurring frequently, and with many unions represented in an area, administrators find it difficult to maintain a balance of power. Therefore, privatization is seen by many as a way to avoid union labor. That thinking does not sit well with the unions, however, and is likely to cause unnecessary confrontations at the bargaining table.

Privatization seems destined to become more the rule than the exception, but with proper boundaries, it should not threaten union labor. If used correctly, money saved by subcontracting could be used to grant other union requests, such as higher salaries and better health benefits.

27. A Cautionary Note

Susan Brown

The increased use of the private sector to deliver state services has exploded since 1978 when California voters passed Proposition 13, a major fiscal containment effort. Since then, other states and localities have passed similar measures. The trend is likely to continue given the current administration's push to invite further private sector participation in delivery of public services and the nonstop fiscal pressure on government budgets at all levels.

How effective has this trend been in curbing costs, in delivering quality services? Under what conditions should a state or local government switch to private contracting? When should it consider reverting to public management of services? Are there situations in which it is more effective to retain public service but improve the delivery process?

Recent work at The Urban Institute, under the direction of Harry Hatry, suggests that innovation should proceed, but with caution. Administrators need to assess each case separately. Although innovative service delivery approaches can reduce costs and improve state services, they can also become inefficient and can have quality problems. The success of any initiative depends on the way it is implemented.

Cost reduction is the primary reason most often given by administrators for greater use of the private sector. Other reasons include reducing the role of government, obtaining special skills, meeting service demands quickly that are beyond current capacity, and increasing service without having to add permanent staff. Occasionally a government negotiates a contract to improve service quality or to experiment with vouchers and nonexclusive franchises to provide citizens with choice as to service provider and service level.

Susan Brown, *"Privatization of Public Services—A Cautionary Note." Reprinted with permission from* Policy and Research Report, *Vol. 18, No. 1, Winter, 1988. Published by The Urban Institute, Washington, D.C.*

Advantages of Contracting

There appear to be three major advantages.

To Add Competition

Government agencies typically are monopolies. Competition introduced by the private sector through approaches such as contracting, nonexclusive franchises, and vouchers tends to motivate organizations to lower prices and sometimes to improve quality.

To Avoid Red Tape and Bureaucracy

It is usually easier for private organizations than for government agencies to hire, transfer, fire, promote, reward, and even out workload peaks. A private organization can purchase new equipment more quickly.

To Take Advantage of Multijurisdiction Economics

Private organizations that operate in more than one jurisdiction can amortize their investments, thereby lowering their unit costs. Multisite private firms can more easily justify new technical equipment, establish new management information systems, and introduce training programs for employees. Their development costs can be spread over each location and they can profit from central purchasing systems.

No Guarantee of Reduced Costs

Despite these advantages, the available evidence does not support the notion that cost savings are guaranteed in a switch to private contracting for public services. Hospital care is one example. A University of California study of public hospitals in a number of counties in California did not find data confirming that management achieved cost savings through contracting. The study did find evidence, however, that the private firms were better at securing revenue. After reviewing several past studies, the National Academy of Sciences found that for-profit hospitals have slightly higher expenses than nonprofit public and private institutions.

The Urban Institute recently worked with two states, Delaware and Maryland, to help them examine innovative service delivery opportunities. The project teams found a majority of the programs under consideration could achieve similar or lower costs through management by public employees. As part of this work, a survey of penal institutions in ten states

that contracted with private firms for inmate food service found six reporting higher costs with contracting, three lower, and one reporting about the
same costs.

Problems May Be Underestimated

Potential problems inherent in using the private sector for the delivery
of public services include increased likelihood of corruption, potential incentives to reduce service quality, possible reduced access of the disadvantaged to the service, and increased chance of interrupted service. These
problems are raised by public employee unions and are usually acknowledged by advocates of privatization. Too often, however, they are treated
only casually.

Corruption

High financial stakes bring with them great temptations to take actions, even illegal ones, to increase gains. Witness New York City's recent
scandals in its parking violations bureau. Sound procurement procedures
can help reduce this potential for corruption.

Incentives to Reduce Service Quality

High financial stakes bring with them a temptation to maximize profitability by skimping on quality. The recent lapses in airplane maintenance
standards that occur when airlines face major financial problems is one example. The principal protections against poor quality are performance contracting and monitoring.

Possible Reduced Access for the Disadvantaged

Private firms have incentives to avoid clients whose payment it is
difficult to secure and those who may be expensive to help — as disadvantaged clients often are. The problem can be alleviated by providing subsidies and requirements in contracts and regulations.

Increased Chance of Interrupted Service

Private organizations, such as contractors, grantees, and firms receiving franchises, are more likely to curtail, interrupt, or cease operations due
to such circumstances as financial problems, strikes, and rebidding of contracts. Such actions could affect client safety or health.

Keys to Successful Contracting

The likelihood of success depends on the particular situation of the public agency involved, its geographic location, and the particular point in time. Success will be greatly affected by performance of the current delivery system, special circumstances such as the number and quality of potential private suppliers, government absorption of displaced employees, and the relationship between employee associations and the government. In addition, without good implementation even the best ideas go awry. A capable contractor and a sound, sustained contract administration and monitoring process are essential to insure successful implementation.

What, then, is the main virtue of the privatization movement? A major advantage, according to Hatry, one that has not been widely recognized, is that competition by the private sector encourages *public* employees to be more innovative and to improve public employee efficiency.

Increasingly, for example, employees and their unions have agreed to changes, such as reductions in the size of garbage collection crews when faced with a city council threat to negotiate a contract to provide the service. Other governments have introduced procedures that involve direct competition between public and private agencies. In another approach, Phoenix and other cities have split work, such as garbage collection, into districts, some of which are served by private contractors and some by public employees. The cities report comparative costs that encourage competition between public and private service delivery organizations.

The message to the public sector should be clear. If a service has problems in efficiency or service quality, the agency will need to improve or will risk being replaced. The net result should be less costly and higher quality services for the public.

28. A Survey of Management Practices

Harper A. Roehm,
Joseph F. Castellano, and David A. Karns

The number of cities contracting essential services has increased in recent years. The major factors accounting for this trend involve the increasing tax pressures associated with financing these services and the importance attached to providing quality services.

The budgetary pressures associated with providing essential municipal services have come primarily from increasing wage rates and capital equipment purchases. In order to meet these rising costs, cities are forced to consider raising taxes, limiting services or some combination of the two. Both options are politically unpopular and, consequently, increase the attractiveness of contracting out the service.

As taxes have been increased to finance essential services, the demands made by citizens for higher quality of service also have grown, as have the number of complaints when expectations have not been met. Contracting of services has afforded cities an option for insuring quality services while minimizing or perhaps eliminating the direct involvement they would have in resolving citizen complaints if they were providing the service.

In order to determine the extent to which cities have been contracting services, the authors conducted a study of municipalities having populations greater than 50,000. The study focused on:

1. determining the services that had been contracted,
2. identifying the methods of selecting contractors and the types of contracts used,

Harper A. Roehm, Joseph F. Castellano, and David A. Karns, "Contracting Services to the Private Sector—A Survey of Management Practices." Reprinted with permission from Government Finance Review, *Vol. 4, No. 1, February, 1989. Published by the Government Finance Officers Association, Chicago, Illinois.*

3. the means for providing initial capital financing,
4. management of displaced worker problems, and finally,
5. cities' monitoring of the quality of contractor services.

Study Methodology

The data collection for the study proceeded in two phases. Student interviewers on the staff of the Consumer and Business Research Center, Wright State University, contacted the chief financial officer or a representative of the finance office in 288 municipalities in July and August 1987. The respondents were asked which services from a list of 12 municipal services were privatized and which were being considered for privatization. Thus, 90 percent of all municipalities with populations of more than 50,000 participated in phase one.

In phase two, a short questionnaire was mailed in the fall of 1987 to the finance officers who reported privatized services, but not county or other government contracted services. The questionnaires included one page for each reported privatized service. One hundred and fifty-two municipalities completed questionnaires in the second phase for a response rate of 52.8 percent.

A few questionnaires were returned with a comment that services were actually contracted to a governmental organization.

Although the term privatization was not explicitly defined in this project, it is an important topic in municipal finance, and the authors believe that most respondents understood the term to involve contracting with a private organization to provide selected services or allowing the private sector to provide selected services rather than the municipality. The survey did not distinguish between services that traditionally, historically, have been delivered by the private sector and those services that municipalities have shifted away from direct provision by the government to provision by contract with the private sector. Few respondents asked for a definition of privatization or returned questionnaires indicating a misunderstanding during the telephone interview.

Table 1 lists the 12 services included in the study and indicates the percentage of respondents who reported privatizing that service. The implicit focus of the study was on those services provided by the private sector and how municipal governments monitor private-sector performance. For each of the 12 service areas considered the study examined the following specific issues:

- Method used to select contractor
- Type of contract with private firm
- Method used to provide initial capitalization financing

- Treatment of displaced workers
- Monitoring the contractor's responsiveness to citizens' complaints
- Dealing with service interruption
- Government influence on pricing, how the service is to be performed, billing and pricing, types of service offered and types of customers served
- City satisfaction with service.

Table 1

PERCENTAGE OF CITIES PRIVATIZING SERVICES

Service	Percentage Privatized
Refuse collection	49.7
Vehicle towing and storage	76.9
Animal control	13.1
Street maintenance	23.7
Transportation	25.9
Health care	26.9
Park landscaping	23.7
Tax collection	4.1
Waste water treatment	8.1
Police protection	1.9
Fire protection	3.1
Building inspection	3.1

(Note: Percentage calculations in Table 1 and in all tables in this article should total to 100 percent. Deviations from 100 percent are the result of rounding to one decimal place.)

Contractors and Contracts

Selection of a contractor is a complex process involving a number of issues. As Table 2 indicates, cost and quality are important to the cities. Furthermore, cities are open to more than one approach. The "lowest bid among qualified companies" approach was used 57.5 percent of the time by cities in selecting a private contractor to perform a service. The "lowest bid" approach was used, on average, for 12.3 percent of the contracts. While "the best reputation" approach was used for only 6.3 percent on average, it was used more frequently (23.8 percent) in contracting the health care functions.

To some extent the selection method employed appears to be dependent on the type of service being contracted. Table 2 shows significant differences between animal control, health care, street maintenance and the other listed services.

Table 2
METHOD USED TO SELECT THE CONTRACTOR*

	Refuse Collection	Vehicle Towing	Animal Control	Street Maintenance	Transportation	Health Care	Park Landscaping	Tax Collection	Other	All Services
Lowest bid	11.9	12.0	–	16.7	15.4	9.5	25.0	–	–	12.3
Best reputation	7.5	4.3	–	–	7.7	23.8	8.3	–	8.3	6.3
Lowest bid among qualified companies	61.2	54.7	37.5	83.3	61.5	33.3	66.7	66.7	50.0	57.5
Other	19.4	29.1	62.5	–	15.4	33.3	–	33.3	41.7	23.9
TOTAL	100.0	100.1	100.0	100.0	100.0	99.9	100.0	100.0	100.0	100.0

Table 3
TYPE OF CONTRACT WITH PRIVATE FIRM*

	Refuse Collection	Vehicle Towing	Animal Control	Street Maintenance	Transportation	Health Care	Park Landscaping	Tax Collection	Other	All Services
Firm fixed price	29.9	46.6	62.5	39.1	44.0	28.6	75.0	66.7	25.0	43.4
Fixed price with escalation	40.3	5.2	12.5	–	8.0	14.3	4.2	16.7	33.3	14.6
Fixed price with incentive	4.5	–	–	4.3	–	–	–	–	–	1.6
Unit price	10.4	32.8	6.3	56.5	28.0	28.6	12.5	–	33.3	25.9
Cost plus fixed fee	1.5	.9	–	–	12.0	–	–	–	–	1.6
Cost plus incentive fee	–	1.7	–	–	8.0	–	8.3	16.7	–	2.2
Other	13.4	12.9	18.8	–	–	28.6	–	–	8.3	10.8
TOTAL	100.0	100.1	100.1	99.9	100.0	100.1	100.0	100.1	99.9	100.1

*All figures given in percentages.

Table 3 examines the types of contracts used for the various functional categories. In a fixed-price contract, the contractor agrees to deliver a certain quantity of service for a set price. While the contractor must absorb any cost overruns, all cost savings accrue to him. An escalation clause which provides for both upward and downward adjustments is frequently added when a great deal of uncertainty exists as to the future direction of labor and material costs. A fixed-price incentive contract includes costs and a percentage for profit; however, there is an agreed upon ceiling price. Usually, any savings as well as any cost overruns incurred while delivering the service are shared between the contractor and the city.

A unit-price agreement allows the contractor to be paid a specific price per unit of delivery. In a cost-plus-a-fixed-fee contract, the fee is fixed as a dollar amount which is added to the actual cost incurred. If the actual cost is lower than anticipated, the percentage fee is higher and if the actual costs exceed what was originally anticipated, the percentage will be lower. In a cost-plus-an-incentive-fee contract, both the purchaser and vendor share in any cost reduction from the original target price. If costs increase, the fee could be eliminated; however, the vendor would be guaranteed recovery of all costs.

Table 3 indicates that on average the "firm fixed-price method" was the most popular, being used for 43.4 percent of the contracts, followed by the unit-price method. The most notable exception was for refuse collection, which used the fixed-price-with-an-escalation-clause method for 40.3 percent of the contracts. One possible explanation for the refuse collection difference is seen in situations where the private contractor must hire unionized employees and is more likely to be subject to the possibility of a change in labor rates and benefits.

Capitalization and Personnel Issues

One of the major advantages cited for contracting out or privatizing a governmental service is that it limits or avoids large, initial capital expenditures for such items as trucks, transportation equipment, facilities, etc.

The findings from Table 4 seem to support this position. The firm providing the private service supplied the initial capitalization in 40.1 percent of the transactions. Normal tax assessment was used for 25 percent and special bond issues used for 5.6 percent. Refuse collection appears to have the most diverse methods of financing; however, 50.9 percent of firms accepting contracts were responsible for their own initial financing.

Personnel problems associated with contracting and privatization have been discussed by Donald Fisk, a well-known researcher on this topic. Generally, unions oppose the municipal contracting of services, and often

Table 4
METHOD USED TO PROVIDE INITIAL CAPITALIZATION FINANCING*

	Refuse Collection	Vehicle Towing	Animal Control	Street Maintenance	Transportation	Health Care	Park Landscaping	Tax Collection	Other	All Services
Special tax assessment	7.5	–	–	–	–	–	–	–	–	1.7
Normal tax assessment	20.8	18.4	44.4	47.4	26.1	12.5	36.8	50.0	22.2	25.0
Special bond issue	3.8	–	–	5.3	13.0	–	21.1	25.0	11.1	5.6
Financed by private firm	50.9	51.3	22.2	26.3	30.4	43.8	21.1	–	11.1	40.1
Other	17.0	30.3	33.3	21.1	30.4	43.8	21.1	25.0	55.6	27.6
TOTAL	100.0	100.0	99.9	100.1	99.9	100.1	100.1	100.0	100.0	100.0

Table 5
HOW CITIES TREAT DISPLACED GOVERNMENT WORKERS*

	Refuse Collection	Vehicle Towing	Animal Control	Street Maintenance	Transportation	Health Care	Park Landscaping	Tax Collection	Other	All Services
Require contractor to hire them	10.1	–	6.3	–	3.8	14.3	–	–	8.3	4.1
Give workers priority for other govt. jobs	11.6	5.2	6.3	30.4	19.2	4.8	30.4	16.7	8.3	11.6
Retain workers	8.7	2.6	–	8.7	3.8	–	4.3	–	–	4.1
Lay off or fire displaced workers	4.3	1.7	6.3	4.3	–	–	–	16.7	8.3	3.1
No government workers involved in service	58.0	87.1	81.3	47.8	65.4	71.4	47.8	66.7	58.3	69.8
Other	7.2	3.4	–	8.7	7.7	9.5	17.4	–	16.7	7.2
TOTAL	99.9	100.0	100.2	99.9	99.9	100.0	99.9	100.1	99.9	99.9

*All figures given in percentages.

clauses within union contracts make this type of conversion extremely difficult.[1] In addition, there may be city ordinances and civil service rules which impact the process. For example, elaborate bumping rights may exist which require that part-time and seasonal employees be laid off prior to full-time employees. Often such issues as employee retention rights, severance pay, vacation pay, sick leave pay and unemployment costs can become prohibitive and prevent the privatization of the service.

In order to minimize this problem, Fisk suggests the following possible approaches: require the contractor to hire the displaced worker, give displaced workers priority for other government jobs or provide for retaining workers.

This survey asked respondents to indicate how the potential problem of displaced workers was handled. As Table 5 indicates, in 69.8 percent of the transactions no government workers were involved in the service at the time of contracting. This could be an indication that governmental units are avoiding contracting out in areas where municipal workers are employed in large numbers. Where government workers are a consideration, in 11.6 percent of the cases those employed were given priority for other government positions. This was particularly prevalent in the street maintenance and park landscaping areas. In the refuse collection and health care areas the private contractor often was required to hire the displaced employees.

Service Issues

A recent survey of 121 public officials found that one of the major goals of privatization was to improve the quality of service.[2] Fisk states that the contractor's responsiveness to citizens' complaints is closely aligned to service levels and quality standards.[3] Table 6 summarizes how the cities in the authors' survey attempted to monitor contractor responsiveness to complaints. The prevalent practice was to require citizens to take the initiative and register the complaint for most of the privatized services, as reported by 74.3 percent for all services. The governmental unit then forwards the complaint to the contractor. Very few cities reported either inspecting or auditing the contractors' performance except in the areas of street maintenance and park landscaping. Even fewer cities conducted surveys to assess responsiveness.

Closely related to the customer satisfaction issue is how governments who contracted a service to the private sector provided for the possible contingency of service interruption by such events as a bankruptcy or a strike. Approaches to minimizing the possibility of a service interruption, shown in Table 7, include checking the contractors' past performance and financial standing (11.6 percent), and requiring a performance bond and a

Table 6
HOW CITIES MONITOR THE CONTRACTOR'S RESPONSIVENESS TO CITIZENS' COMPLAINTS*

	Refuse Collection	Vehicle Towing	Animal Control	Street Maintenance	Transportation	Health Care	Park Landscaping	Tax Collection	Other	All Services
Complaints go to government officials to track contractors' performance	76.5	83.2	75.0	50.0	69.2	63.6	57.1	100.0	75.0	74.3
Assess monetary penalties for complaints	4.4	1.8	—	—	—	4.5	—	—	—	1.6
Offer bonus for no complaints	—	—	—	—	—	—	—	—	—	.3
Survey citizens to assess responsiveness	2.9	.9	—	—	3.8	—	—	—	6.25	1.6
Use formal inspection system	8.8	5.3	—	45.8	11.5	13.6	38.1	—	6.25	12.2
Other	7.4	8.8	25.0	4.2	15.4	18.2	4.8	—	12.5	10.0
TOTAL	100.0	100.0	100.0	100.0	99.9	99.9	100.0	100.0	100.0	100.0

*All figures given in percentages.

Table 7
HOW CITIES DEAL WITH SERVICE INTERRUPTION*

	Refuse Collection	Vehicle Towing	Animal Control	Street Maintenance	Transportation	Health Care	Park Landscaping	Tax Collection	Other	All Services
Have not thought about it	15.2	11.3	31.3	8.3	25.0	22.7	4.5	16.7	31.25	15.4
No concern—service interruption is minor inconvenience	4.5	19.1	25.0	16.7	—	—	18.2	33.3	12.5	13.2
Check contractors' past performance and financial standing	16.7	6.1	6.3	—	20.8	36.4	9.1	16.7	6.25	11.6
Require performance bonds and termination penalties	48.5	20.0	25.0	66.7	41.7	18.2	36.4	33.3	25.0	33.1
Retrain equipment and cross train personnel	7.6	2.6	12.5	—	8.3	—	9.1	—	12.5	5.1
Divide service among contractors	7.6	40.9	—	8.3	4.2	22.7	22.7	—	12.5	21.5
TOTAL	100.1	100.0	100.1	100.0	100.0	100.0	100.0	100.0	100.0	99.9

*All figures given in percentages.

termination penalty (33.1 percent). Neither of these approaches addresses directly the issue of how to quickly reestablish service in a satisfactory way. Some cities reported dealing with this problem by cross training personnel (5.1 percent) and others by dividing the service among different contractors (21.5 percent).

It would appear from these responses that cities have done little to provide for continuation of service after a disruption. Only 26.6 percent either have cross trained or divided the contracts among different contractors so that if one provider ceases, another can fill the gap. Among those concerned with a potential service interruption, most seemed to prescribe a preventive approach: 33.1 percent attempted to guard against it by requiring a performance bond and a termination penalty.

The responses varied considerably depending on the area of potential disruption. An average of 15.4 percent of the cities had not thought about the potential problem—even in the area of refuse collection. Approximately 13 percent thought that most types of interruptions would have minor consequences to the public and, therefore, were not concerned with this potential problem.

Influence on Service Provision

Tables 8 through 10 summarize the respondents' answers to questions dealing with how much influence the units had in the areas where services have been contracted to the private sector. An examination of these tables clearly shows that government units have been able to influence the price charged for services: 57.3 percent reported moderate, major influence or total control as shown in Table 8. Considerable influence also was noted on the types of service to offer: 71 percent moderate influence or more, shown in Table 10. Only in the area of billing and collection (Table 9) was a declining degree of government influence noted.

In terms of particular services, the results were mixed. It appears that governments have the least influence in areas where technical expertise is required, such as animal control, health care and park landscaping. Even in these areas, governments exert significant influence in the pricing, types of service and types of customers served. Governments have more influence for those functions which will affect larger numbers of the public such as refuse collection and transportation.

Table 11 summarizes governments' satisfaction with privatized services. Of the governments responding, 52.7 percent reported that they were very satisfied, on average, with the services that had been privatized. Those somewhat or fairly satisfied totaled 43.6 percent. The highest degree of satisfaction was noted in such areas as refuse collection, street maintenance

Table 8
INFLUENCE A GOVERNMENT HAS ON PRICING*

	Refuse Collection	Vehicle Towing	Animal Control	Street Maintenance	Transportation	Health Care	Park Landscaping	Tax Collection	Other	All Services
No control	28.1	25.0	14.3	33.3	20.0	31.8	52.4	33.3	16.7	27.7
Slight influence	12.5	15.5	21.4	23.8	12.0	13.6	14.3	16.7	8.3	15.0
Moderate influence	9.4	15.5	35.7	19.0	16.0	27.0	4.8	–	25.0	15.6
Major influence	26.6	22.4	7.1	19.0	8.0	22.7	14.3	16.7	25.0	20.5
Total control	23.4	21.6	21.4	4.8	44.0	4.5	14.3	33.3	25.0	21.2
TOTAL	100.0	100.0	99.9	99.9	100.0	99.6	100.1	100.0	100.0	100.0

Table 9
GOVERNMENT INFLUENCE INVOLVED ON BILLING AND COLLECTION*

	Refuse Collection	Vehicle Towing	Animal Control	Street Maintenance	Transportation	Health Care	Park Landscaping	Tax Collection	Other	All Services
No control	25.0	38.5	21.4	52.6	16.0	38.1	58.8	–	33.3	34.9
Slight influence	14.3	15.6	21.4	5.3	12.0	19.0	5.9	40.0	16.7	14.8
Moderate influence	8.9	14.7	42.9	21.1	12.0	19.0	–	–	16.7	14.1
Major influence	19.6	15.6	–	5.3	32.0	23.8	11.8	40.0	8.3	8.3
Total control	32.1	15.6	14.3	15.8	28.0	–	23.5	20.0	25.0	25.0
TOTAL	99.9	100.0	100.0	100.1	100.0	99.9	100.0	100.0	100.0	97.1

*All figures given in percentages.

Table 10
GOVERNMENT INFLUENCE ON TYPES OF SERVICE TO OFFER*

	Refuse Collection	Vehicle Towing	Animal Control	Street Maintenance	Transportation	Health Care	Park Landscaping	Tax Collection	Other Services	All Services
No control	7.8	27.0	14.3	15.0	11.5	13.6	26.3	16.7	25.0	18.8
Slight influence	15.6	9.6	7.1	10.0	3.8	4.5	5.3	33.3	–	10.2
Moderate influence	18.8	14.8	28.6	10.0	23.1	27.3	5.3	33.3	25.0	17.8
Major influence	25.0	27.0	14.3	35.0	30.8	45.5	21.1	–	25.0	27.1
Total control	32.8	21.7	35.7	30.0	30.8	9.1	42.1	16.7	25.0	26.1
TOTAL	100.0	100.1	100.0	100.0	100.0	100.0	100.1	100.0	100.0	100.0

Table 11
CITY SATISFACTION WITH SERVICE CURRENTLY CONTRACTED*

	Refuse Collection	Vehicle Towing	Animal Control	Street Maintenance	Transportation	Health Care	Park Landscaping	Tax Collection	Other Services	All Services
Very satisfied	76.5	44.9	26.7	52.2	52.0	36.4	50.0	40.0	58.3	52.7
Somewhat satisfied	7.4	28.8	33.3	34.8	16.0	31.8	25.0	–	16.7	22.6
Fairly satisfied	16.2	22.9	33.3	13.0	24.0	22.7	20.8	40.0	25.0	21.0
Somewhat dissatisfied	–	2.5	6.7	–	4.0	9.1	–	20.0	–	2.8
Very dissatisfied	–	.8	–	–	4.0	–	4.2	–	–	.9
TOTAL	100.1	99.9	100.0	100.0	100.0	100.0	100.0	100.0	100.0	100.0

*All figures given in percentages.

and transportation. Animal control, towing and health care results were good but not as high as the areas just noted. Overall, governments appear to be extremely satisfied with their efforts towards privatization.

Summary

The primary purpose of this article has been to provide data about some of the management practices in contracting and privatizing being used by cities with populations in excess of 50,000. The survey data documented, as was to be expected, that practices vary from management area to service area, but that there appears to be for each area of interest a predominate approach.

The "lowest bid among qualified companies" was the most popular method for selecting the contractor. The "firm fixed price" was the most common type of contract. Approximately 40 percent of the services were financed (capitalized) by the private firm and 69.8 percent of the contracted services did not involve government workers. By far, the most common way to monitor citizen's complaints was to have complaints go to government officials for tracking contractors' performance. In general, cities attempted to minimize the possibility of a service interruption by examining the contractor's past performance and financial standing. In terms of government influence, governments appear to have the least influence in areas where technical expertise is required and the most where large numbers of the citizens are affected. Even in those areas where an expertise is required, governments exert significant influence over contractors in pricing types of service offered. Finally, cities appear to be very satisfied with services privatized.

Part Five: The Future

29. Considerations for the Future

Patricia S. Florestano

The Movement Toward Privatization

During the 1960s and 1970s, city, state, and national governments expanded their activities enormously, creating new initiatives that ranged from civil rights to environmental protection and employment and training. Political goals focused on individual economic security, equality, and governmental responsiveness.

Currently the political goals appear to be economic growth and individual choice. Charges of governmental ineffectiveness have led to efforts to restrain government spending, limit taxes, reduce regulation, and redefine the basic scope and direction of governmental activity. Changing perceptions of public priorities and problems have led politicians and citizens alike to argue that government is no longer the solution to everything. In the words of President Reagan, "Government is the problem." While we can argue over what precisely caused this major shift, several changes in attitude have emerged.[1]

1. Government is doing more than it ought to be doing, that is, it is intruding too much into our lives.
2. Government cannot act effectively or efficiently.
3. Public officials and agencies are not sufficiently responsive, not so much to the weak or disadvantaged but to the middle class and the business community.
4. Government makes excessive resource demands, that is, it spends too much.

Patricia S. Florestano, "Considerations for the Future of Privatization." Reprinted with permission from Urban Resources, *Vol. 2, No. 4, Summer, 1985. Published by the Division of Metropolitan Services, University of Cincinnati, Cincinnati, Ohio.*

Government officials have adopted a number of strategies in the face of this altered political atmosphere. First, there is a shift in the scope and direction of government activity. Budgets decline or fail to grow; public programs are eliminated or reduced. The second reaction is the movement toward privatizing government activity, a movement which has challenged profoundly both what government does and how it does it. In this context, privatization has several different meanings: government should ignore some problems, leaving their resolution to the private sector; government should make more extensive use of market-available solutions to problems; and government should create markets for the production of public services.[2]

Eight techniques were identified by HUD during its capacity-sharing projects to study privatization and the alternatives for service delivery. They are:

1. contracts with the private sector.
2. arrangements for service delivery by/with other governments.
3. subsidies/grants.
4. vouchers.
5. franchises.
6. voluntary personnel.
7. self-help.
8. limiting demand (fees, user charges).
9. regulation and tax incentives policies.

All that is left is to reduce or eliminate the service.

"Is the Bloom Off the Rose?"

Privatization is quite old. One need only think of the Hessians to see an example of contracting out from about two hundred years ago. Mercenaries were a veritable private industry in the time of classical Greece, and contract management of cities was a fact of life in Renaissance Italy. But until the Reagan administration, interest in contracting for services (as opposed to goods) and other forms of privatization was not at the top of our political agenda. The Reagan administration triggered an avalanche of privatization activities, studies, ordinances, etc. Governments rushed in where they had previously feared to tread. Ray Hunt, writing in *PAR,* said that such a positive response lies in the fact that the contract state is a *distinctly American style of operating — a way of having an ideological cake while also eating it: broadly speaking, it harmonizes with American individualism and anti-socialistic biases and comports with customary American preferences for reliance on the private sector for goods and services.*[3]

However, it may be that the euphoria which has surrounded the notion for the last four years is premature. (Is the bloom off the rose?) During the '70s, accounts that could be found were glowing but few; more recently serious studies of various forms of privatization are becoming increasingly available. During the '80s these case studies are more disparate—and in some cases they reveal relatively infrequent usage of some of the privatization techniques. Nonetheless, if we want to be more hardheaded about these options, perhaps we should look ahead coolly and dispassionately at the implications of current and future trends for privatization.

Predicted Trends in American Society[4]

Social Changes

A tremendous number of Americans are now involved in quasi-public volunteer work. A major proportion are in health care and education: hospital work, rescue squads, fund raising, work with the elderly, the PTA, and school board service. There is reason to believe that in the near future, the activist, volunteer impulse in our citizens will coincide with a desire to get more involved in the governmental process.

A subtly changing emphasis from a representative democracy to a participatory democracy is a second major social trend. Other social trends include the increased influence of religious beliefs, the importance of women's perspectives, and widespread active concern about the environment.

Structural Changes

The experts are less agreed about the permanency of these trends, which include the apparent evolution from centralized management and decision-making in the public and private sectors to some decentralization of these processes, as well as the decentralization of populations in cities and urban areas. A third structural change is reflected across the country in a growing number of partnerships between business and governments, described as the "blurring" of lines between the public and private sectors. A fourth structural change lies in the evolving nature of the federal system and its fiscal patterns, with less federal money but more devolutions of responsibility going to state and local governments.

Technological Changes

Run-away trends, not only irreversible, but synergistic, include: the shift from an industrial to an information-based, service-oriented economy, with the emergence of communications as the most important industry under a broad umbrella of various services. Closely related is the growth and intrusion of computers into all facets of our lives. This growth in computers coincides with the pressure from taxpayers to improve productivity and efficiency. In fact, computers offer many possibilities to enhance the success of government programs, with the added potential to reduce manpower needs in government agencies and lower financial burdens on taxpayers.

Finally, think of the impact of universal cable on our lives. Ultimately we will all have access to from 40–100 channels with the cost low enough that equity of access will not be a problem. We will also have interactive or feedback cable which, because of its democratizing effect, will be very supportive of human networking. The advent of this two-way cable TV will likely provide a sort of "instant electorate."

Demographic Changes

This is the pre-eminent set of trends and includes: an increasing percentage of older citizens, paralleling a decrease in the proportion of young people; an overall increase in the total population; mobility continuing at a rate slightly lower than that of the last decade; and an increasing number of households and minorities.

Employment Changes

Fewer hours will be devoted to work and fewer years will be worked. It has been suggested that medical advances could affect longevity so much that following retirement we would face 40 to 50 years of non-work, a period of high needs and fewer resources for public services. At the same time, high-demand jobs will require specialization beyond the reach of most governmental units. In this context, the experts predict the decline of labor unions together with the continuation and growth of unemployment as well as conflicts between those who work and those who don't.

Economic and Fiscal Changes[5]

Market patterns will be fragmented, with consumers and or voters showing more diversification and more specialization in their tastes. Large centralized facilities/services will no longer provide automatic payoffs, because the cost of capital will continue to skyrocket. Inflation will continue, partially because it is built into the economic system by indexing. Major increases in sales and income taxes, rather than those on real property or business activities, are likely, in essence representing a shift from business and property to consumption and income revenues.

These demographic, technological, economic, structural, and social changes will have an impact on government's ability and will to deliver services through either traditional or alternative means.

The Future: What Does All This Tell Us?

The inescapable conclusion is that the movement toward privatization is not going to disappear any time soon. Reconsider the factors that stimulated the trend: 1) a concern for the costs and effectiveness of government; 2) a dislike for government intrusiveness; and 3) a growing desire for more individual self-reliance, which is to be buttressed hopefully by economic growth. Do these factors show signs of dissipation? Not now, certainly — all of these factors are among the major reasons for the Reagan victory.

Not in the future, either, if we can believe the trend forecasters: self-help and volunteers; participatory democracy; decentralization; public-private partnerships; less federal largesse coupled with more state and local responsibility; a service-based economy; robots, computers, and cable; more elderly, more minorities, and more people; unemployment; and consumer-citizen specialization. In the face of these sorts of trends, government will continue to withdraw from selected activities.

It's happening now as citizens and public officials question the extent to which particular services must necessarily be delivered by a public agency. It's happening now as public officials, because of fiscal limitations, struggle to set priorities among various activities. It's happening now as services are being reduced or eliminated in response to revenue and spending restraints. This last election saw more fiscal restraint measures on ballots across the country than at any time since the passage of Proposition 13.

In addition to reductions in activities and altered financial arrangements, we are seeing and will continue to see an increased role for private enterprise in providing public services. Nationally, the number of partnerships between business and governments will continue to grow, further blurring the lines between the public and private sectors.

The trend toward volunteerism and self-help in all areas of our lives will be especially evident in the provision of public services. A parallel trend lies in the growth of community involvement in local governments' decision-making. Professional managers and public employees are increasingly realizing that they have to involve the citizens in the solution of public problems. Our system of governance will be less bureaucratic, less expensive, and more inclined toward partnerships with groups and toward sharing in the delivery of services.

In the light of the Reagan victory, "privatization" is a key word for the conservatives. Press reports note the existence of plans, either drawn up or proposed, to transfer to the private sector numerous functions now performed by the federal government, such as insuring bank deposits and controlling air traffic.[6] Conservatives have suggested ending the federal government's monopoly of mail boxes and mail slots, so that private mail services could have access to them. An idea that is reportedly being tested in several cities would result in government turning over the management or ownership of public housing projects to tenants and tenant associations. If the conservative philosophy prevails at the national level for the next four years and beyond, it is likely to have a massive impact on state and local governments also.

Generally, the impact upon career employees is negative. As Bill Timmons noted, impacts include career disruption and dislocation, erosion of merit systems, and undermining of trust and credibility. At a meeting on "The Revitalization of the Public Service," we noted the generally negative impact of privatization on the employee. This can only be balanced by the potential for positive impact on the agency.

If public agencies are able to discard responsibility for services and activities that bear only indirectly on their public mission, they may be able to concentrate more directly on the essential activities of government. It may also be that cost reductions resulting from following a market delivery approach for appropriate services can reduce the pressure on services that are *not* susceptible to the market approach. If we are forced to think more clearly about which public activities actually produce public, as compared to private, benefits, we may be able to concentrate on those things that only government can do and improve the doing of them.

30. The Business
of Local Government

Kate Ascher

Contracting out the delivery of services has become a familiar item on American municipal agendas. Like other aspects of the broader privatization trend, contracting out has generally been portrayed as a "public versus private" issue — the assumption being that one mode of delivery is more appropriate than the other. Such a portrayal carries with it very high political stakes and has therefore prompted a reaction from trade unions, conservative think-tanks and other lobbying organizations. All too often the participation of these groups in the debate has led to an unsettling, and indeed unnecessary, level of controversy surrounding local service delivery decisions.

The problem with the "public versus private" dichotomy is not simply that it is controversial. More disturbing is that this controversy has acted as a smokescreen, calling attention to the political symptoms — rather than to the underlying economic causes — of recent shifts in service delivery modes. Municipalities have tended to base delivery decisions more on political than on economic realities, and in doing so have failed to make maximum use of new, private approaches to service delivery.

It's time we changed the way we think about contracting out public services. Rather than view it as an isolated political development, we need to see it as part of a broader economic question — one which concerns the relative benefits of internal delivery versus those of external or market provision. That question is as relevant to private companies — who must continuously make decisions as to which goods or services they will produce

Kate Ascher, "The Business of Local Government — An Alternative View of the Privatization Debate." Reprinted with permission from The Privatization Review, *Vol. 3, No. 4, Fall, 1987. Published by The Privatization Council, Washington, D.C. (Printed by Maxco Publications, Inc., Little Falls, New Jersey.)*

themselves and which they will purchase from an outside supplier — as it is to public agencies. The difference, of course, is that private firms recognize these decisions as economic or commercial ones and have therefore not hesitated to make efficient use of market alternatives, while public agencies' inability to view the issue in other than political terms has prevented a timely response to new market offerings.

This article attempts to put the contracting out debate into appropriate historical and economic perspective in an effort to encourage more professional and less political approaches to the issue on the part of the public agencies. The first section considers the trends in service provision over the past 60 years, focusing specifically on the relationship between developments in the private and public sectors. The second section uses the lessons drawn from recent history to construct a framework for analyzing current service provision decisions.

An Alternative Perspective

It is only recently that market provision of services has achieved a measure of popularity in either public or private sectors. For many years, internal or direct provision of services was the norm in nearly all organizations. In the private sector, internal provision of professional and support services was to a great extent born of organizational growth and the presence of considerable economies of scale. As the size and complexity of the workload expanded, many firms found it cheaper to hire lawyers, accountants and caterers directly than to contract with an outside firm. Even those firms which were too small to achieve any economies of scale often provided services directly, due to the difficulties in finding a suitable external provider. (Cleaning is a good example of a service which many firms were forced to provide themselves in the years preceding the birth of the contract cleaning industry.) Internal provision of services also provided a measure of flexibility in labor deployment allowing corporations to respond quickly to changes in the commercial environment.

The growth of direct provision in the public sector shared similar origins. As government grew, both in terms of size and responsibility, economies of scale developed in certain functional areas. Many of the new responsibilities of government (such as welfare disbursement or the provision of low-income housing) could not be provided on other than an internal basis, as they required administrative expertise unavailable in the market place. In the few areas where commercial alternatives did exist, accusations of political corruption and patronage often kept contracting out to a minimum. Furthermore, agencies saw government employment as one way of bolstering the labor market, particularly during the economic dislocation of the 1930s and the war effort of the 1940s.

But this overwhelming preference for internal provision of services was not to last, and the past 20 years have witnessed dramatic changes in approaches to delivery decisions—most visibly in the private sector. Far from assuming that new or additional services will be provided internally, many private firms now start from just the opposite assumption: that they will take on direct responsibility for delivery only if the market cannot provide them with an adequate service. The reasons behind this shift in both behavior and attitude are numerous and diverse.

At least two "organizational" reasons can be identified. One was the growing inefficiency associated with direct delivery of services. As organizations continued to grow, economies of scale were no longer widely realized. Size frequently led to cost excesses. Budgets became swollen due to continued calls for additional resources and to the persistence of programs and operations beyond their useful lives. New administrative layers associated with direct provision distorted existing networks of communication, pushing senior management further out of touch with both operational procedures and with the workforce.

Continued organizational growth also brought inflexibility. As programs and people became entrenched, many organizations found themselves unable to react swiftly to changes in client needs or in other aspects of the external environment. Sizable workforces in both public and private sectors provided fertile ground for trade union recruitment. As membership grew and bargaining power increased, these unions place substantial constraints upon the methods, and thus upon the costs, of doing business.

Three "environmental" reasons also contributed to increasing interest in external provision. One was the rapid development of technology and the specialization in the marketplace which accompanied it. As technology developed, both the need for new forms of expertise and the number of firms able to provide these services increased. Organizations soon found that in relying on internal staff, they often fell behind the state of the art and risked compromising their competitive position.

Development in the technology industries was a reflection of a larger trend—the growth of the service sector as a whole. Whereas previously there had been no viable alternative to direct provision in many areas, suddenly there were whole industries capable of carrying out a range of both technical and non-technical tasks. Entry barriers to most of these service industries were negligible, which meant competition was fierce and prices were low. This caused many organizations to examine the cost-effectiveness of the internal operations as a first step in reviewing their resource deployment decisions.

The third, and perhaps the most significant, change in the environment was the realization that continued economic growth was unlikely and that a period of retrenchment would be necessary to maintain both our standard of living and our competitive position in the world's economy. In the private sector, the combination of shrinking profit margins (characteristic of mature industries) and increasing competition from low-wage producers abroad focused management attention on the need to cut costs. A similar cost-consciousness developed in the public sector, though for different reasons. The aftermath of the 1973 oil crisis and the growing strength of the "taxpayers' revolt" put great pressure on elected officials at all levels of government to scrutinize expenditures more closely. Not surprisingly, given the inefficiencies noted above, service delivery was among the earliest areas to come under the magnifying glass.

The coincidence of these organizational and environmental factors stimulated reappraisals of service provision on a wide scale throughout the 1970s. But even before that time, the private sector had begun to look to the market for the provision of non-essential support services. In the late 1950s and early 1960s, a number of companies began experimenting with contract cleaning and catering services. The success of these arrangements had two effects: it prompted other companies to consider market provision of similar support services, and at the same time it encouraged the pioneering firms to experiment with external provision of other, more critical factors of production. Significant cost-savings were achieved and, as internal inefficiencies became more apparent, the popularity and appeal of market solutions grew. By the early 1980s, the phenomenon of outsourcing had become both widespread and well-accepted in manufacturing industry.

The public sector was much slower to react to changes in its operating environment, and contracting out did not gain notoriety as an approach to service delivery until the late 1970s and early 1980s. In one way, its arrival on the scene paralleled the experience of the private sector. Contracting-out techniques were initially limited to the provision of support functions such as catering or cleaning — services important to the day-to-day operations of the agency, but not directly related to client outputs. Yet the public sector did not move as quickly as the private to allow contractors to take on more critical client-related responsibilities. While it has occurred in isolated cases, such as garbage collection or ambulance services, the political controversy surrounding the issue has prevented a wider appreciation of what the market has to offer.

Towards a New Approach

The lessons we can draw from recent history provide an important foundation for a more modern approach to public service delivery. They suggest strongly that contracting out cannot be viewed as a unique political development but must be seen as part of a larger economic trend. Contracting out in the public sector and outsourcing in the private are much like fraternal twins — born of the same parents but with different names and appearances. Both have resulted from changes in economic relationships and in the economy as a whole, and both share similar motives: maximizing flexibility and responsiveness while minimizing cost. Far from a public *versus* private issue, reliance on market solutions is a public *and* private development, and one which can only be evaluated against an economic — not a political — canvas.

Even without the political smokescreen, however, evaluating market alternatives is a complex process which needs to be tackled both systematically and objectively. Numerous factors must be considered and weighed before reliable provisions choices can be made. Although in practice the number and relevancy of these factors will vary from case to case, it is possible to draw up a checklist of variables which can provide a general framework for the evaluation process.

Cost

Among the most significant factors which need to be evaluated is the comparative cost of alternative modes of provision. This is not always as straightforward an exercise as it sounds. While it is relatively easy to identify the cost of an outside contract, it is much more difficult to identify the true cost of existing internal operations; functional budgets rarely take account of overhead costs such as senior management salaries, physical space requirements or payroll and accounting support. Additional costs associated with external contracts — such as transitional and monitoring costs — also need to be factored into the cost equation.

Divisibility of Services

Some services will be more difficult to split off from the body of the organization than others. Services like computer programming or data processing may require familiarity with the organization's accounting or financial systems and are therefore poorly suited to contractual arrangements. In contrast, support services such as catering or cleaning generally require little knowledge of internal operating procedures, and demand minimal communication with other functional areas. However, even a service such as cleaning, if it takes place in a sensitive environment like a hospital, may present difficulties due to the technical knowledge required and to the inevitable contact with patients.

Market Alternatives

As we saw in the preceding section, the growth of contracting out was to some extent driven by events in the marketplace — specifically by the proliferation of new service companies offering highly competitive prices. While both agencies and firms now have greater choice of suppliers than ever before, it is still important to evaluate carefully both the nature of the supplying industry and the individual companies within it. The size of the industry is critical; a small number of suppliers can lead to a monopolistic situation, while a larger number will greatly increase the bargaining power of the purchasing organization. Other important factors are the level of experience and financial strength of supplier firms. In many cases, the presence of new and inexperienced firms in an industry has led to loss-leader pricing and ultimate default on the contract.

Confidentiality

Market provision of certain services may put outsiders in close proximity to sensitive information. In the private sector, this is likely to raise serious competitive issues and result in a bias toward direct labor. The consequences of unwanted public sector disclosures are different, but equally dangerous.

Security of Supply

Market solutions necessarily entail a higher degree of risk than direct provision, as it always possible that a supplier will be unable to fulfill its contract. It is up to each organization to evaluate both the likelihood and the impact of any interruptions in service. In the private sector, delays in the provision of goods or services will have a detrimental impact on revenues and may affect customer loyalty toward the product and or the company. In the public sector, failure to provide continuous service may have more dramatic consequences. Refuse collection, emergency services and social welfare programs are obvious cases in point.

Difficulty in Specifying Output

Not all services lend themselves easily to contractual arrangements, due to the difficulties in specifying outputs and the importance of quality in determining customer satisfaction. Gardening, for example, is a task which can be detailed and scheduled fairly easily. Provision of corporate medical services, however, presents a more difficult case in terms of both specification and measurement. Many public services fall at the difficult end of the spectrum, with services such as education, safety and public health posing significant problems of measurement.

These six factors are by no means the only ones that an organization should consider in evaluating market provision. Issues such as corporate culture and industrial relations, for example, may warrant equal or even greater attention than those highlighted above. But despite its limitations, the framework suggested above can help us begin to understand both the complexity of service provision decisions and the need for a more sophisticated cost-benefit approach to analyzing them.

Consider the case of major oil companies, many of whom have found that they can purchase oil on the spot market at a lower price than that which it costs them to produce it internally. Though the incentive is there to maximize profits by purchasing large quantities of oil and reducing the amount produced directly, few companies will do this because of the risks involved in over-reliance on external suppliers. The quality of spot market oil cannot be guaranteed, and firms are likely to lose the flexibility to have as much oil as they want when they want it. As a result, most firms limit their spot market purchases to a reasonably small percentage of their total needs.

Similar issues arise in a public sector context. Privatizing refuse collection, for example, may prevent the municipality from exerting direct control over the quality of the service provided. It also involves an element of risk, for if the contractor fails to perform up to standards or withdraws from the contract, the city or town is left with disgruntled citizens and dirty streets. Yet a number of cities have found that the cost savings associated with contracting out are substantial enough to offset the risks. The result has been a series of successful experiments with contract collection in metropolitan areas across the country.

These examples are useful not only in highlighting the complexity of the decision process but also in demonstrating that the utility of market solutions is situation-specific. What is an acceptable risk in one functional area may not be acceptable in another. As a result, service delivery decisions need to be handled individually. In each case, a modified form of cost-benefit analysis must be undertaken, one which reflects both the needs and objectives of the organization at a particular point in time.

The most likely outcome of this discrete form of decision-making in any organization — be it public or private — is a mixture of delivery modes: certain services will be resourced internally and others will be provided by the marketplace. This balance between delivery modes may shift from time to time due to changes in the market or to internal organizational changes, and it is important that flexibility be built into the system. As one American municipal administrator with significant experience in managing private contracts noted, "anything a city is doing in-house ought to be contracted,

anything contracted should be done in-house, and every five years you
should switch." The point is not that there is any inherent advantage in
alternating modes of provision, but that services which remain unchanged
for long periods of time are likely to become inefficient and unresponsive
to citizen needs.

Concluding Remarks

The preceding pages have attempted to show that what is often referred to as the privatization of municipal services is not — contrary to
popular belief — a "private versus public" issue. Instead it is a question of
the relative advantages of internal and external provision in a given situation, a question similar to that facing private firms in many aspects of their
operations. The issues facing public sector agencies may be more complex
than those in the private sector, due to the delicate nature of certain public
services and to the fact that public sector outputs are often difficult to
specify. But that does not mean that the evaluation exercise undertaken by
public agencies should be any less rigorous. To the contrary, the complex
nature of public services demands an even more rigorous and more professional approach to evaluating delivery options than we might expect to see
elsewhere.

To date, however, the public sector has shied away from any such
rigorous form of analysis, and "business-like" approaches to delivery decision have been more prevalent in board rooms than in town halls. While
this may not be particularly surprising, it is worrying from the standpoint
of democratic theory. It suggests that private companies have been more
responsive to customer needs and to changes in the commercial environment than local agencies have been to citizen needs and to change in their
own economic environment. We owe it to ourselves to change this little
situation by bringing a little more professional discipline — and a little less
political posturing — to the business of running our cities.

31. The Choice Between Privatization and Publicazation

Jerry Frug

Privatization is a fashionable idea these days in some state and local government circles. In theory at least, any governmental service could be delivered by a private business under a government contract. Garbage collection, ambulance services and health care are familiar candidates for privatization, but there is no reason to stop there. Public schools could be replaced by private schools as long as students are given government-subsidized vouchers to pay for them. Police departments could be replaced by private security guards, judges could be replaced by professional arbitrators, and fire departments could be replaced by private emergency businesses. Some states are even considering transferring their prison systems to private hands. Indeed, once you begin to take the idea of privatization seriously, you can quickly come to the view that government could be reduced to the performance of three tasks: the collection of revenue by taxation, the decision of which services this revenue should buy, and the negotiation and drafting (and, perhaps, the monitoring) of contracts with private businesses for the delivery of the chosen services. In fact, some of these jobs could be contracted out too. For example, government could hire a collection agency to enforce its tax laws, a private management consultant to determine what services to provide, and private lawyers to negotiate and draft its contracts. Taken to its limits, then, privatization could transform government simply into a revenue-generating mechanism run by a few people whose job would be to begin the process of contracting out, choosing the consultants and lawyers who, in turn, would continue the

Jerry Frug, "The Choice Between Privatization and Publicazation." Reprinted with permission from Current Municipal Problems, *Vol. 14, 1987–88. Published by Callaghan & Company, Wilmette, Illinois.*

cycle of contracting and re-contracting. As a means of employment and delivery of services, the state really could wither away.

Why, however, would anyone *want* to go down this road to privatization? The usual answer people suggest is that private businesses are more efficient and better-run than governments are. But what do the terms "efficient" and "better"-run mean when they are invoked in this way? To some extent, private businesses are "efficient" because they do not have to comply with hundreds of laws that routinely are applied to governments, laws ranging from civil service and competitive bidding requirements to the demands of the Bill of Rights. But if any of these laws serve a valuable purpose, one would think that they should be applied to the managers of publicly funded prisons, schools, and fire departments whoever they are; conversely, if these are not good ideas, they should not be applied to anyone. Why should "private" prisons, financed solely by tax dollars, be exempt from the constitutional requirement that prisoners be treated in accordance with due process of law? Why should the constitutional restrictions on the arbitrary expulsion of students be applied only to schools labelled "public" and not those labelled "private," when both kinds of schools would be paid for by tax revenues and charged with the task of educating the locality's population? I think the answer to these questions is that both kinds of institution should have to comply with the Bill of Rights. Moreover, I think that there is no more reason to fear corruption in a state-run police department than in a privately run police department, and that there is no more reason to tolerate abuse of employees in a "private" hospital operating pursuant to a contract with the government than in a city-run hospital. But if these contentions are true, the "efficiency" gains derived from private exemption from requirements imposed on government do not support a move to privatization. If any of these requirements are unnecessary, one should relieve governments from having to comply with them; if the requirements are desirable, one should apply them to any entity that performs a service offered in the public interest and supported by publicly generated revenue.

Indeed, any argument for privatization based on the notion that the private sector is more "efficient" than the public sector can be answered by proposing to reform the public sector instead. Some people claim, for example, that the incentive system in the private sector makes employees more productive than does the system adopted by government. But even if this is true (and its truth is much debated), the difference between their incentive systems is attributable simply to the legal rules that require government to operate differently from the way business operates. If schools would be run better if they competed against each other, such a competition could be arranged in public schools as well as in publicly financed private schools. If employees and managers in prisons and police departments could be led to act more efficiently by bonuses or profit-sharing, such a system could be installed in government as well. If private firms run better because they pay their executives more money than the government is permitted to pay, the government could revise its wage scale instead of contracting out its services. After all, it's the taxpayer who pays the bill in either case. Slogans like "competition" or "the profit motive" cannot determine the choice between having services performed by the public or private sector.

Even if the private sector is found to be more "efficient" in some sense of the word, it doesn't follow that privatization would be a good idea. Some people assert, for example, that privatization is desirable because services are cheaper when they are run by private businesses rather than by government. Before transferring services to a private concern, however, we need to find out why they are cheaper (if, indeed, they are). If the services are cheaper because private employers cut the wages or benefits of workers from below the levels offered by government, we need to determine whether such cuts promote the public interest. It's by no means obvious that the public interest is advanced by paying workers less or by providing them less adequate health or retirement benefits. Similarly, if private costs are lower because employees work harder out of fear of being fired, we need to decide whether we want to use public money to create that kind of workplace or whether, alternatively, we think that job security better contributes to a sound working environment. Fostering certain values is often worth the cost. (And—to repeat—if we find the values not worth fostering, the alternative system could be adopted in the public sector itself.)

In my opinion, privatization has become an attractive idea these days because the reform that can readily be seen as an alternative to privatization—transforming government itself—appears to be much more difficult than the process of contracting out to a private concern. Reforming government is a formidable task not only because making the tough choices about the best way to operate services is hard but also because, even after people have decided what to do, they have to get their ideas adopted. This requires dealing with state legislatures, city councils, unions, and interest groups. When confronted with such an arduous task, it's not surprising that people say, "Who needs it? Let's just contract the services out." In the current debate about state and local government services, proponents of privatization have shifted the burden of persuasion to those who favor retaining services in the public sector. The question on the public agenda has changed from "how do we make government better?" to "why not contract out?"

Posing the issue of privatization in these terms, however, does not adequately capture what is at stake in the privatization debate. That this is true can be seen just by looking in a dictionary. According to Webster's Third

New International Dictionary of the English Language (the 1981 unabridged edition), the verb "privatize" means "to alter the status of (a
business or industry) from public to private control or ownership." One
might think, therefore, that the noun "privatization" would, in a parallel
fashion, mean the alteration of a business' status from public to private
control. This seems to be how people (including me, so far in this essay)
are using the term these days. But look what the dictionary definition for
"privatization" actually is:

> The tendency for an individual to withdraw from participation in social and
> esp[ecially] political life into a world of personal concerns usu[ally] as a
> result of a feeling of insignificance and lack of understanding of complex
> social processes.

In his famous survey of America in the 1830s entitled "Democracy in
America," Alexis de Toqueville found that taking an active part in political
life was an American's "most important business and, so to say, the only
pleasure he knows.... If an American should be reduced to occupying
himself with his own affairs, at that moment half his existence would be
snatched from him; he would feel it as a vast void in his life and would
become incredibly unhappy." Since Toqueville's time, the decrease in participation in public life has contributed, as Toqueville predicted, to individual feelings of insignificance and to a sense that no ordinary person
can deal with the complex social problems of the modern world. These feelings have led, in turn, to further decreases in participation in public life,
generating still more "feeling[s] of insignificance and lack of understanding
of complex social processes." This cycle of privatization could accelerate
if states and localities transferred control of their important public services
to private entities. Traditionally, the political world has offered a way to
engage with others that is different from private life, a form of engagement
known as democracy. The sense of empowerment that we gain whenever
we become participants in the creation of our social and political world will
be lost if we withdraw even further into our private lives or commercial
dealings. To combat this trend toward privatization—to prevent this kind
of de-privation—we need to revive the sense of public involvement and connection engendered by engagement in political life. I shall call the process
of reviving participatory political life "publicazation." This is not just an
unfamiliar concept in the privatization debate; it's not even a word at all
(according to Webster's unabridged dictionary).

These days, popular involvement in government is limited primarily to
participation in the election of those who control the delivery of public services. Even those who want to transfer government services to private
business seek to retain this feature of public life. The people who would

provide public services would no longer work for an elected official, but they would work for someone chosen by an elected official. Such a change would attenuate, but not cut, the ties that link the electorate with the delivery of public services. But even the ties that now exist do not adequately allow for public involvement in the delivery of government services. Today our state and local government services are run bureaucratically, not in a participatory manner; if transferred to private hands, they would be run bureaucratically as well. A move toward publicazation requires more than simply the maintenance of a status quo. Government operations must be reformed in a direction opposite to that of privatization, encouraging not withdrawal from political life but more active, participatory politics.

There are various forms that publicazation could take in the operation of government services. Those who work in the public sector could be encouraged to participate more actively in the decisions about how their workplace operates. Self-government will become a meaningful contribution to people's sense of themselves only if it is part of their ordinary, day-to-day lives; workplace democracy is, therefore, an important aspect of publicazation. The increasing interest in employee self-management in the United States has not yet adequately taken hold in the delivery of government services. But there is no reason why employee self-management is more appropriate in industry than in a school system. Indeed, allowing teachers to take a greater collective role in the management of their schools could be a first step toward publicazation.

Moreover, public services could be provided in a way that involves members of the public in their planning and management. In the 1960s, public involvement in government decisionmaking took the form of citizen review panels for police departments, citizen advisory boards for public hospitals, and federally sponsored programs that required the maximum participation of those affected in the planning of specific federally funded services. Publicazation could build on the virtues, and learn from the mistakes, of these experiments in participatory decisionmaking. Crime watch neighborhood organizations, community-based schools, and citizen involvement in city planning and development are examples of possible forms of public participation in the delivery of government services.

Finally, some government services could be managed by groups formed on a participatory basis. Publicly funded housing projects, for example, could be organized in a way that encourages those who live in the housing to assume some of the responsibilities of its management; experiments of this kind are already taking place in a few American cities. In a similar fashion, publicly funded programs that provide food to the poor could help recipients organize community-based, popularly run food cooperatives in neighborhoods in which grocery stores are being closed down. Participation could even occur in such an unlikely place as a prison system. In the political prisons of El Salvador, the political prisoners currently participate in a number of the management decisions that affect their areas of the prisons.

To be sure, the future of publicazation does not turn on whether control of public services is in the hands of the government or the private sector. The suggestions just made for government services — workplace democracy, consumer involvement in management decisions, and decentralized, participatory management of service delivery — could take place whether the services are run by government or by business. Publicazation and privatization — in the sense of transferring government services to private businesses — need not be thought of as opposites. Both could happen simultaneously. The critical choice between publicazation and privatization, therefore, is not whether government or business should run public services. The critical choice instead is whether we want public participation in the delivery of public services whoever provides them — whether we want to foster the values of publicazation. In my view, only by taking a share in governance can citizens learn how to deal with people with whom they disagree, how to wield and limit power, and how to affect the complex social processes that affect their lives. Only by taking a share in governance can a citizen overcome the feelings of insignificance and powerlessness that constitute privatization. Of course, publicazation would not be an easy undertaking, either in the government or in the private sector. But the difficult work of reformation can itself become a vehicle for citizen participation. Indeed, organizing to make government and business more participatory could become the initial project of publicazation.

32. The Private Market Can't Always Solve Public Problems

Robert Kuttner

In the public donnybrook between Chrysler Corp. Chairman Lee A. Iacocca and Interior Secretary Donald P. Hodel over who is the worse commercializer of the Statue of Liberty, neither man came off looking like Mother Teresa. Iacocca had auctioned off exclusive commercial use of Miss Liberty's logo, and Hodel wants Ellis Island, of all places, to include a four-star hotel. The spat invites reconsideration of the appropriate boundaries between things public and things private.

Lately a new word has entered political discourse: privatization. The idea is that private is invariably more efficient than public, that government ought to stay out of as many realms as possible, and that even where government gets involved, government should contract-out tasks to private firms or give people vouchers rather than provide them services directly. President Reagan wants to sell off public lands and public dams and get the government out of the mortgage insurance, legal aid, and veterans' health business. Down the road, some of his advisers hope to supplant public schools with private education vouchers and Social Security with "super–IRA's." In local government, one sees privatized garbage collection, park maintenance, and even privately operated prisons.

But there are both philosophical and practical difficulties with this conservatives' utopia. First, in certain areas of life the criteria of the private market seem inappropriate. That is because human beings are not solely economic creatures. They have social attachments, patriotic stirrings, religious commitments, family bonds, and psychological needs, some of

Robert Kuttner, "The Private Market Can't Always Solve Public Problems." Reprinted with permission from Business Week, *Issue No. 2936, March 10, 1986. Published by McGraw-Hill, Inc., New York, New York.*

which contradict the textbook view of economic man. It offends us, as citizens, to have national symbols auctioned off to the highest bidder.

Votes and Love

In organized society, we counterpose certain public values to those of a pure market. Some things aren't supposed to be bought and sold. It is against the law to sell votes, although interest groups do try to buy influence. You are not supposed to buy love, though prostitutes merchandise sex. It is against the law to buy and sell people, although many babies are virtually purchased for adoption. But such breaches of our stated values show that society holds dear things besides markets.

In short, maintaining a political democracy in a private economy requires a set of compromises between the two incompatible principles of political equality—one-person-one-vote—and economic inequality—one-dollar-one-vote. Even in the strictly economic realm, our society has decided to stop somewhat short of pure Social Darwinism, which holds that the race belongs to the swift and too bad for the laggards. We believe that all children, as American citizens, deserve an education, apart from whether their parents can buy it. We believe that nobody ought to die for lack of access to medical care. A pure economist might term these only examples of "rational" responses to cases where the market has failed, but that explanation trivializes them, for the underlying concerns that these social arrangements reflect are civic values, not market values.

As a practical matter, once society departs from the principle of one-dollar-one-vote, things get messy. If people qualify as citizens for services that they could not afford as consumers, then somebody has to decide who gets what. In a purely private transaction, the criterion is automatic: If you have the cash, you get to buy the product. End of debate. But in the public realm, we are always having to decide subjective issues such as per-pupil outlays or hospital reimbursement formulas.

It must be noted, however, that once a social commitment is made—to health care, for example—even private insurers and private providers have to wrestle with such issues as who stays how long in the hospital, and at what charge.

Age-old Question

Similarly, the appeals of contracting-out government become less apparent when one takes a closer look. In theory, contracting-out government services brings to the public realm all the virtues of the private market—

flexibility, innovation, and competition. In practice, however, contracting-out government begs the ancient political question: *Quis custodiet ipsos custodes?* (Who will watch the watchers?)

The gross inefficiency of Pentagon contracting—probably the most "privatized" portion of government—is hardly an advertisement for the superiority of privatization. In local government, there is evidence that when too many public services are contracted out, there are just not enough public officials and too little public-sector *esprit de corps* to keep the process honest. A study by the conservative Massachusetts Taxpayers Foundation investigated state government contracting-out of social services and concluded that the state had lost "fiscal and program control" to a "provider-dominated system." Beyond a certain point, government-by-contract couples the inefficiencies of the public sector with the less savory aspects of the private sector.

The market, the late economist Arthur Okun wrote, "needs a place, and the market needs to be kept in its place." Amen. We Americans are not just buyers and sellers; we are also citizens.

Chapter Notes

Notes to Chapter 4

1. Harry P. Hatry, *A Review of Private Approaches for the Delivery of Public Services* (Washington, DC: Urban Institute, 1983), p. 70.
2. Also referred to as "load shedding" or "exiting."
3. Hatry, *Private Approaches*, p. 73.
4. John C. Goodman, "Preface," in *Dismantling the State: The Theory and Practice of Privatization,* by Madsen Pirie (Dallas, TX: National Center for Policy Analysis, 1985), p. viii.
5. Madsen Pirie, *Dismantling the State: The Theory and Practice of Privatization* (Dallas, TX: National Center for Policy Analysis, 1985), p. 29.
6. Service shedding is only sporadically referred to in the literature on cutback management. More than cursory discussion occurs only in Lawrence H. White, "Privatization of Municipally Provided Services," *Journal of Libertarian Studies* 2 (Winter 1978): 187–97; "Demunicipalization of Services," *Policy Report* 2 (July 1980): 1, 3–4; Mark Frazier, "Privatizing the City," *Policy Review* 12 (Spring 1980): 99–108; E.S. Savas, *Privatizing the Public Sector: How to Shrink Government* (Chatham, NJ: Chatham House, 1982), pp. 118–124; Hatry, *Private Approaches,* pp. 66–77; Hartley C. Fitts and Earl W. Lindveit, "Alternative Service Delivery Approaches Used by Local Governments," U.S. Department of Housing and Urban Development, Office of Policy Development and Research, n.d., pp. 19–20; and Stuart Butler, *Privatizing Federal Spending: A Strategy to Eliminate the Deficit* (New York: Universe Books, 1985), pp. 52–53.
7. John M. Griener and Harry P. Hatry, *Coping with Cutbacks: Initial Agency-Level Responses in 17 Local Governments to Massachusetts' Proposition 2½* (Washington, DC: Urban Institute, 1982), p. 130.
8. Fitts and Lindveit, p. 5.
9. E.S. Savas, "Municipal Monopolies Versus Competition in Delivering Urban Services," in Willis D. Hawley and David Rogers (eds.), *Improving the Quality of Urban Management,* vol. 8 of *Urban Affairs Annual Review,* p. 488.
10. Idem., *Privatizing Public Sector,* p. 122.
11. Hatry, *Private Approaches,* p. 67.
12. See Hatry, *Private Approaches,* pp. 68–9; and Fitts and Lindveit, pp. 19–20.
13. Pirie, pp. 17–23.
14. Hatry, *Private Approaches,* pp. 74–76.
15. White, "Privatization," p. 187; "Demunicipalization," p. 4.
16. For example, Savas suggests closing senior citizens' centers before or at the same time as day-care centers to free up the elderly for child-care functions. *Privatizing Public Sector,* p. 120.
17. While this might be appropriate as an interim or second-best measure, a better alternative would be to regulate health and safety through civil-law adjudication. See Bruce M. Johnson and Tibor R. Machan (eds.), *Rights and Regulation: Ethical, Political, and Economic Issues,* with foreword by Aaron Wildavsky (Cambridge, MA: Ballinger Publishing Co. for the Pacific Institute, 1983), especially chapters 1–3, 6 and 10.

18. Hatry, *Private Approaches,* p. 73.

19. White, "Privatization," p. 193; and Savas, *Privatizing Public Sector,* pp. 121–122. See especially Frazier, "Privatizing the City," pp. 91–108.

20. Robert W. Poole, Jr., *Cutting Back City Hall* (New York: Universe Books, 1980), pp. 65–70, 82–85; James T. Bennett and Manuel H. Johnson, *Better Government at Half the Price: Private Production of Public Services* (Ottawa, IL: Caroline House, 1981), p. 47; and White, "Privatization," p. 193.

21. See Jonathan R.T. Hughes, *The Governmental Habit: Economic Control from Colonial Times to the Present* (New York: Basic Books, 1977).

22. Charles N. Glabb and Theodore A. Brown, *A History of Urban America* (New York: MacMillan, 1967); John C. Teaford, *The Unheralded Triumph: City Government in America, 1870–1900* (Baltimore: Johns Hopkins University Press, 1984); and Samuel P. Hays, "The Politics of Reform in Municipal Government in the Progressive Era," *Pacific Northwest Quarterly* 55 (Oct. 1964): 157–169.

23. See, for example, George W. Hilton, "The Rise and Fall of Monopolized Transit," in *Urban Transit: The Private Challenge to Public Transportation,* Charles A. Lave (ed.), foreword by John Meyer (Cambridge, MA: Ballinger Publishing Co. for the Pacific Institute, 1985), pp. 31–48.

24. Teaford, p. 189.

25. Ibid., p. 268.

26. See Frank Tariello, Jr. *The Reconstruction of American Political Ideology, 1867–1917* (Charlottesville, VA: University Press of Virginia, 1982).

27. Glabb and Brown, p. 175.

28. For example, by a prominent transportation economist of the World Bank, Gabriel Roth. Roth is scheduled to preside over the International Conference on the Roles of Private Enterprise and Market Processes in the Financing and Provision of Roads, sponsored by the Transportation Research Board, July 8–11, 1986, in Baltimore, Maryland.

29. (New York: Universe Books, 1980), pp. 26–30 and 95–106.

30. Savas, *Privatizing Public Sector,* especially pp. 29–52.

31. Ibid., pp. 118–131.

32. See note 7.

33. James M. Buchanan and Robert D. Tollison (eds.), *The Theory of Public Choice: Political Applications of Economics* (Ann Arbor, MI: University of Michigan Press, 1972), pp. 22–23.

34. Pirie, pp. 17–23.

35. Ibid., pp. 24–29.

36. Ibid., p. 3.

37. Ibid., pp. 30–115. For a brief review of these methods and how they might apply to local government, see Philip E. Fixler, Jr., "Britain Leads the Way in Privatization," *Fiscal Watchdog* No. 103 (May 1985).

38. Pirie, pp. 30–52.

39. Karl Peterjohn, "Dumping the Garbage Monopoly," *Reason* (November 1980), pp. 43–47.

40. Although this research has not come across any articles or reports citing specific examples, the data from the 1982 International City Management Association's (ICMA) alternative service-delivery survey indicates that the three local governments had to shed the operation of their convention centers/auditoriums to for-profit firms and one government has shed this activity to a non-profit association. The ICMA data resides on the Local Government Center's Privatization Database.

41. Theodore J. Gase, "Getting Street Wise in St. Louis," *Reason* (August 1981), pp. 18–26.

42. Dick Bjorseth, "No-Code Comfort," *Reason* (July 1983), pp. 43–47; and Thomas Hazlett, "They Built Their Own Highway," *Reason* (November 1983), pp. 22–27.

43. See note 7.

44. Steve Hanke, "Privatization: Theory, Evidence, and Implementation," in *Control of Federal Spending,* C. Lowell Harriss (ed.), *Proceedings of the Academy of Political Science,* vol. 35, no. 4, 1985.

45. Peterjohn, pp. 43–47.
46. Hatry, *Private Approaches,* p. 73.
47. Ibid., p. 70.
48. Griener and Hatry, p. 104.
49. HUD Officials advised the author that some ICMA surveys had mistakenly indicated that the same service activity was both "shed" and "contracted-out," due to a confusion over the meaning of "service shedding." In order to ensure the reliability of that portion of the data relating to service shedding, the Privatization Database omits all ICMA service shedding data wherein the respondent reacted positively to any other mode of service delivery relative to a particular service.
50. For example, White, "Privatization," p. 192.

Notes to Chapter 7

1. *Privatization in the U.S.: Cities and Counties,* National Center for Policy Analysis (NCPA) Policy Report no. 116 (Dallas: NCPA, June 1985), 7.
2. Robert W. Poole, Jr., and Philip E. Fixler, Jr., "The Privatization of Public Sector Services in Practice: Experience and Potential" (Paper presented to the Conference on Privatization of the Public Sector, Department of Public Policy and Management, Wharton School, University of Pennsylvania, Philadelphia, Pennsylvania, 18–19 Sept. 1986), 3. Conference papers are to be published in a forthcoming issue of the *Journal of Policy Analysis and Management.*
3. James L. Perry and Timlynn T. Babitsky, "Comparative Performance in Urban Bus Transit: Assessing Privatization Strategies," *Public Administration Review* 46 (Jan./Feb. 1986): 61, 63–64.
4. Barbara J. Stevens, ed., *Delivering Municipal Services Efficiently: A Comparison of Municipal and Private Service Delivery* [Summary], a report prepared by Ecodata, Inc., for the U.S. Dept. of Housing and Urban Development, June 1984.
5. James C. Mercer, "Growing Opportunities in Public Service Contracting," *Harvard Business Review* 61 (March April 1983): 178.
6. Harry P. Hatry, *A Review of Private Approaches for Delivery of Public Services* (Washington, DC: Urban Institute, 1983), 20.
7. Robert W. Poole, Jr., *Cutting Back City Hall* (New York: Universe Books, 1980), 161.
8. *Compendium of Privatization Laws* (New York: Privatization Council, April 1986).
9. Sandra Rosenbloom, "The Taxi in the Urban Transport System," in *Urban Transit: The Private Challenge to Public Transit,* ed. Charles A. Lave (Cambridge, Mass.: Ballinger Publishing Co. for Pacific Institute, 1985), 194–95.
10. Harry P. Hatry and Eugene Durman, *Issues in Competitive Contracting for Social Services* (Fall Church, Ill.: National Institute of Governmental Purchasing, Inc., Aug. 1985), 10.
11. Theodore Gage, "How to Buy Cops," *Reason,* August 1982, 23–28.
12. John D. Hanrahan, *Government for Sale: Contracting Out – The New Patronage* (American Federation of State, County and Municipal Employees [AFSCME], 1977); and *Passing the Bucks: The Contracting Out of Public Services* (AFSCME, 1983).
13. Poole and Fixler, 13–14.
14. John Tepper Marlin, ed., *Contracting Municipal Services: A Guide to Purchase from the Private Sector* (New York: John Wiley & Sons, 1984).
15. Hatry, 72.
16. *Compendium of Privatization Laws.*
17. Madsen Pirie, *Dismantling the State: The Theory and Practice of Privatization* (Dallas: National Center for Policy Analysis, 1985), 43–47, 49–50.
18. Privatization Concerns Task Group, *Employee Incentives for Privatization* (Washington, DC: U.S. Office of Personnel Management, 1986), 19; and "FED CO-OP," Washington, DC: July 1986.

Notes to Chapter 10

1. For a detailed discussion of creative financing options see *Creative Capital Financing,* John E. Petersen and Wesley C. Hough, Municipal Finance Officers Association, 1983.
2. *Government Financial Management Resources in Review;* September 1984, Government Finance Research Center, Washington, DC.
3. Harvey Goldman and Sandra Mokruvos, *The Privatization Book,* Arthur Young International, New York, NY 1984.

Notes to Chapter 13

1. T. Kolderie, "The Two Different Concepts of Privatization," *Public Administration Review,* July/August 1986, Vol. 46, No. 4, p. 287.
2. M.A. Schulman, "Alternative Approaches for Delivering Public Services," *ICMA Urban Data Service Reports,* October 1982, No. 14.
3. C.F. Valente and L.D. Manchester, "Rethinking Local Services: Examining Alternative Delivery Approaches," *ICMA Special Report,* March 1984, No. 12, p. xi.
4. See Schulman, 1982.
5. S. Martin, "The Arvada Volunteer Story," *Public Management,* October 1982, Vol. 64, No. 10, pp. 13–14.
6. See Shulman, 1982.
7. R. Warren, M.S. Rosentraub, and K.S. Harlow, "Coproduction, Equity, and the Distribution of Safety," *Urban Affairs Quarterly,* June 1984, Vol. 19, No. 4, pp. 447–464.
8. J.L. Brudney, "Local Coproduction of Services and the Analysis of Municipal Productivity," *Urban Affairs Quarterly,* June 1984, Vol. 19, No. 4, pp. 465–484.
9. W.E. Bjur and G.B. Siegel, "Voluntary Citizen Participation in Local Government," *Midwest Review of Public Administration,* June 1977, Vol. 11, No. 2, p. 142.
10. J.L. Brudney, "Coproduction: Issues in Implementation," *Administration and Society,* November 1985, Vol. 17, No. 3, pp. 243–256.
11. See Brudney, 1984.

Notes to Chapter 17

1. "State Prisons Around Nation Scramble for Relief as Overcrowding Mounts," *New York Times,* September 28, 1983, p. A16.
2. National Institute of Justice, *Assessing Needs in the Criminal Justice System* by Abt Associates Inc. (Washington, DC: USGPO, 1984), pp. 9–10.
3. National Institute of Justice, "Prisoners vs. Space: The Case for More Determinant Corrections Planning" by Abt Associates Inc. (unpublished draft, 1984).
4. "Financing Clean Water," *Engineering News Record* 209:15 (October 7, 1982), p. 48.
5. U.S. Census Bureau, *Governmental Finances in 1972-73* and relevant preceding issues.
6. James A. Maxwell and J. Richard Aronson, *Financing State and Local Governments* (Washington, DC: The Brookings Institution, 1977), p. 214.
7. John Vogt and Lisa Cole, "An Introduction to Municipal Leasing," *Municipal Financing Journal* (Summer 1983), p. 223.
8. John E. Petersen and Wesley C. Hough, *Creative Capital Financing for State and Local Governments* (Chicago: Municipal Finance Officers Association, 1983), p. 82.
9. California Department of Corrections, "Report to the Legislature: Alternative Financing of California Prisons" (January 1, 1984), p. 6.
10. John J. Hampton, *Financial Decision Making* (Reston, VA: Reston Publishing, 1976), p. 471.
11. E.F. Hutton, *Innovative Alternatives to Traditional Jail Financing* (New York, 1983).
12. Frieda K. Wallison, "Tax Exempt Lease Financing Gains Attention as Economic Conditions Change," in Petersen and Hough, *Creative Capital Financing,* pp. 178–179.

13. Shearson Lehman/American Express, *Financing Alternatives for State and Local Correctional Facilities* (New York, 1984), p. 3.

14. California Department of Corrections, ."Alternative Financing," p. 13.

15. Remarks at 1984 ACA Winter Conference (January 9, 1984).

16. Wallison, "Tax Exempt Lease Financing," pp. 179–180.

17. E.F. Hutton, *Innovative Alternatives,* p. 9.

18. Interview with John W. Gillespie, Jr., Shearson Lehman/American Express, Public Finance Division (February 15, 1984).

19. "Jail Issue Uses Lease-Purchase Backing to Take Advantage of a Floating Rate," *The Bond Buyer* (June 22, 1984).

20. Statement of Financial Accounting Standards, No. 13, "Accounting for Leases" (Stamford, CT: Financial Accounting Standards Board, 1976). See also, Lisa Cole and Hamilton Brown, "Municipal Leasing: Opportunities and Precautions for Governments," *Resources in Review* (January 1982).

Notes to Chapter 23

1. Charles M. Tiebout, "A Pure Theory of Local Expenditures," *Journal of Political Economy* (October 1956): 416–24.

2. Albert O. Hirschmann, *Exit, Voice and Loyalty* (Cambridge, MA: Harvard University Press, 1970).

Notes to Chapter 25

1. William Shonick and Ruth Roemer, *Public Hospitals Under Private Management: The California Experience,* Institute of Governmental Studies, University of California, Berkeley, 1983, Chapter 5.

2. Bradford H. Gray, Editor, *For-Profit Enterprise in Health Care,* National Academy Press, Washington, DC, 1986, p. 93.

3. Barbara J. Stevens and E.S. Savas, "The Cost of Residential Refuse Collection and the Effect of Service Arrangement," Graduate School of Business, Columbia University, September 1976.

4. See, for example, John D. Hanrahan, *Government for Sale,* American Federation of State, County and Municipal Employees, Washington, DC, 1977.

5. *Ibid.,* p. 116.

Notes to Chapter 28

1. Donald Fisk, "Issues in Contracting for Public Services from the Private Sector," *Management Information Service Report,* May 1982, pp. 5–6.

2. Jonathan N. Goodrich, "Privatization in America," *Business Horizons,* Jan.-Feb. 1988, p. 16.

3. Fisk, p. 4.

Notes to Chapter 29

1. Edward T. Jennings, Jr., "Public Choice and the Privatization of Government: Implications for Public Administration." Paper prepared for presentation at the Symposium on Revitalization of the Public Service, University of Missouri–Columbia, Lake of the Ozarks, October 26–27, 1984, pp. 3–4.

2. Jennings, p. 2.

3. Raymond G. Hunt, "Cross-Purposes in the Federal Contract Procurement System," *PAR* (May/June 1984), p. 248.

4. See Bayard Cetron and Thomas O'Toole, *Encounters with the Future* (1982); George Gallup, Jr., *Forecast 2000* (1984); Herman Kahn, *The Coming Boom* (1982); John Naisbitt, *Megatrends* (1982); and Daniel Yankelovitch, *New Rules* (1981).

5. 1983 Annual Survey of the Joint Economic Committee of the Congress, reported in the *National Civic Review* (September 1984), p. 412.

6. Dan Morgan, "Now the Real Revolution?" *The Washington Post,* 4 November 1984, D5.

About the Contributors

Affiliations are as of the time the articles were written.

Kate **Ascher,** Assistant Director, Port Development, Port Authority of New York/New Jersey, New York, New York.

Robert W. **Bailey,** Assistant Professor, Political Science Department, Columbia University, New York, New York.

Susan **Brown,** Editor, *Policy and Research Report,* The Urban Institute, Washington, D.C.

Jeffrey L. **Brudney,** Associate Professor, Department of Political Science, University of Georgia, Athens, Georgia.

Karen B. **Carter,** Associate Editor, *Journal of the Water Pollution Control Federation,* Water Pollution Control Federation, Washington, D.C.

Joseph F. **Castellano,** Professor of Accountancy, School of Business Administration, Wright State University, Dayton, Ohio.

Kent J. **Chabotar,** Lecturer, School of Education, Harvard University, Cambridge, Massachusetts, and Chief Financial Officer, The Williamson Group, Inc., Charlestown, Massachusetts.

Lisa A. **Cole,** Vice President, Eden Hannon & Company, Alexandria, Virginia.

Thomas B. **Darr,** a free-lance writer based in Pennsylvania, was Deputy Secretary for Legislative Affairs to former Pennsylvania Governor Richard Thornburgh.

Philip E. **Fixler,** Jr., Director, Local Government Center, The Reason Foundation, Santa Barbara, California.

Patricia S. **Florestano,** Director, Institute of Government Service, University of Maryland, College Park, Maryland.

Jerry **Frug,** Professor of Local Government Law, Harvard Law School, Cambridge, Massachusetts.

Harvey **Goldman,** Executive Vice President and Chief Financial Officer, Air & Water Technologies Corporation, Branchburg, New Jersey.

Harry P. **Hatry,** Director, State Policy Center, The Urban Institute, Washington, D.C.

Jody **Hauer,** Research Fellow, Public Services Redesign Project, Hubert H. Humphrey Institute of Public Affairs, University of Minnesota, Minneapolis, Minnesota.

Edward C. **Hayes,** President, Metro Associates, San Diego, California.

Douglas **Herbst,** Manager, Capital Finance Advisory Services Group, Arthur Young & Company, New York, New York.

David A. **Karns,** Director, Consumer and Business Research Center, School of Business Administration, Wright State University, Dayton, Ohio.

Lanny **Katz,** Manager, Capital Finance Advisory Services Group, Arthur Young & Company, New York, New York.

Roger L. **Kemp,** Adjunct Professor, Graduate School of Public Administration, Rutgers University, Newark and New Brunswick, New Jersey. Additionally he is an author and consultant as well as being a full-time city manager for over 12 years.

Ted **Kolderie,** Senior Fellow and Director, Public Services Redesign Project, Hubert H. Humphrey Institute of Public Affairs, University of Minnesota, Minneapolis, Minnesota.

David **Krings,** County Administrator, County of Peoria, Peoria, Illinois.

Robert **Kuttner,** Economics Correspondent, *The New Republic,* The New Republic, Inc., Washington, D.C.

Charles **Martin,** Executive Director, Data Processing Services, County of Peoria, Peoria, Illinois.

John R. **Miller,** Partner and National Director, Government Services Practice, Peat Marwick Main & Co., New York, New York.

James **Mills,** Consultant and former Chief Executive Officer, National Contract Sweepers Association, which later merged with the National Solid Wastes Management Association, Washington, D.C.

Sandra **Mokuvos,** Manager, Arthur Young & Company, New York, New York.

Joe **Morris,** Associate Editor, *American City & County,* Communication Channels, Inc., Atlanta, Georgia.

Terry **Peters,** Research Analyst, Texas Research League, Austin, Texas.

Robert W. **Poole,** Jr., President, The Reason Foundation, Santa Barbara, California.

Harper A. **Roehm,** Professor of Accountancy, School of Business Administration, Wright State University, Dayton, Ohio.

Larry J. **Scully,** former Vice President, Eden Hannon & Company, Alexandria, Virginia, and President, Scully Capital Services, Washington, D.C.

David **Seader,** former Executive Director, The Privatization Council, New York, New York, and Vice President, Privatization Financing, DnC America Banking Corporation, New York, New York.

Ralph L. **Stanley,** Administrator, Urban Mass Transportation Administration, Washington, D.C.

Terry **Stone,** Associate Editor, *American City & County,* Communication Channels, Inc., Atlanta, Georgia.

Christopher R. **Tufts,** Senior Manager, Peat Marwick Main & Co., Washington, D.C.

John A. **Turner,** Director of Public Relations, Rural/Metro Corporation, Scottsdale, Arizona.

Eugene J. **Wingerter,** Executive Director, National Solid Wastes Management Association, Washington, D.C.

Frances E. **Winslow,** Administrative Assistant, Police Department, City of Irvine, Irvine, California.

Index